W9-DJN-653

SOLON H. BORGLUM

Solon Hannibal Borglum
1868–1922. *Library of Congress*

Solon H. Borglum

"A MAN WHO STANDS ALONE"

A Biography by

A. Mervyn Davies

"What is Art but life upon a larger scale"

PEQUOT PRESS

Chester, Connecticut

62207

To Emma

What is art
But life upon a larger scale, the higher,
When, graduating up in a spiral line
Of still expanding and ascending gyres,
It pushes toward the intense significance
Of all things, hungry for the Infinite?

E. B. Browning

Contents

List of Illustrations

Preface

The name Borglum in sculpture has become so synonymous with the creator of the four great heads of presidents on Mount Rushmore my first point must be that this book is not about that Borglum. It is not too well known today that there was another Borglum sculptor, Gutzon's younger brother, who signed his work "Solon H. Borglum." This is the first full-length biography of Solon Borglum.

Solon Borglum leaped to the forefront in Paris at the turn of the century in the period of America's emergence as a world power. If only for this, his story is worth telling. In a very real sense he not only represented that moment in time, he embodied it. His unique identity as an artist was spotted by the French, who dubbed him *Le sculpteur de la prairie*, according him a special interest apart from those of greater reputation. He was born in the West, lived there till manhood, was a living part of the subjects he depicted. When the critics studied his work, they saw something that was "untrammelled by convention."

Solon Borglum's triumph at the *Exposition Universelle* in Paris in 1900 was no flash in the pan. It was repeated at the Pan-American Exposition in Buffalo the following year, the Louisiana Purchase Exposition in St. Louis in 1904, and then in opposite corners of the South with two equestrian monuments in 1907. His fame had become international. Even in Denmark, the native country of his parents, he was accorded recognition. During those years photographs of his work frequently illustrated articles, and it is a question whether any artist at the time received greater attention in the press. The strength and realism of his work, its beauty, truth, tenderness and poetry, struck strong chords of sympathy. As Charles H. Caffin wrote in 1904, Solon Borglum was "probably the most original sculptor that this nation has produced."

The second point I need to make is that this work is not an art book, but the biography of a man who can be regarded as a great artist. A subtle but very profound difference. Naturally I like to think that I am putting Solon Borglum in his rightful place as an artist, but my chief concern is different and I believe greater. I do not think that Americans, speaking generally, are sufficiently aware of the part that citizens like Solon Borglum have played in the national life. Here is the difference between an art book and the biography of an artist, which needs to be underscored. An art book is not primarily concerned with more than art. It is written by a specialist, one who may be, and often is, a college professor of art history. The aim and method of the biographer are different. His primary concern is not with his subject's art. He uses the latter to a wider end, the enlargement of a personality through the goals of art. What the biographer attempts is the projection of that personality onto a larger screen, the screen of American life and history.

This is specially true in the present instance. Before Solon Borglum became an artist he was a cowboy ranchman. He was already thirty when he made his debut in Paris. And then during World War I he gave up a full year of his all too brief life to serve his fellow man in a quite different capacity.

There is another aspect that makes the biographical approach essential in this case — the separation of Solon Borglum's work into two distinct periods, his Westerns and his works of universal significance. This becomes a genuine stumbling block to historians when they attempt to classify him. There can be little doubt that his reputation has suffered in consequence of that change. The shortness of his sculptural career after the change points up the fact that he did not live long enough, nor produce enough work, to establish himself on his new course.

The result is puzzlement for anyone trying to place Solon Borglum. If their interest is only in Western Art, their concern with him lapses after ten years. On the other hand, if their interest is not exclusively in Western Art, there is relatively little Solon Borglum art for them to examine, scarcely more than a dozen pieces, though these happen to be, in my opinion, among his finest creations. (In comparison, at the end of a long and active career, Paul Manship left well over 600 works.)

My third point is my own personal qualifications for this undertaking. These I have the temerity to claim are substantial, despite the fact that previously I devoted my life to research and writing on history, politics, constitutional affairs, religion and church history — everything, you might say, but art!

Preparation for such a different field of inquiry began in my impressionable years when privileged to enjoy the friendship of a very rare kind of person, an artist similar in spirit to Solon Borglum, Fred C. Richards, R.E., ARCA, the distinguished Welsh etcher and designer, of whom I will only say here that no artist could be more "impractical" or less typically a man of the world. As though it were yesterday I can recall the "new eyes" of appreciation "Dick" gave me at the age of seventeen when in the course of a personally conducted tour of the little city of St. David's on the Welsh Pembrokeshire coast he pointed out to me the difference between the "Bishop's Palace," with the patina of age on its ancient walls, and the more popular gothic Cathedral, restored in the Victorian way, which was not always the happiest.

With that lesson in aesthetic appreciation, one that I would never forget, I believe this book had at that moment its psychological inception. So I take this opportunity to pay tribute to "Dick." Both Fred Richards and Solon Borglum epitomize for me the genuine, dedicated artist. A further similarity in their lives was the comparative brevity of their careers; both died at the age of fifty-three, ten years apart.

I came on the American scene too late to know Solon Borglum in the flesh, but I had the inestimable advantage of knowing intimately several of his co-workers as well as his widow, Emma Vignal Borglum. During the last ten years of her life I came to appreciate Mme. Borglum's many fine qualities. Her courage and devotion to truth were outstanding and her Parisian culture, keen mind and learning attracted the friendship of some of America's intellectual leaders. The dowry she brought to her pioneer husband was an infinite knowledge of arts and letters.

R. Harold Paget, after Solon "dean" of the Silvermine colony, was the respected New York editor, scholar, author, and literary agent. He was "Editorial Director" of the five-volume *Outline of Christianity* and actually its entire inspiration, as became immediately evident when he, too, died prematurely. Harold Paget, aware of the importance of Solon Borglum's work, took the first essential steps to preserve the records of his life and his achievement. He it was who organized the *Solon H. Borglum Memorial Committee*, a group of leading sculptors that sponsored the belated publication of *Sound Construction*, an art textbook that Solon Borglum worked on for the last ten years of his life. To the importance of the publication of *Sound Construction* can be added the record of statements made by the sculptor's fellow artists and friends, which define Solon Borglum's dominant position in sculpture at the time of his death.

I was well acquainted with that stalwart warrior of Saint Mark's in-the Bouwerie in New York, Dr. William Norman Guthrie, whom to know at all could be esteemed an honor. By maintaining an "experiment station" in his church, Dr. Guthrie made himself an ecclesiastical pioneer as well as a great Christian, though certainly an unconventional one. Dr. Guthrie and Solon worked closely together during the last five years of the sculptor's life.

It was my privilege to know personally members of the original Silvermine group of artists, the Howard Hildebrandts, the Brinleys, the Cassels. John Cassel, editorial cartoonist of the New York *Evening World*, unconsciously played an important role by successfully persuading Solon to submit to an interview with a colleague, which stands today as a valuable document of the sculptor's ideas at the end of his life. The painter Carl Schmitt, his wife the former Gertrude Lord, and Marguerite Hamilton, daughter of Hamilton Hamilton, even now enjoy recollecting those far-off days in rural Silvermine. Fred Buttery, close friend and neighbor of Solon, descendant of a long line of operators of the historic sawmill on the Silvermine River, still vigorous and filled with memories of early Silvermine, willingly shared his intimate knowledge with an interested listener, which I always was. In this way I was given glimpses of a unique way of life that still existed half a century ago. In my research nothing has been so remarkable as the way faces lit up at the mention of Solon Borglum's name, one of the unsolicited dividends of my task.

For the last ten years I have been living in the remodeled studio-barn in Wilton, Connecticut, that Solon Borglum used to create some of his finest pieces — which gives me the feeling that if atmosphere can rub off on a writer it has done so for me.

I have conscientiously tried to comprehend the various problems peculiar to the sculptural craft, beginning with the sculptor's dire need of space, as much space as he can get, and ending with what so often happens to his work after it is completed. If some sculptors appear to live in palaces it is not because they have palatial tastes. And if they are more inclined to destroy precious plasters and unsold works than to store them, it is for the same reason, lack of the one essential of their chosen career — space. A museum director is under the same handicap. He may want to do much more than he is doing toward proper public display of the nation's heritage in sculpture, but he too is plagued with the physical problem of space. Not infrequently a sculptor's name gets detached from his masterwork as soon as it leaves the studio, and his ego has to find some other support than the praises of the world. How many, for instance, of the millions who visit the National Lincoln Memorial in Washington each year can name either its sculptor or its architect?

The biographical approach is most of all dictated in the present instance by the nature of the man of whom I write and the materials out of which the life and art of Solon Borglum sprang, grew to maturity and flourished for a very short while. Solon seems to have been a man forced by circumstances to accommodate himself to situations which might have destroyed another lesser man. To study him sympathetically both as man and artist is to be brought face to face with unpublished material that has been withheld for years. This has been a profound experience, leading me to say, "What a man, to be able to survive those emotional stabs and arrows, to laugh and be gay through it all and still achieve greatness!" I regret if some of the facts revealed are in direct opposition to those published by established authorities. This is unfortunate but inevitable when adhering as closely as this narrative does to original sources.

The resulting biography is the end product of an endeavor that began some fifteen years ago. Then it was that my wife Monica began with her brother Paul the immensely involved task of dealing with the lamentable state in which their distinguished father's affairs were left by his sudden, premature death, followed as it was by the total if temporary eclipse which affected most American artists of the period. There were pieces of Solon Borglum's finest work that still lay only in plaster. There were plaster models which had been cast in bronze but in inadequate numbers. The confusion caused by the simultaneous existence of two Borglum sculptors, with his brother Gutzon's sudden, enhanced fame following Solon's death, further complicated the work. The consequence was that Solon's name and art had passed behind a cloud of neglect if not into actual oblivion. This, with her brother's help, Monica sought to rectify.

Success in this endeavor has been notable. Four important exhibits have been held to date, the last in the nation's capital at the Smithsonian's National Collection of Fine Arts, which closed December 3, 1972. And groundwork laid for a permanent representative collection of Solon Borglum sculptures. Most of the necessary casting has been done, the endless details involved together with supervision of the work of the foundries close to completion. The majority of his drawings have been deposited in The National Collection of Fine Arts, Washington, D.C. A collection of photographs of the sculptor's work has been made and deposited in the Library of the N.C.F.A.

This manuscript can be considered a vital, comprehensive element of the whole project. Everything that has gone into it from the intimate knowledge of the artist, the experience gained at the art foundry, the many hours of research at the Library of Congress, which now houses both the Gutzon and Solon Borglum papers, conversations with artists, particularly sculptors, and not least, going through and reading the mass of letters and other data in the family archives — nothing has escaped a thorough screening as my wife and I have worked together, Paul, her brother, having died in 1968.

A biography is clearly enriched if it has the aid of members of the family. If there is bias here an experienced writer can spot it and make the necessary allowances. In this case I do not feel there has been undue bias or partiality, the motive being to clarify what obviously needed clarification. My aim has been to state accurately and simply what the facts were, letting the chips fall where they would.

Paul Borglum, my brother-in-law, was always most helpful and cooperative in his lifetime, making numerous suggestions and corrections, and I am deeply appreciative of his assistance. Harriet Borglum Faidy, youngest of the nine children of the Borglum family, was intensely interested in what began as her niece's project. The last of her generation, she was eager to correct the many misstatements that had appeared in previous published accounts, particularly relating to family history. She had hoped to put on paper her own recollections but death intervened. However she spent many days in our home and in her home in Chicago, going over packages of letters from various members of the family, some dating back many years. I have yet to find an error in what she supplied. Since her death her son Fjor has shown the same interest.

To these foundations have been added the contributions made by Professor George Borglum and his wife Imogene. As George's father August married Lucy Vignal, Solon's wife's only sister, a singularly close relationship existed among them all, made even closer by American residence of the two families. The contribution by George and Imogene of letters exchanged between members of the family added much of importance. George was formerly Professor of French, Wayne State University, and long a writer, producer of documentary films and "artist" in the fields of literature and language education. Following a recent study of the manuscript he renewed his encouragement and extended his grasp of its documentary importance, not only in setting the family record straight, but in illuminating a previously little-known chapter of art history in general, and of American pioneer history as well. He has supported these interests with his scholarship and editorial experience to sharpen in significance and appeal this account of yet another great American artist and personality.

Monica began to research the life of her father when we lived in St. Louis. I accompanied her on most of her errands, never realizing then that my name and not hers would appear as author of the published work.

While on a visit to the art academy in Cincinnati where Solon had studied, we encountered the last survivor of Solon's generation of students. And from that chance meeting a train of thought developed. After displaying one of his classmate's earliest plasters H. H. Wessel raised this question: *Which* Borglum, "your father, or your uncle," had all those successes in Paris? It was a provocative question.

In Paris, we walked along the rue Boissonnade, passing No. 16, which we stopped to photograph because it was here that the two art students, Solon Borglum and Alphaeus Cole, had shared a studio. We talked to Mrs. Murray MacKay whose husband had had a studio opposite theirs in those far-off days, which she recalled with much nostalgia. And here I want to thank "Mimi" Vogel for the diligent way she researched the Paris archives, obtaining data about both brothers' exhibits from the Office de Documentation, Bibliothèque Nationale.

We spent an entertaining and illuminating evening with Professor Gilbert Fite, who had just published his history of Mount Rushmore. Professor Fite told us much about his experiences while compiling the data.

Our trips to America's Far West, which took us back to Solon's early years of struggle and privation, were particularly rewarding, despite Doug Perham's greeting: "If only you had got in touch with us when my parents were living," a reminder of how few there were who could recall the days when Solon was an itinerant painter in southern California. In Sierra Madre Mrs. Pictor Nelson gave us fascinating recollections of accompanying her parents as a child in pigtails to the Gutzon Borglum "At Homes"; she remembered the studio home, built in the French style, with so few rooms that Solon, the younger brother fresh from the ranch, slept outdoors.

Merton Hinshaw, then director of the Bowers Memorial Museum in Santa Ana, was our obliging host and took us to various spots of interest to anyone studying that early phase of Solon's career. We saw the actual house in Orange County where Solon had stayed for several months, and the location of the Perham house in Santa Ana, at West Broadway and Washington.

In Ogden, Utah, Solon's birthplace, we visited the A. J. Knapps, Lamont herself being a sculptor who had studied Solon's career. In South Dakota we joined the countless admirers of Gutzon's work on Mount Rushmore. We saw places where the Borglums had gone when Solon took his Paris bride on their postponed honeymoon. (I was made sharply aware that Emma's diary of that fabulous trip was not only first-class source material but excellent reading.) On our way home we were able to traverse the Nebraskan red sandhill country made famous by its association with Willa Cather and Mari Sandoz, and also Solon Borglum, who had spent many years cattle-ranching along the banks of the Loup River. We decided that the land had changed but little.

In St. Louis I was fortunate to meet Paul Manship, who had come there to judge a sculpture exhibit. I saw him many times thereafter. There were always dividends to what he had earlier supplied Monica, on how he had begun his own distinguished career with Solon as a youth fresh from Minnesota, living with the family. And it was a pleasure to see his widow, Isabel, who first knew Solon as an art student in Paris, whom Paul had met and courted at the Borglum home in Silvermine, as well as other members of his charming family. His son John Manship and John's wife Margaret Cassidy, both rising artists, have alike been generous in giving me access to their specialized knowledge. Both have read the manuscript. Also while in St. Louis and since their move to the east, we enjoyed knowing the late Carl C. Mose, sculptor, and his wife Ruth, to whom I owe a marked stimulation of my interest in what had been for me a rather esoteric form of art. And whatever else our removal from St. Louis to Silvermine, Connecticut, had to commend it, we were brought closer to the scene, as it were, to persons who knew Solon in the latter part of his life.

I will always remember the way Laura Gardin Fraser, James Earle Fraser's widow and herself a sculptor of note, came down from lofty scaffolding in her Westport studio to greet us. She it was who told Monica that a biography of her father was "long overdue", and she it was who passed on to us the story of how the National Sculpture Society and Gutzon Borglum parted ways. I still recall her strong indignation as she spoke of Gutzon's disregard of the principles of the Society's founding, which it was trying to uphold: "These were men who were trying to establish a code of ethics in this new field of creative endeavor."

Other sculptors whom I came to know were Walker Hancock of Gloucester, Massachusetts, and Gertrude B. Lathrop, Falls Village, Connecticut. Gertrude, a former student of Solon Borglum, made some excellent photographs while with him, which she has printed especially for our use and for which I am grateful. Walker has been most encouraging from the start, saying that this was a much-needed book that filled a gap in the history of American art. He felt that no effort should be made to water down either the enthusiasm or the frank account of personal relations. Truth would not be served in this way — and "isn't truth the point of a biography?"

Monica and I spent many happy days as guests of another student who played a large part at Rocky Ranch, Mildred Nash Bly, Solon's student assistant before World War I. We stayed with Mildred many times at Rockport, Massachusetts, and I never left without a sense of what a remarkable man she had worked with and a deepened conviction of the importance of the assignment I had given myself.

Louise Durant Rice of Sheffield, Massachusetts and Frances Kent Lamont are other friends who knew Solon Borglum in the later days of his career, having been students and in Frances' case taught in the School of American Sculpture in New York. Both gave me pictures of his teaching methods and his personality.

There are others whom I wish to take this opportunity to thank. Their contributions have been varied and all of them welcome. Chester Beach wrote what he knew of the abortive Archer Huntington scheme for the beautification of the American Geographic headquarters in Manhattan. Jim and Alice King, then of Silvermine, recalled a somewhat different side of Solon's personality when he came home from his wartime experience in France, "mellowed" but still determined that American art must be truly American. Marguerite and Hélène Daggy told of the happy times their parents had with Solon and Emma. Alphaeus Cole, whose fine portrait of Emma Vignal still hangs on our wall and always attracts attention, told of his studio-mate in Paris, stressing his generosity and perhaps naïveté. Louis T. Rebisso III, grandson of Solon's friend, patron and teacher at Cincinnati, told of the Academy's star pupil and his dreams of accomplishment when he went to Paris; he also recalled Solon's generosity. Ruth Mary Collings M.D. of Greensboro, North Carolina, belonging to a family who had known Solon in Santa Ana, was able to show us some of his early work, a piece of sculpture and several water colors, which she treasured.

Those who have been kind enough to read some version of the manuscript and make constructive suggestions include many of those named. I wish here to thank them all, but especially our niece Linda Fry and daughter Gwyneth Kelley, whose encouragement has been constant and helpful suggestions many. Other members of the Borglum family who have made valuable contributions include Jean Brinkema, daughter of Solon's "twin" brother Arnold, who recalled Solon's first show in the basement of his father's house in Omaha.

Also, in addition to those mentioned, Floyd and Ruth Noble, Dorothy Ashe Thompson, David Robinson and his wife Adele Klair, Mrs. Alice Belward, and Mrs. Oscar Johnson of St. Louis, closely associated with the early Silvermine days through her annual visits to her sisters Mrs. Dye and Miss Walter, intimate friends of Solon and Emma Borglum. Charles Ferguson of the New Britain Museum of American Art is another who was good enough to read the manuscript and whose judgment I value.

A recent addition to this list, Phil Kovenick of Los Angeles, presently working on an extensive and much-needed index of Western artists, like myself became captivated by what he learned of the personality and artistry of Solon Borglum and generously shared with us some of the fruits of his own research including several photographs. I am particularly indebted to him for what he found regarding Lisa Borglum, Gutzon's first wife, who understandably has heretofore been a shadowy figure.

A number of public institutions have been extremely helpful. I want to thank the following: in Washington the Library of Congress, especially Dr. Mearns, and the Archives of American Art; in London the British Museum and the Royal Society of British Artists; in New York the Public Library and the Metropolitan Museum of Art; in St. Louis the Missouri Historical Society, the Public Library and the City Art Museum Library; the Cincinnati Art Museum and Library, the Detroit Institute of Arts, the Nebraska State Historical Society, the Charlotte M. Hall Museum Library, Prescott, Arizona.

A final point. Some may question my treatment of Gutzon. But I am taking him at his word: he once said to his friend Rupert Hughes who was doing a short biography of him, "I ask only one favor: for God's sake don't cover me with the twaddle and gush usually written about artists." (Gilbert C. Fite, *Mount Rushmore*, p. 21.)

I do believe that a truer picture of Gutzon Borglum emerges from this treatment; he was a great man — warts and all!

A. MERVYN DAVIES

Wilton, Connecticut
May, 1974

SOLON H. BORGLUM

CHAPTER I

The Borglum Brothers

John Gutzon (1867–1941)   Solon Hannibal (1868–1922)

The true story of Gutzon and Solon Borglum, full brothers in an originally Mormon family[1] whose seven other children were their half brothers and sisters, has never been told. Their relations in particular are an untold story. One reads of a conventional relationship, with the elder brother making pointed reference to his affection for his "little brother" [2] and his policy of never competing with him.

Why did Gutzon go out of his way to make such statements? Why did he emphasize something that never existed, except possibly in his own mind? Solon competed with other sculptors as a matter of course. Why then should he and his brother *not* compete? Fifteen months' difference in age is nothing. Solon was Gutzon's younger brother but not his "little brother." Statements of this nature arouse the investigator's curiosity.

It will be no surprise to learn that brotherly relations were acutely strained on occasion, beginning with their first experience of trying to work together as artists in the same studio in Sierra Madre, California, and quite possibly earlier. The clash at Sierra Madre[3] was so severe, in fact, that it became a crucial episode in the life of each. Both had been captivated by the romantic challenge of being "great artists doing great things together . . ." The dream was never realized. At Sierra Madre painting was their medium, Gutzon being ahead of Solon because of his earlier start. They planned to work together, Solon taking instruction and criticism from his elder brother. But it did not work out that way.

After more than half a century since Solon's death and over thirty years since
Gutzon's, it is time to get at the truth. It has profound relevance, particularly for
Solon.

An incalculable hindrance to getting at the truth is the fact that Gutzon, in
the company of many famous people, was not just impatient with, but frequently
oblivious to, factual accuracy.[4] In Morris West's novel *The Devil's Advocate*
however the words, "You can never bury the truth so deep that it cannot be dug
up," seem to apply particularly well in the present instance.

In April 1922, three months after Solon Borglum's sudden untimely death,
a news feature appeared in a leading newspaper of the nation under the head,
"Gutzon Borglum—A Sculptor of the West,"[5] by Robert Alexander Horwood,
accompanied by a familiar cut of Gutzon. Without mistake however the article
itself was a well-informed one on the life, personality and achievements of Solon!
The editor's ignorance, or carelessness, foreshadowed the transposition to come in
the reputations of the brothers. Even the phrases "Sculptor of the West," "The
Plainsman,"[6] became Gutzon's, to the layman at least, for eventually Gutzon
would purchase a ranch in South Dakota and stock it with cattle. In effect,
Gutzon, who had grown to manhood despising frontier life, contemptuous of
Solon's loyalty to the wilderness and the free, open life of the range, found
himself in middle age playing the role of his brother.

Just ten years before, in 1912, a full-page illustrated article had been
published in the New York *Sun* with the title, "Solon Borglum, The Sculptor,
Once a Cowboy."[7] It reminded the reader that although Solon was doing
monumental work in different parts of the country he had first risen to fame in
Paris, where he had exhibited his sculptures of the West in the Salon, in the
Exposition Universelle, and in private showings. This was a retell of the success
story widely published in the early years of the century. After a decade or more it
still had news value. Solon was currently working on the monument of Jacob
Leisler for New Rochelle, to be unveiled the following year.

In the previous year, 1911, publication of a new edition of the *Encyclopaedia
Britannica* gave an account of Solon's life and achievement, which ended with
two lines devoted to his brother: "His elder brother, Gutzon Borglum, born in
1867, also shows himself an artist of some originality." At that time Gutzon had

been in New York for nearly ten years. He had exhibited at the St. Louis Exposition, where he had been awarded a gold medal for a small group, "Return of the Boer," [8] done in England and exhibited in Paris and London several years before. By 1909 Gutzon had already conceived and executed his General Sheridan Monument and a remarkable bust of Lincoln, both works in the nation's capital. The former is a strong and original work. The latter grips the visitor to the Capitol Rotunda with its unique depth of feeling. As works of art — and subsequent years have not dimmed their importance — these two sculptures alone deserved attention, far more than the two lines in the *Britannica*. Why was this very solid achievement left without mention at the time?

An attempt to answer this question is essential for it contains the key to much that has been previously suppressed or omitted in writing about Gutzon Borglum, whose personality has never been fully understood. Why was he what he was? To tell the life of Solon with integrity, omitting Gutzon and the occasions when their lives and careers touched and clashed, is as impossible as to try to tell the life of Gutzon without dealing with Solon's influence upon him.

It is well to begin by identifying the two men as personalities. So far as the general public is concerned, confusion has been at the heart of the problem. The sculptors of the period were familiar with Solon's work and most of them knew him personally. Many had been eyewitnesses of his success in Paris. By Augustus Saint-Gaudens and others he was well liked and had quickly been welcomed into the fraternity of sculptors both in Paris and New York. The critics too were generous[9] in their judgment of his work. The New York *Sun* of November 4, 1902, said it "has brought into the somewhat effete domain of modern sculpture a whiff of fresh invention as invigorating as the air of the Western plains."

Gutzon Borglum was a problem, however, and still is. Today, thirty years after his death, despite his great achievement, there exists no adequate biography. Adored by his admirers, hated by many, he continues to be an enigma to those who would make a true appraisal.

Paul Manship, not long before his death, was hard put to describe Gutzon Borglum. The words did not come easily. Finally, curling his lips in disapproval he said, "Oh, he was . . . a go-getter.[10] He liked to be in the news. He followed important people." This was the best that Paul Manship could do for Gutzon!

Another New York sculptor, when asked to answer charges that Gutzon had made, exclaimed, "Borglum? I won't discuss him.[11] That man is too much in the newspapers. He's always seeking publicity."

A remark attributed to Daniel Chester French is another illustration of the attitude of some of his fellow sculptors: "I see that Borglum[12] is making molehills out of mountains again."

There is more pique than justice in these comments. They overlook the solid achievements of the sculptor, expressing disapproval of his "tactics" with considerable likeness of feeling. It appears that Gutzon Borglum may never really have enjoyed good relations with most of his fellows, at least not until a new generation appeared which did not associate him with the early years of trying desperately to establish himself in New York as a sculptor, frequently at the expense of his brother.

The fact is that Gutzon had a highly controversial personality which, though it often fascinated the layman, affected his standing in business as well as professional circles. If French could make his alleged remark, a non-artist could do the same.

Paul Bellamy of South Dakota, who had become acquainted with Calvin Coolidge during the summer of 1927 when he was still in the White House, was visiting the former President at his Northampton home. Said Coolidge, "do you see Mr. Borglum very often?" [13] Bellamy replied that he frequently saw the sculptor during the summer months. "How far is it from Northampton to Rapid City?" asked Coolidge. "Oh, about two thousand miles, Mr. President," replied Bellamy. Coolidge looked pensively out the window, blew a puff of cigar smoke, and said, "You know, Mr. Bellamy, that is just about as close to Mr. Borglum as I want to be."

One could seldom be neutral about Gutzon Borglum. He was either admired or disliked, both extravagantly. Admirers saluted him as a genius and lavished romantic hyperbole to express their feelings. Opponents, particularly those who had clashed with him, always a violent experience, had difficulty finding words to describe their detestation. Stanley King's biographer,[14] Claude M. Fuess, relating the "egotistical" sculptor's behavior at the time of the aircraft corruption charges brought by Gutzon in 1918, called him "an uninhibited and unmitigated nuisance," irrational and intemperate.

The distinction between the brothers was felt by those who had never come in contact with them. An English businessman who traveled extensively in this country identified Gutzon by calling him "the notorious Borglum," while Solon was for him "the famous Borglum." The relevance of this distinction becomes clear when it is recalled that it occurred at the time of the Stone Mountain blowup with its almost daily headlines.

The Stone Mountain project justly commanded headlines. It promised to be a "first" for this nation and judging by the prophesies made at the time it would be a "first" in the world or at least worthy of a place among the great monuments of the past. But in the end it was not only President Coolidge who would wish to put two thousand miles between himself and Gutzon, but also the citizens of Georgia. Many of them had started out believing they were dealing with Solon, who in 1907 had given them their handsome General John B. Gordon Monument in front of the Capitol in Atlanta. But as the world knows, it was Gutzon who went down to Atlanta in 1916[15] to take up the commission. As the world does *not* know, the great project was originally, according to members of the Venable family and those close to Solon, to have been a joint enterprise of the brothers.[16] When the blowup came there were puzzled citizens who, remembering Solon's courtesy, patience and willingness to cooperate with committee members, relatives and individual experts, concluded it was the war that had changed their sculptor, making him difficult if not impossible to work with.

Laura Gardin Fraser, widow of Solon's intimate friend James Earle Fraser, stated no more than the truth when she pointed out that from the beginning of Solon's rise to fame the brothers were different, and recognizably so. In a lecture on American sculpture she called the two Borglums "as distinctly opposite[17] as two persons can be, brought up as they were in the same environment on the plains west of the Mississippi."

Solon can be seen distinctly. He was the idealistic, unworldly artist, serious, sincere and hardworking, without being a plodder. Down to earth in his simple philosophy of life, he had no tolerance for shams and hypocrisies, made friends easily wherever he went and was beloved by artists and laymen alike. When he died tributes to his rare personality filled the press, typified by what Raymond V. Ingersoll, his YMCA superior during World War I, wrote: "Though Solon Borglum was a most unassuming man,[18] his strong personality was felt even by those who met him only casually . . . showing in exceptional combination many of the noblest elements of American character." Lorado Taft, representing his fellow sculptors, called him one of America's "best-loved artists." [19]

In contrast, some of Gutzon's best-known works trailed trouble, some were conceived in trouble. Still, his courage, cleverness, resourcefulness and disregard for the feelings of others brought him through on top. He knew how to keep his name before the public, turning friction into eye-catching headlines.

One cannot minimize nor bypass the amount of confusion that reigned in the business art world when in the fall of 1901, separately and independently, both Borglums reached New York from Paris within a few weeks of one another, each claiming to be "Borglum the Sculptor." Solon's change to New York was natural and inevitable, following the years of expanding recognition as a sculptor that began in the Cincinnati Art Academy in 1897. This was not so for Gutzon.

During those years and earlier, Gutzon was making every effort to reach greatness in the field of painting. He was ambitious to become a fashionable portraitist, and on the advice of friends had gone to London to achieve his aim.

Lorado Taft, art critic and sculptor, in his *History of American Sculpture* published two years after Gutzon had arrived in New York, correctly placed Gutzon among sculptors of "European birth, or under the influence of the Old World." [20] This is significant in the clarification of the two brothers' work at that time. Although Gutzon was on the scene and had done a little sculpture, he *was not yet included among those Americans striving to establish a truly American art*, where Solon was generally placed. Charles H. Caffin devoted [21] a whole chapter to Solon Borglum among his eleven *American Masters of Sculpture* (1903), but Gutzon's name is hardly mentioned in that work.* Even as late as 1910, Gutzon himself confessed his own "powerful bias toward Italian art," [22] his admiration for the Classical "more than all else." This would never be true of Solon.

Gutzon's biographers pay little attention to this period, except for its successes, such as they were. It was anything but a happy time for him and explanations can neither be fabricated nor avoided. He was experiencing all the frustrations of one who wanted to get ahead fast but was unable to determine in which direction and in what style to apply his skill. In contrast to Solon,

---

* In a general discussion about the American Indian sculpture, Caffin says merely: "Gutzon Borglum in his statuettes has represented with realism and vigor its actualities."

Gutzon's work was as yet unsettled. He could be looked upon as an eclectic in search of an identity.

In attempting to pull away from the old, and influenced by it at the same time, Gutzon was producing another kind of art than Solon's. Circumstance naturally plays its part, but the answer is more deeply imbedded in the contrasting nature of the two artists. Not only was their art different, their approach to art was different. What was Gutzon and where was he going? No one seemed to know, perhaps least of all Gutzon himself. Even what name he should use professionally remained a problem.

It is clear that what successes he had in Paris as a student in 1891–1892 were not repeated. In London he was making his way. There are records of exhibits and sales from time to time. There are portraits of well-known figures, social events in which he played a part. But the fact has been missed that, *by his own calculation,* success of a magnitude to satisfy his need of recognition eluded him. He leased a handsome villa in famed St. John's Wood, a section of London popular with artists, then enlarged it for giving big parties. Among the latter Isadora Duncan's debut was the most important. But despite this artistic and social activity Gutzon's name does not appear in a listing of those belonging to the clique of painters[23] known as the St. John's Wood Artists. The English "Annual Register" of 1901 states: "The first year of the new century was not remarkable for fresh developments in the world of art. No new reputations were formed, no painter or sculptor of note travelled out of his beaten track or surpassed within it his own earlier achievements."

Gutzon was frankly miserable, emotionally upset, running aground more than he would admit. He was well past his youthful target date for "greatness," having boasted that he would be great "by the time he was thirty." [24] In 1897 he *was* 30.

If Gutzon Borglum felt crushed and discouraged, what could be more likely? While there was Solon across the Channel,[25] receiving plaudits Gutzon so desired for himself! If ever a contrast of fortunes could engender jealousy of a younger brother, there it was.

In 1898 a lucrative contract from the Midland Railway Company for the execution of large murals for the Queen's Hotel in Leeds temporarily revived Gutzon's spirits. He wrote at the time to his Los Angeles patron, the widow of General John C. Frémont, Jesse Benton Frémont, that he looked upon the work as the beginning of a new era in his career. Indeed it was, if only because it gave him temporary economic independence from Lisa, his first wife.

It is necessary at this point to introduce Lisa Borglum, an artist in her own right[26] who had been Gutzon's teacher in California. Elizabeth Jaynes Putnam, granddaughter of Judge William Green of Green Hill, Worcester, Massachusetts, had been educated in Boston and New York. She had studied art and music with the leading teachers of the time both in the East and in San Francisco, where she was particularly referred to as the pupil of William Keith. Within a year of her marriage to Gutzon she was awarded a gold medal by the Western Art Association, and when they were later in Paris her work was accepted by the Société Nationale des Beaux-Arts along with her husband's. Eighteen years her husband's senior, she had come into his life when he was a raw, unsophisticated youth, fresh from the frontier. Lisa spotted in her young husband, whom she married in 1889, many of his rare qualities. He was alert and vital, ambitious and clever, and quickly responded to attention and instruction. She set herself the task of uniting her own experience, technical knowledge and established position as an artist, with his developing talent. Having received instruction in both the East and the West, with social connections which she did not hesitate to use in his behalf, it appeared she had everything to offer him, advice, guidance, teaching, collaboration. Soon she was openly claiming that he was indeed a "universal" genius, one that would be great perhaps earlier than his own target date of thirty. Thus for some ten years Lisa was a central figure in Gutzon Borglum's life and career as a rising young painter. Yet this extraordinary marriage and the effect it must have had on the young artist has been largely by-passed in the accounts of Gutzon's early life.

When the time came, as was inevitable, for Gutzon to break away from Lisa's influence it was another instance of the lives of the brothers touching dramatically. An impending second contract[27] with the English railroad for murals for a Manchester hotel put money in his pocket at an opportune moment. Irked by his slow reception in London, despite the fact that he was now an exhibiting member of the Royal Society of British Artists,[28] and plagued with doubts about his "new era," he decided to move his residence from London to Paris. He exchanged their modest *pied-à-terre* on Boulevard Arago for an elegant villa in the rue de Port Royal.

If the years 1897–1901 were crucial for Solon, and they were, they were no less so for Gutzon. If they brought success and domestic happiness for Solon through his marriage to the charming daughter of a French Protestant minister in Paris, these same years must have brought Gutzon to depths of misery. To top everything, this younger brother, always content with so little, was now having a family, a blessing Gutzon himself yearned for. Indeed, only one totally without sensibility can look at such a moment in Gutzon's mature life and not feel for him the greatest compassion. Solon did not condemn his brother's behavior at this time,[29] which was on occasion unspeakable; or wrongs done him in Sierra Madre, a near-crushing experience; nor would he those that lay in the future.

As Gutzon was preparing in 1901 to occupy his new home in Paris his heart was already leaving the scene, deserting an intolerable situation in which he was yoked in marriage to a wife he no longer loved and, just as intolerable, one who was holding him tethered to an art that no longer inspired him.

Today as then, Gutzon Borglum's emergence as a sculptor in New York marks for him the end of an era[30] and the start of another, but it has been overlooked how much of his new career was to be modeled on Solon's. His sister Harriet, who had come with her mother from Omaha for a sightseeing trip abroad and to see the Paris Fair, recalled Gutzon's fascination with his brother's work. He would return again and again to Solon's life-size group, "Stampede of Wild Horses," which had been so strategically placed at the entrance to the American Pavilion at the *Exposition Universelle*. Eighteen-year-old Harriet, standing beside him, saw his undisguised admiration of Solon's work. "Oh," she said, "he admired Solon's work." [31] She was convinced of this. As he stared into the action of the plunging animals he must have asked himself, "How did Solon do it?" Studying the various exhibits of other sculptors, he must have pondered the question, "Where am I in all this?"

Where indeed? If his conclusion was that he represented an outgoing era, it was inevitable. He could recall impossible days in Sierra Madre when he and Lisa attempted to "refine" Solon's work and Solon's irritation at their "interferences," for Solon had already developed a mind of his own in art and knew what he was after. He had not come under the influence of Thomas Eakins for nothing.

The position was simple but explosive. There was Solon, who had no regard for Lisa and her teaching. There was Lisa, who was jealous of Solon[32] and feared his influence on her husband. Gutzon was caught between two warring artists with very different ideas about art.

Now, after five years, the situation had not changed except that in 1901 Solon had something tangible to show for his stubborn adherence to his own convictions. In spite of all efforts to deflect him, Solon had emerged. He was now a respected member of the American colony in Paris, looked upon as a genuine artist with a great future. The name Borglum was his. For Gutzon all this was hard to swallow, perhaps impossible. The unpretentious "little" brother who had chosen to rough it in the mountains rather than remain under his and Lisa's roof in Sierra Madre, *how had he done it?* It must have been the question of questions that Gutzon asked himself at the *Exposition Universelle*.

The year of Gutzon's great awakening was 1901. It was consistent that the coup de grâce to the Old World and all that it had meant to him should be administered by Lisa herself, in Paris at a family gathering. When Lucy, August's wife — August was a brother who had spent a year in London studying music — remarked that a certain work at the Salon had been described by Solon as "great art," Lisa burst out in a frenzy, never to be forgotten by those who witnessed the scene, *"But what does Solon know about art?* [33] *He is not an artist!"*

Not long afterward Gutzon was on the high seas returning to America.

Gutzon Borglum was a great man. His works, all attesting to his varied and exceptional qualities, proclaim the fact and give distinction to the American scene. He was versatile and only that kind of artist could have met and mastered the many obstacles and hazards involved in bringing the carvings of Mount Rushmore to triumphant completion. That monument is not only notable portraiture, it is even more an engineering feat. As historian Gilbert Fite concludes, it is a phenomenal achievement, "one for the ages." [34] Its very large size bears witness to this, for Gutzon believed that art, to be American, had to be large and meaningful else it would not represent adequately the dreams, ambitions and accomplishments of the robust American republic. But at the time of Solon's death, that best known work of Gutzon was still in the future.

Gutzon Borglum had an instinct for greatness. It was part of his nature. Largeness and lavishness characterized everything he did, in the way he spent money, ran up debts, bought immense properties, designed studios, entertained associates, sent his father to Europe to research and if possible enhance the family name. The Stone Mountain Memorial to the Confederacy was not only going to show the gigantic figures of Lee and his staff on the face of the enormous, elliptical monolith, but the semblance of a whole regiment trailing away in the distance behind. What he came to do had to be breathtaking. The title *Give the Man Room* most aptly describes Gutzon Borglum.

If Gutzon could only have been less ruthless in fulfilling his ambitions, set bounds that did not exclude Solon — or fellow artists for that matter — this story from the very beginning would be different. One feels that neither man ever reached the full stature of his creative potential. Gutzon's life, stormy as it always was, could have been less so had his conscience not been troubled over Solon. Because of their different natures the dream of two brothers collaborating some day, as any psychologist could have told them, was more idealistic and sentimental than realistic. As a tie binding them together it was present all their lives. In the torment of his own making the truth may be that Gutzon killed his own dream.

In George Grey Barnard's "Struggle of the Two Natures of Man" the Metropolitan Museum of Art in New York possesses one of the great works of a sculptor who has been compared in profundity to Michelangelo and Rodin. There is no victor depicted in this struggle, no triumph is visible on the face of the standing figure, nor defeat on that of the recumbent one. Victor Hugo is said to have supplied the idea with his line, "Je sens deux hommes en moi"; in the words of Saint Paul, "the good that I would, I do not; but the evil which I would not, I do." Was this the answer?

Solon Borglum did not wear his hair long, nor disdain the ordinary conventions of society. In many ways he was definitely conservative, perhaps foolishly so.

His wife wrote that during their engagement she learned "what a good man Solon Borglum was." Clearly that opinion did not change. The words were written several years before she died. But in that very fact lies one of the prime difficulties of telling his story convincingly, for a good man is always difficult to portray. One is encouraged however by the fact that Coleridge, speaking of Milton, once said that every truly great poet had to be a "good man." In the same sense in which he used the word "good," the same is true of artists; and it was very definitely true of Solon Borglum.

Along with this quality of goodness was an astonishing gaiety which seldom deserted him. Despite the fact that Solon was a very serious person embarked on a serious enterprise and his whole life lived on that plane, the spirit of fun, revealed by some of his photographs, lurked just below the surface.

No one valuing success by the standards of the business world would have surrendered the advantages of residing and working in New York, nor pursued with so much diligence his work in the rustic environment of the Silvermine of that day, nor freed himself so uncompromisingly from economic considerations by his willingness to accept, as he was known to do, the very smallest remuneration for a commission he really wanted.

Above all, Solon was master over self-pity, not allowing defeats and frustrations to shake his faith in himself. In the light of what we know today to have been the circumstances he frequently faced, his fortitude was remarkable.

Formal church membership was not for Solon Borglum. As Emma explained when requesting a transfer, her husband was still "at heart a member of Bishop Hare's mission church in South Dakota." His friend, admirer and co-worker in Solon's last art project, William Norman Guthrie, rector of Saint Mark's in-the-Bouwerie, said of him: "He believed profoundly, and therefore he could conceive greatly." [35] These words were inspired by a truly religious figure depicting the aspiration of man.

Solon's life illustrates many fundamentals of American freedom. Without apparent racial prejudice his friendships included Booker T. Washington, and the black painter, Henry O. Tanner, whose work is receiving fresh attention today, and he had a very special feeling for the red man. America for him was no exclusive land of race and class, but a place that must welcome all. In World War I in France he saw the relevance of the "melting pot" to those peoples who had fought side by side for an ideal. Writing to Emma, he said that his heart filled with a new happiness as he passed out his cups of coffee and chocolate to the weary soldiers returning from the front: Australians, French, British, Senegalese, Tunisians, Algerians, Canadians, and black and white Americans.

CHAPTER II

A Child of the West

Legend has it[1] that the Borglum family tree was planted by a crusading twelfth-century knight, one Conrad Reinfeldt, who accompanied his liege the emperor Frederic Barbarossa, to the Holy Land in 1190. On the way he saved the emperor's life in a wild boar hunt, for which act of courage he was awarded the hereditary title of *de la Mothe*, "the One of Courage."

The spread of the *de la Mothe* family across Europe can be followed through the appearance and reappearance of the honorific appellative. It is seen, for example, in the full name of the celebrated French theologian and writer of the seventeenth century, François de Salignac de la Mothe Fénelon, archbishop of Cambrai. As critic of the policies of Louis XIV, who in 1685 revoked the Edict of Nantes guaranteeing freedom of worship to Protestants, and as defender of the offbeat Quietist movement within the Church, he acted with unostentatious courage. Such are the presumable descendants, like the Borglums, of the original *de la Mothe* ancestors.

Close to the Western Sea in windswept Jutland, the most northerly province of Denmark, stands an ancient, white stone monastery known as the Borglum Kløster. It emerged from the Middle Ages as a center of learning, one of its priors during the Reformation being Niels Sorenson Mothe, who, on becoming a Lutheran, married a former nun. From this union the Borglum family can be traced in an unbroken line, acquiring the surname when, by royal decree, the former prior's descendants were required to assume the name of the monastery.

The Borglum Kløster, Jutland, Denmark

The American story begins[2] with Jens Møller Haugaard Borglum, born in Hjorring, April 18, 1839, twenty-five years of age when he emigrated to America. One account has it that the step was motivated by a desire to escape conscription, war with Prussia having just broken out. Another gives dissatisfaction with the settlement of an inheritance as the reason. The records, however, of the Church of Jesus Christ of the Latter Day Saints in Salt Lake City, that he had become a Mormon convert, are quite clear.

Denmark, like all Scandinavia, was the scene of much Mormon missionary effort. Converts to the new faith numbered thousands. Summer after summer from 1850 onward pioneers crossed the Great Plains, making their painful, often hazardous way to the promised land. Missionaries affectionately called it the New Jerusalem where, beside the Great Salt Lake, they would build their Zion.

In the Civil War year of 1864, Jens Borglum was among them. He can be seen with some clarity as the most desirable of colonists, young, strong, idealistic, intelligent and dedicated, a tested "saint" who had survived all manner of persecution during eight years of "laboring" for the faith in his native land. As if these were not qualifications enough, he was a woodcarver by trade and a restless searcher for "the truth." In later years he described himself as a "very studious person[3] who early formed his own opinions." A proud and independent man, these traits all served Jens in the trials that lay ahead.

Jens arrived in the English port of Liverpool April 27, 1864, where he married Ida Mikkelsen, daughter of a Copenhagen furrier, who was traveling with her seven-year-old brother, John. On April 28 they joined a party of 973 converts led by Patriarch John Smith, and set sail for America in a ship called "Monarch of the Sea."

On reaching New York after a voyage of thirty-six days, they journeyed by rail and river steamer to the village of Wyoming,* Nebraska, then the starting point of some of the wagon trains. Here they joined Captain William B. Preston's company, but the luxury of a place in a wagon was not for them. So scarce was space in the covered wagons during these days and so numerous the pioneers that many were forced to improvise ways to cover the distance, independent of the wagons yet attached to them for protection and subsistence.

---

* No longer on the map, Wyoming was a freighting point on the Missouri. During the latter part of the Mormon migrations some three thousand wintered there.

Hundreds walked, their belongings in pushcarts, and among them were Jens and Ida. When news of their safe arrival on September 15, 1864 reached relatives back home, Jens and Ida were joined the next year by other members of their families, including Christina, Ida's eighteen-year-old sister. On crossing the Plains, this party was not blessed with the same good fortune as the first. Led by Captain Minor Atwood, it encountered most of the terrors which made the crossing of the Great Plains a fearsome experience. Many of its members were lost and the rest did not reach Salt Lake City until the second week of November.

Upon the sisters being reunited, Jens took Christina as his second wife, in accordance with the precepts of the Mormon Church at that time. Christina bore her husband two sons. The first, John Gutzon de la Mothe, known during his early years as "Johnnie," was born March 25, 1867, in Ovid, Idaho, high above Bear Lake in the Wasatch range. The second, christened Solon Hannibal de la Mothe, was born December 22, 1868, in Ogden, Utah, where the family had moved in the meantime.

In this wholly new relationship whose emotional pressures could not possibly have been foreseen, there developed an incompatibility between the sisters which was not conducive to happiness and domestic peace. As the clouds gathered Jens became increasingly tormented by doubts until, after three years and by mutual consent, Ida, Christina and he each made their renunciations twenty years in advance of the official banning of plural marriages. With the dissolution of the second marriage the family gave up its membership in the Church and in the community.

Jens' position with the Mormon Church is authentically reviewed by one who knew him both earlier in Denmark and at the time. Jens Borglum "was a man of good address[4] and attractive in appearance and made friends wherever he went. He frequently visited my father's house while laboring as a missionary. . . . So much is known to me, that Bro. Borglum became dissatisfied with conditions in Utah, went to Idaho and later to Omaha, Nebraska. . . . Your father [the inquirer was Solon's brother, Frank] having been a man of prominence in the Church before emigrating, no doubt had to pass through the unpleasant experience that many others have passed through when first arriving in their adopted country on this side of the Atlantic. They were handicapped by lack of knowledge of the language, and before becoming used to the habits and customs of the people here, became discouraged. But I venture to say that there is nothing in your father's life that caused him to leave the Church of which you need to be ashamed."

Some six months after Solon's birth, another son arrived. Arnold was born to Ida, also in Ogden, Utah. As soon as the new baby "was old enough to travel," Jens took the entire family east as far as Omaha. Here Christina rejoined her parents,[5] who had also emigrated, leaving her two boys to be brought up by her sister Ida. The traveling this time was by the newly-arrived railroad, the Golden Spike having been driven at Promontory, May 10, 1869. Later, Christina remarried.

Patently, Jens' character would direct him toward a life of service to his fellowman. This became apparent when, with the treeless plains' greater need of physicians than woodcarvers, his thoughts turned to the study of medicine. A sympathetic doctor eased his way with the loan of books and other assistance until he received his M.D. degree at the Missouri Medical (homeopathic) College in St. Louis, February 19, 1874, at which time he anglicized his name.

Dr. James Miller Borglum hung out his first shingle in the little prairie town of Fremont, Nebraska. The settling of Fremont was similar to that of scores of towns in the Mississippi River basin. Most of its twelve hundred inhabitants had deserted the Overland Trail and settled at this point because of their fears of the trek across the seemingly endless Plains with their attendant and multiple dangers.

Solon was a normal child and his boyhood was happy. He had a passionate fondness for the outdoors, which he had ample opportunity to indulge. He was the chief, perhaps the only, member of his family to appreciate fully the advantages of Fremont. A stable full of horses, which the country doctor maintained, provided endless challenges to a venturesome boy. Solon "could ride before he could walk," and his passion for horses gained him the reputation of being a daredevil, for which honor he paid with the scar of a mustang's hoof that marked his forehead for life.

Solon was also known as a youngster given to pranks and to mischief. Chores didn't bother him, especially if they were outdoors. He was strong and sturdy, reveling in action. He was positively enthusiastic over his first paid job, an early morning paper route on which he left the house before breakfast, happily whistling along his way. All his earnings went to his father as a matter of course.

In later years Gutzon recalled his brother's "insatiable curiosity[6] about life and his utter confidence and belief in the harmlessness of everything and everybody in life," traits that can be found in the mature man.

An early description states that Solon was "hardy and quick and clearheaded,[7] fit for action and hardship, an integral part of the rough life around him. And because he was a quiet, sensitive, imaginative boy he was unconsciously akin to it all."

Nothing suggests that Solon was a model pupil. Truancy was certainly indulged in by many pupils, including Solon and his brothers. It must have been now, by the way he pitted his mind and strength against the shackles of the schoolroom, that he gained the reputation of being a "frank failure."

The culmination of revolt against the schoolroom was a scheme developed and carried out with two of his brothers. The railroad was an exciting novelty with tremendous appeal for adventurous boys. One day Johnnie, Arnold and Solon decided it was more important to fight Indians than attend school. The story, which has persisted, embroidered through the years no doubt, had it that they were running away from home on the theory that they were men, and wanted the fact recognized. Boarding the train in a moment when no one was looking, they hid in a boxcar and remained long enough to put many miles between themselves and Fremont, long enough also to cause terrible fears among those at home. When finally discovered they were made to walk the rails all the way back. Sufficient punishment, one would think, but an irate and anxious father cannot be blamed if he gave vent to his emotions by chastising the boys one by one in the traditional manner.

Dr. Borglum compensated in his own way for the shortcomings, such as they were, of the Fremont grammar school. It was his practice, as he made the rounds of scattered ranches and cabins, long, wearisome drives at best, to take along one of his boys to care for the horse and hold the reins as they drove over the prairie, often far into the night. This was a tour of duty each boy took in turn, each believing himself to be his father's best companion.

When it was Solon's turn, he not only acted as groom for the horse and companion for his father, he soon qualified as his assistant, unaware that he was preparing himself for his life on the plains. In this school he was a ready learner, acquiring the skills of a practical nurse and witnessing the facts of life — birth, physical suffering, death. He developed a proficiency in attending a newborn infant which was later to amaze and delight his wife, who proudly boasted that it was her frontier husband who taught her how to hold their first child.

These were not the only benefits Solon derived from the long drives. Horizons widened as he accompanied his father to Indian tepees as well as to the cabins of white men. He grew up, in fact, among Indians, sharing the companionship of their children, sometimes staying overnight. Out of these associations came a human bond which persisted and deepened through life. Dr. Borglum did not miss the opportunity to impart to his sons the wisdom of his accumulated experience. He was the kind of pioneer doctor about whose concern for the welfare of humanity was said, "No night too dark, no road too long, no home too humble." Solid foundations were thus laid in the formative years of Solon's life — his respect for ethical principle, for such values as loyalty, patriotism, devotion to home, service to others, the gift of life.

Solon's early learning must be described as a haphazard experience of reality and formal schooling, the latter a useful but relatively small part. When the house in Fremont was sold and the family moved to Omaha, Solon showed, by what he achieved in his one full year of serious schoolwork, that the term "frank failure," which pursued him endlessly, had to be descriptive only of his boyhood school days in Fremont. The records of Creighton College,[8] Jesuit institution in Omaha, show "premium" for excellence in Christian Doctrine, "first honors" in arithmetic, "distinction" in grammar, history and geography. With these promising results Solon was entered for another year, but he did not return.

Gold Coast fever was epidemic and members of the family did not escape. Dr. Borglum and Ida became the parents of their last child, Harriet, born in Omaha November 24, 1882, by which time Gutzon, aged fifteen, had given up St. Mary's Academy in Kansas City[9] and left home for good. He had decided to take up art and had apprenticed himself to a Los Angeles lithographer while pursuing his art studies. Miller, the eldest brother, was also in Los Angeles, associated chiefly with Helen Hunt, author of *Ramona*. His task was to drive the novelist around the city while she sought material for her romances.

The restless doctor himself succumbed for a while to California's attractions, so much more varied than the cattle and distribution center which Omaha was at that time. Putting together what cash he could, James Borglum made the trip, doubtless dreaming of better prospects, but his hopes were not fulfilled and he returned to Omaha.

One solid result of his visit, however, was a land deal — six thousand acres of undeveloped Nebraska soil acquired in exchange for a property he owned in Pasadena, an exchange that had special consequences for Solon.

For Solon the trip to the West Coast yielded an extended period of exhilarating freedom in a land where nature seemed to have contrived perfection. In all his boyhood dreams he had encountered nothing to match the extraordinary terrain of that time with its mountains, valleys, forests, shores, and mesa, the great Sierras on one side, the sparkling Pacific on the other, separated by a still unconquered wilderness. What outdoor boy could it fail to have thrilled and challenged?

In the year or more Solon spent in California he learned a trade. Already at home on any horse and unafraid to take on the worst, he was also by this time an old hand with the lasso. He still had to learn the serious business of large-scale ranching, but there was no problem here. Reasoning that a cowboy should want to move up to managing his own ranch, he was able to persuade his father to let him go back east and develop the recently acquired acres in the Nebraska sandhills.

Solon's chief companion up to this time had been his brother Arnold, born in Ogden, Utah, June 2, 1869. So inseparable were they that close friends and family called them "the twins." Traveling together on this wonderful trip they stopped at their birthplace in Utah, climbed mountains, ventured through canyons, putting together matchless tales of adventure. Everyone thought of them as two starry-eyed would-be cowboys. Nevertheless, at the end of the working year, Arnold declared that roughing it was not for him and that he had had it with cattle and horses and open lands and wilderness. He urged Solon to come work with him for the railroads, whose business was booming everywhere. "No," said Solon, "I'd be as bad there as I was in school." So each of "the twins" went his own way but their close bond remained. During the years when Solon was struggling to become a painter, Arnold helped out by sending a few dollars from time to time. This was typical of Arnold. It is a notable fact that all his available earnings at this time went to members of the family — a practice that ended with his marriage.

Little is known about the relationship between Solon the cowboy and Johnnie the aspiring painter. By stringing together a few facts, however, attitudes

Arnold and Solon 1883.   "The Twins"

can be established from which probable conclusions can be drawn. This period is generally overlooked as it relates to Solon except for the obvious fact that he mastered the skills of his calling in California, which brought him back to Nebraska and the ranching life that was to provide him with a chief source of material for his later work. Apart from the escapade several years before of going "to fight the Indians" with Arnold and Gutzon, no incident nor dependable anecdote fills in the story. Yet, during the year 1883–84, after they left home, Solon and Gutzon, 15–16 and 16–17 respectively, must have seen one another on occasion. In *Give the Man Room* we read: "On a ranch somewhere in the vicinity was Solon Borglum. Of all the family he was the closest to Gutzon because he had shown interest in art." Another reference suggests the probability of some contact: Solon helped Gutzon pay for his first lessons in art.

Gutzon clearly had a head start on Solon, a slight one in age, and a greater one in art experience. He was volubly ambitious but friendless and with little money. Charles Lummis' description, written several years later, reminds one that Gutzon Borglum was not exempt from the testing period of struggle that makes a man what he aspires to be, or destroys him along with his ambitions. He was "a green, serious lad [10] belaboring canvas in a bare room on what was then Fort Street. He had no money and not many friends."

In these circumstances it is quite certain that Gutzon longed for the companionship of his brother, who was on a ranch "somewhere in the vicinity."[11] So much of an age, bound together by poignant circumstances, having a common interest in painting and ambitious to be important in the eyes of the world, they surely met whenever possible. It is further quite probable that, just as he had turned over his paper route earnings to his father, Solon now helped Gutzon[12] from his cowboy pay, Gutzon passing on his knowledge of techniques as he acquired them. This could be the basis[13] of a later claim that Solon had been his pupil.

The date of Solon's return from California is not known except that it was toward the end of 1884 or in the first part of 1885. The one tangible marker in this misty period is an entry in the Omaha City Directory of 1885: "Borglum, Solon H., painter, res. 2415 Caldwell."

What was then the status of the boys' grandiose plan to become great artists together, the vision which continued to haunt them the rest of their lives?

We know only that, for the time being, a home, a herd of cattle, ranch hands, horses and a lasso in the wilderness took precedence for Solon over easel, canvas and brushes. Solon had made up his mind to become a cowboy rancher. He, unlike his brothers, had resolved that he would be happy doing just that.

CHAPTER III

The Epic of the Plains

One hot summer's day a teen-age prospector could be seen crossing the treeless, trackless plains of Nebraska's sandhill country, seated in an old, creaky wagon, driving a tired horse while a still tireder cow plodded behind. His own body, target of the blazing sun, was so weary that each fresh jolt from the uneven ground served only to further depress his lagging spirits.

As the traveler himself recorded in later years, using the third person, his strong body would not permit the thought of stopping. First he had to find the right place for his shack. His determination will not be lost on the reader. This was an experience the teen-ager of that day would never forget. The youthful pioneer was resolved to set up a cattle ranch on virgin land.

He had not chosen an auspicious moment for such a venture. The grasshopper, early scourge of the settler, had spent itself but the historic droughts and terrifying blizzards of 1887–88 lay just ahead. Solon was in good time for them both. Cattle were to die in heaps, owners calculating their losses as two-thirds of their herds. Many of the settlers lost heart altogether. Solon was not of their number, sticking to his ranch until 1893. Only as a hardened veteran of twenty-four did he surrender it in exchange for what he had discovered to be his true vocation.

Actually, in the climate of the time, there was nothing very remarkable about the teen-ager's feat, as Solon would have been the first to admit in later years. In seeking to establish a ranch he was only following the trend of his day, taking advantage of a favorable situation. At the very doorstep of his home in

Omaha lay the broad state of Nebraska with its countless acres of virgin soil and abundant pasturage. It was the moment in time when the great cattle drives from the South — Oklahoma and Texas — were opening up the whole area to the homesteader. Solon had the qualifications for responding to the urge of his generation.

Background is the single most vital element for understanding Solon. His heredity and the environment in which he grew up were different and cannot be taken lightly. He was American and a Westerner and there is always a Bunyan somewhere in the Westerner's makeup, Solon not excepted. Even after he left the West, pioneering remained the essence of his life. Its influence can be seen in his addiction to hard work, in the hours he kept and many other characteristics of the rancher's way of life. His disregard, too, of physical comfort and material things, his driving ambition to make something of himself, his easy acceptance of life's hazards, his cheerfulness and serenity in the face of adversity were all hereditary traits that responded to environment. Even his choice of a sophisticated Parisian wife, so different from himself, was approved by a primitive wisdom, an instinct stemming from a Nordic heritage that combined courage, daring, imagination, resourcefulness, ingenuity, and tenacity. Stubbornly independent and determined, he could be mulishly obstinate, and this too is Nordic.

Life at Loup River began to take shape as the young ranchman established his home and recruited helpers, "frontiersmen, desperadoes and hard-drinking cowboys," his future wife called them. At this point Solon's plans might have crashed had he not found among these men, so much older than himself, one who became his foreman, dependable Joe Andrews, who was as interested in the success of the ranch as he was. "With this strong and good man," wrote Emma, "he accomplished much." Together, he and his foreman dug the well, planted the corn, cut the wild grass for hay, built the bunkhouse, bought a minimum of stock and were in business.

Several hundred cottonwood trees were planted as windbreaks, for shade and for a touch of beauty. Solon watched these trees grow and, years later, as he and Emma were passing down the rue de Sèvres near the Egyptian fountain in Paris, he spotted a fine, tall cottonwood. His eyes lit up with excitement as he told her that his cottonwood trees at Loup River would now be as big as the one they were looking at.

At first the rancher was not seen by anyone. His days were fully occupied with his "boys," his horses and his herd, except on the rare occasions when supplies had to be fetched from Cairo, the nearest town. The "boys" knew him as a "quiet, decided good fellow," exhibiting nothing of the boss to hamper ease and freedom of communication, always possessing their respect, and experiencing no difficulty maintaining authority. "It was merely," [1] according to one early account, "part of the day's work for him to tell them what to do. Unconsciously he made his rude estate a typical democracy. He had his duties, and the boys and ponies their work . . . all were equal in the eyes of the great real world about them. The same storm beat upon each and the same hot sun. Such a philosophy was unconscious and inevitable . . ."

Above all, it was practical. "A boy his age does not impose his will on frontiersmen, even when he is the master," says Emma. "I am sure that his strength lay in his lack of fear and his knowledge of the boys . . ." Just as he was not "boss," so he did not carry a gun, nor drink strong liquor. However, on making a judgment that a man had to leave, the man had to leave. Solon was firm. An anecdote, known to all members of the family, illustrates this: Riding a coach one day, he was accosted by a drunken Irishman who demanded his place. Solon refused, and in defense of his seat had to throw the man down, then quietly returned to his place with studied unconcern. According to Arnold, Solon was so strong he could down a man twice his size.

Such circumstances were rare, Solon usually being an observant and contemplative person. "Many a time," [2] we are told, "he would urge or lead his pony up some undiscovered ridge and, reaching the top, he would sprawl on the sandhill and watch the wind mow paths in the bunch grass below. Or looking over the stretch of silent plain and hill to the illimitable blue beyond, he would unwittingly know himself a part of a great inexplicable something that he could not understand or express. Or after a stampede, as he sat in the saddle or stood beside his horse at night alone, with the sweating flank of the herd before him, and the hills and his cabin back of him somewhere in the blackness, the fierce epic of the plains wrote itself into his heart while he knew it not."

It was a period of rapid change. The Great Plains were filling up. A land boom was developing. Retired businessmen arrived from the east, usually despised as tenderfeet. The coming of wire put an end to the open range. The census bureau declared the frontier closed in 1890. The tragic events of the end to

Sioux freedom, the Ghost Dance and the death of Sitting Bull, occurred only a few miles farther north. The last round of bitter bloodshed took place on December 29, 1890, one week after Solon's twenty-second birthday.

Every settler still had to make up his mind how to view his redskinned neighbor, as a friend or as a menace. Solon could have been no exception. His mind might have been made up ever since he had accompanied his father on errands of mercy to the tepee. Those sympathies, however, could have been greatly strengthened at this time by the friendship of a remarkable man whom he met on the ranch. Bishop William Hare, Episcopal missionary, was exactly the kind of man to make a deep impression on an idealistic youth, as he traversed his vast diocese of Niobrara in utter disregard of physical comfort and the dangers to be encountered along the way. Echoes of his influence on Solon are heard from time to time.

Solon was looked upon as a veteran by his new neighbors and they elected him sheriff. As he was always modest about himself, one would not expect to hear him boast of any exploits in that office. One feels instinctively that his interpretation of his role would have been that of a peacemaker. Once he had to drive a demented woman to the hospital, and this could have been a test as it put a fighting woman beside him and a skittish horse in front. He also told of a problem with a gun-happy rancher who had gone berserk. He took such experiences for granted.

There is additional reason for this view of him. Solon once wrote an article for *Youth's Companion* on "Our Vanishing Types," in which one of the types he described was the sheriff. He wrote this: "The sheriff has been portrayed as a bloodthirsty daredevil. He is almost always a daredevil, almost never blood-thirsty. The man who has done more than any other to purge the frontier of the lawless characters that infested it for years was invariably the antithesis of those he hunted. They were brutal, blustering, drunken; he was gentle, quiet, sober." Solon went on to say that the sheriff was "invariably good-natured and brave," not a boaster, who did his capturing whenever possible without using a gun. "His pride was to go out and take a desperado single-handed and without bloodshed." [3]

The cowboy was viewed in a similar light. Here Solon's opinion is worth quoting at some length. He called the cowboy the most misrepresented of all the "vanishing types":

The people of the East have been led by ignorant or careless writers, painters and sculptors to confuse him with the cattle "rustler" or raider. He has been pictured as a desperado, going about "shooting up" towns and leaving a trail of carnage behind. Such characters have existed and do exist in connection with the cattle industry of the West, but they are not the dominant type. There is the cowboy who comes to the ranch in the spring and fall, and at all other times is a vagabond. This is a type that the people of the East have had thrust before them.

The cowboy first got his bad name from the practice of speculators years ago. These men used to go as far west as possible, buy a small bunch of cattle, and drive them east to the markets of Omaha, St. Louis and Kansas City. The bunch in its progress eastward used to absorb all stray cattle, increasing like a snowball as the result of raids upon unprotected herds. Also, vast herds of cattle were driven from the Texas ranches to the northern markets. These enormous bunches required many men to attend them. In the mixing of herds and brands, fighting frequently occurred. Subsequently, laws were passed compelling the fencing in of great ranches, and this took away the more romantic feature of the occupation of the soldier of the plains. He was made a mere fence-rider. Science is crowding out the old type of desperado cowboy. A better breed of cattle is being developed, and the men selected to care for them must know their business. Science has taught that to promote the welfare of cattle they must be made comfortable.

If there is anything that a first-class western man resents, it is the assertion that the disreputable cowpunchers are natives of that section. As a matter of fact, these ruffians almost invariably drifted from the cattleyards of the eastern markets. To be sure, they ran things for a time with a high hand, but just as soon as the western communities felt that they were strong enough, they organized vigilance committees and drove the intruders away.

Solon's interest in art showed when his brother Frank, aged eight, visited the ranch in 1887, sent there by his father to recuperate from a serious illness. Solon helped the boy wile away the time sketching. A few of young Frank's drawings are still among Solon's papers.

No phenomenon of the Plains made a deeper impression on any settler during the winter months than the blizzard; the blizzards of 1887 and 1888 are historic, and the blizzard is a recurrent theme of Borglum art, occurring in several of his best-known works. The way the storm would descend without warning, and with terrifying power and fury, were characteristics he chose to catch and depict again and again.

There is a marble entitled "The Last Roundup," which shows a saddled but riderless horse caught in such a storm, struggling for life. A graphic account of this event exists among the Borglum papers.[4]

The January morning was mild, ominously so to the experienced eye, and the rancher on Loup River took advantage of the brief break in the winter to send his boys out to round up strays. After they left he rode over to see a neighbor, one of the retired tenderfoot ranchers from the East, who had asked for his help. Finding the "old man" on the point of going after his own strays, Solon did his best to dissuade him, suggesting that his own boys could easily do the job for him. But the old man insisted on going himself. Shortly after Solon left for home the blizzard struck without warning and with fullest force.

In telling the story Solon characteristically uses the pronoun "we" to include his horse: "The snow was so thick and blinding I knew my only hope was in our being able to keep the direction of our place in our minds. This and nothing more would take us the right way. We might as well have been in the dark as far as our eyes were concerned. And if the distance had been very great we would soon have lost the feeling of the right direction with that blinding storm square in our faces."

Solon and his boys had the know-how for this kind of emergency — avoid the dry runs since they are the first to fill, keep moving, and give direction with pistol shots — but not the elderly tenderfoot. Later in the cabin as the boys related their experiences, an ominous hush quieted their lively talk when one of them, Anderson, began telling of a riderless pony that had kept working its way toward his group. A little closer, they saw the outline of a fine, big, Western saddle. "We all with one distressed voice cried, 'It's the old man's pony!' There it stood high above the cattle, plunging in the snow in its effort to get to us . . .", Anderson continued, "I told the boys to keep up a little shooting and I would go up the dry run and see if I could find anything. . . . Suddenly I came across some horses almost buried at the bottom of the dry run, with no track of any kind around. The snow was filling in at what seemed a ton a minute." He turned back in fear. When he reached the boys he said, "Come on, or this will be *our* last roundup!"

"The Last Roundup." A riderless pony working its way toward them. Marble. Height approx. 13½ in. 1902. *Walter Russell.*

And so life beside the Loup River continued. Each year Spring arrived with its eternal promise, fresh and beautiful, but at the season's end Solon had nothing to report to impress his concerned father. Yet, unfailingly, he would greet the oncoming season with a new burst of enthusiasm, "Next year will be different." He loved it.

Life under the best circumstances was hard and could be cruel for any pioneering ranchman. But for Solon it suggests that Nature had marked him for her own. It seemed that in her most violent moods she had laid odds against him, determined to halt his progress and drive this youthful intruder from the Plains along with the indolent and the discouraged. By turns she employed drought and flood, cyclone and blizzard, all with redoubled force in her effort to break his stubborn spirit. Then, failing, it was as though she relented and initiated him into the secrets of her power. When he was ready he would leave the Plains, but never would he abandon this close-knit relationship. He would never forget what he had learned. He would relate these experiences — they would be called "anecdotes" — through his work as a sculptor.

CHAPTER IV

The Vital Decision

"Solon, you should be an artist." [1]

These were the catalytic words that may have reawakened Solon's artistic ambition. Spoken by Gutzon when he visited the ranch in 1890 on his way to Europe, they were never forgotten by Solon. They provided a permanent basis for gratitude, and possibly inhibited later resentment when Solon had cause to feel anything but gratitude.

They must be read, however, in the light of past history. They must be interpreted in the context of that earlier description of Solon and Gutzon, teen-age boys, on their own, struggling to prove themselves men in Southern California. The words have been interpreted differently, but it is difficult to escape the conclusion that Solon was being urged by them to abandon his present life. He had shown Gutzon some of his sketches, done from time to time, and Gutzon, who had gone ahead with his art, was determined to reawaken those teen-age ambitions in Solon. Gutzon was shocked by Solon's present way of life, his hand-to-mouth existence, and the rough men who were his companions. All this cowboying on that unprosperous ranch was abhorrent to Gutzon's nature.

Things had gone well with Gutzon since the Los Angeles days. He had attended art school in San Francisco, where he had attracted some attention; he was married to one of his art teachers, Elizabeth Jaynes Putnam,[2] "Lisa," and they were now on their way to Europe to continue his studies. Ambitious, buoyed by the purchase of his canvases by the local tycoon George W. Liniger, clearly headed for big things, Gutzon's words to Solon have a ring of jubilation. And their effect was instant, the transition from ranchman to artist began immediately. Solon was soon combining art instruction in Omaha with management of the ranch, attending classes taught by J. Laurie Wallace.

His sister Harriet recalled how he would drop her off for dancing class on his way to art school. Mark Pollack, a fellow student, never forgot one sketching expedition which was interrupted by a family of skunks and the excitement and hearty laughter that accompanied the adventure. Another, Mrs. Orr, recalled Solon's studiousness and sincerity.

Miller, eldest among the family's children, had given up in Los Angeles and was back home. At loose ends, he joined Solon on the ranch. The brothers did not hit it off but Miller's widow throws some light on Solon's personality by saying that her husband could never understand his brother's urge to get out into a storm as it broke. "It always puzzled him the way Solon had to make pictures in a storm." Unknowingly, she was describing one of Solon Borglum's favorite themes. One has only to remember how often Solon used the wind as protagonist in his dramas of life on the Plains to see significance in the Miller Borglum anecdote. Throughout his life he was to love storms and tempests, whose violence seemed to engender in him an inner serenity. One cannot imagine his fleeing from any storm, for part of his affinity with the Plains Indians lay in their kindred response to natural phenomena and instinctive understanding of nature's ways. Once, years later, he was discovered standing against high rocks that faced Long Island Sound, wrapped in a blanket and blissfully content. A storm was raging with waves lashing the shore. Solon had exchanged the warmth and shelter of his host's house for the great display taking place outside.

On another occasion — Solon's wife never tired of telling this story on herself — he and Emma encountered a hurricane while returning from America. He managed to prevail upon her to leave the security of their cabin, carrying her in his arms in order to view the awesome sight. One look at the waves and she fainted dead away!

Three years passed while Solon wavered between his two vocations. As the French critic Henry Bargy[3] would put it, "Tantôt à cheval, tantôt au chevalet." Which would take control of his life, the horse or the easel? For one who loved horses and the Great Plains as much as did Solon Borglum, it was a cruel choice.

The clearest signal of an impending decision came one morning when some of his Omaha family arrived at the ranch expecting to be entertained but found their rancher so thoroughly engrossed in a picture that he had forgotten the planned outing. It was obvious to all that the ranching days were numbered.

Doubtless the decision would have come of itself but it was hastened by an invitation from Gutzon, who again triggered the crucial step toward his brother's future career.

Gutzon's return from Europe was a memorable event in the Borglum family, especially as he was now able to prove that art was not the foolishness some of them thought. Gutzon was at last happy and at ease, with the goal that meant most to him being realized and success crowning his efforts.

On the first evening the account of his European experiences held all who heard it spellbound. In Paris his work had been accepted by the Salon and by the so-called 'new' Salon. A year in Spain had proved equally rewarding, culminating in a one-man show in Madrid. They had seen a number of the great picture galleries of the world. Time to think on the way home had produced vaulting ambitions for the future. He and Lisa were about to open a studio in California where the paintings he would do would be on the order of the wonderful frescoes that had so captivated him in Spain. His theme was to be the Conquistador epic.

The homecoming was made the occasion for a notable family portrait in which Gutzon and Solon can be seen standing with their brothers, Miller, August and Arnold, all offspring of the Mormon period. Gutzon's wife Lisa is chic, and Dr. Borglum, seated opposite Ida, is a distinguished figure with full beard and frock coat, befitting his professional status. In front are the three youngest, Theodora, Frank and Harriet. Anna is seated with her husband, Alfred Darlow, who holds the first grandchild on his knee. A Great Dane lies in the foreground, revealing significantly the new importance of its owner. Gutzon had brought back with him four Great Danes and a Spanish manservant to care for them. He had previously warned[4] his father that they were bringing home five Great Danes. He, of course, was the fifth! The sensation the dogs made, as all had come bounding off the train in Omaha, was tremendous. It was very adroit showmanship, to be repeated at every stop along the line to Santa Anita, where the startling arrival was reported in the local paper.

The vistas of glory and renown achieved through art that Gutzon described entranced none of his listeners more than the one whose ambitions now also lay in that direction. Not one word of the spellbinder's discourse was wasted on

The James Borglum family. From left standing: Arnold, August, Alfred Darlow (husband of eldest daughter Anna) holding first grandchild Ida, Solon, Miller, Gutzon. Seated: Ida (Mrs. James Borglum), Anna, Harriet, Theodora, Frank, Dr. Borglum, Lisa (first Mrs. Gutzon Borglum). In the foreground a Great Dane. Courtesy George Borglum.

Solon. He was fascinated, happy and ready. Solon hastened to show his brother
what he himself had accomplished during those three intervening years.

Solon had hung his one-man show in the spacious basement of his father's
home. "There were pictures everywhere," [5] said one, retelling the experience to a
younger generation — landscapes, portraits and, above all, horses. Gutzon, who
also remembered the occasion, spoke of it years later:[6] "On scraps of wrapping
paper he had recorded with photographic truth [the] movement, walking,
trotting, single-footing, galloping, of horse, steer and lesser animals of the
prairie." Enthusiastic over what he saw and in his typical open-hearted way,
Gutzon immediately invited Solon to follow him to California, where they would
open a studio together. In Gutzon's own words: "I pleaded with him to give up
his ranch and follow art, and this he shortly did and joined me in California."

The impact of this basement show upon his friends and family, particularly
upon his brother, determined Solon's next step, to sell his share of the stock and
give up ranching, which he did without even waiting for a favorable market. His
mind now made up, all his thoughts were concentrated on Gutzon's warm
invitation.

The Sierra Madre experience, however, remains today, as it was in their
lifetimes, a disastrous episode veiled in mystery.

With the advantage of time and subsequent happenings it is clear that the
person of prime importance in the situation was Gutzon's wife. Apparently she
had not been consulted! Not only as Gutzon's teacher but as one who had
exhibited her own work, she was considered an artist of talent. She did not
conceal her feelings about Gutzon's "genius." She had dedicated herself to
making him a great painter. Already her young husband had made his personality
felt in Los Angeles. He had been described with accuracy and without lack of
respect as "a rough Nebraska boy — sturdy, energetic and interesting." [7] A
ménage à trois, from Lisa's viewpoint, would clearly be an arrangement to avoid.
Another "rough Nebraska boy," this one with ideas so different from her own,
would destroy the foundations of her relationship with her pupil and husband.

Solon was a product of the revolutionary Thomas Eakins school. Solon's
Omaha teacher, J. Laurie Wallace,* was a successful pupil of the Philadelphia

---

* J. (for John) Laurie Wallace, 1864–1953. Born in Ireland of Scottish parentage. Came to
this country as an infant. Studied at Academy of the Fine Arts in Philadelphia under Thomas
Eakins, with whom he formed lasting ties of friendship and influence. Came to Omaha in 1890.

artist and a sensation in local art circles. Wallace started his art classes in Omaha very soon after his study with Eakins and Solon must have been among his first students. There is, in fact, nothing in Solon's art that runs counter to the tenets of Eakins' teaching.

Gutzon, on the other hand, perhaps influenced by Lisa, practiced a different form of painting, one in which the romantic idea lingered. It was still the vogue in California at this time, its school being the offshoot of the Hudson Valley school, whose roots were in British landscaping. The conflict between the two concepts of art is part of the history of American painting.

If Solon had had hopes of getting instruction either from Lisa or Gutzon, he was soon convinced that as artists they and he were poles apart. In her journal Emma mentions Solon's only comment relating to his Sierra Madre experience: "There were too many interferences." And in later years Lisa's own words are on record that she had no opinion of Solon's art. To that must be added the fact that Solon never blamed his brother for the difficulty, but Lisa. Clearly, Gutzon was caught between his wife, his brother and the changing art climate of the time.

In her brief account of her husband's life, Emma states that Solon, finding no guest room in the Borglum studio, took to sleeping outdoors, which was no hardship since he was used to roughing it. She describes him waking up at dawn amid the inviting mountains at Sierra Madre's very doorstep and returning to the studio in time for the day's activities. But one morning he did not return. Instead, he picked up the blanket Lisa had lent him with a request for its return and took off up the trail, leaving behind no word of his intention, only some canvases and heavy equipment, purchased for their joint enterprise.

And there were the dogs, the Great Danes, whose responsibility had become Solon's, following the departure of the Spanish servant. The pungent smell of the dog mash as it cooked and the stench of the kennel developed in him a lasting aversion to the breed as well as a hateful memory added to an already unhappy experience. Years later, when Monica was offered a fine Great Dane pup, her father returned such an explosive "No!" that the surprised daughter prevailed upon her mother for an explanation. As for the dogs, out of hand and neglected, they all came to a bad end. One was shot by an irate neighbor. The rest were poisoned.

During the next few months Solon can best be described as an itinerant painter. The climate of southern California makes vagrancy feasible, the teeming game of those days made it practical, and to one of Solon's temperament it was agreeable . . . but who shall say, as his daughter puts it, that he was not heavy-hearted?

In the fog that shrouds this crisis in Solon's life, his next definite appearance was in Los Angeles as a sidewalk artist. This is established by the fact that he was there during the railroad strike of 1893, and we have his drawings of the picturesque adobe houses of the old city.*

One day the owner of a racing stable in the vicinity stopped to watch him sketch, then asked, "Would you be interested in painting my portrait?" As the question was accompanied by an invitation to stay with the owner while the portrait was being done, Solon eagerly accepted.

The visit lasted four months, affording a welcome break from Solon's now standard diet of crackers and oatmeal cooked on a portable stove. Happy once more to be among friends, he spent much time studying the play of muscle as the horses exercised on the track.

We find Solon next staying with a fruit grower in Orange County, painting his host's grandfather, the Reverend Amasa Stanton, from a daguerrotype. This frame house can still be seen, in an orange grove at the entrance to Silverado Canyon leading to "Old Saddleback," a favorite haunt of Solon's for the next few months.

Close at hand lies the thriving city of Santa Ana, then a spot of considerable charm and natural beauty with some claim to culture, having as its chief attraction an opera house specially built for the celebrated Mme. Modjeska, whose mountain ranch was a local landmark. In Santa Ana the wandering abruptly ceases. The itinerant artist had evidently reached a decision.

Solon Borglum's first studio — if it can be called that — was a small, windowless room with a skylight which Solon rented for $2 a month. Having no furniture, he took possession by spreading his blanket on the floor. It must have required some breathtaking optimism, however, to tack the sign on the door: LESSONS IN ART. After a week with no pupils, another notice appeared under the first: SATURDAYS ONLY. With that, Solon took off to roam the mountains of the Santa Ana range from Sunday morning to late Friday.

---

* These drawings are in the National Collection of Fine Arts, Smithsonian Institution, Washington, D.C.

Early settlers well knew the peaks of those mountains. One in particular, "Old Saddleback," [8] was so etched against the sky that it was for them a symbol of hope. As a local account has it, "each day's tasks and trials and joys were marked by the rising of the sun over Old Saddleback. To it in the quietness of early morning they looked and received inspiration, and in the twilight when the day's work was done, they found the sun's rays suffusing the old mountain in a soft glow of light." So it could have been for Solon at this time of acute testing.

In the years ahead, as a teacher of teachers, Solon was to lay stress on a student's need of "bread before cake." "Don't be afraid," he was to tell his hearers, "to give your students coarse bread." He emphasized this, even to those who thought they had exceptionally gifted pupils. "Remember the minute apprenticeship even Michelangelo went through." It could be that he was remembering also his own experience. Frémiet was to say to him, "You are lucky, sir.[9] Many young men go to art school and come out polished with nothing to say. You lived, you had something to say, then you began to think about art."

An account written at the time of Solon's death, inspired by fellow artists who had known him intimately, reads: "His early years[10] on the path of studentship hold no romantic story of the strivings of genius; they were stark suffering, but suffering which stamped him as one who had passed undismayed, ever glorying, through the refiner's fire."

"Stark suffering." As the personality of Solon Borglum emerges, one realizes that the reference would not have been to any suffering caused merely by physical hardship. Privation of that sort was always something he could take in stride, as though it were the ordinary lot of anyone wanting to get out of the rut and achieve. But anguish of the spirit — psychological suffering — this was something else, although Solon would have been the last to speak about it in such language.

Saddleback has twin peaks, Sandiago and Modjeska, a mile apart. The canyons leading up to them are almost impassable, with slippery slopes covered by thorny masses of tangled vine. Once the top is reached, magnificent views extend in all directions from either summit. To the northwest the plain of Los Angeles stretches away to the sea. In clear times one can see the islands in the Pacific, a hundred miles distant. To the north lie the snowcapped Sierras; to the northeast, the spreading San Bernardinos; below, a tangle of cliffs, canyons, primeval forest, streams, and waterfalls.

Was this Solon's "country"? One cannot be sure. He spent much time in it, but he once got lost and spent days finding his way back to a trail leading somewhere. He contrasted it with the country he knew better, his familiar sandhills. "Mountains are wonderful," he once said to Emma, "when you are on top. Otherwise, they are viewstoppers."

In his weekly wanderings Solon encountered some interesting characters. The fast-disappearing day of the frontier was leaving behind a remarkable flotsam of old prospectors, stranded miners from worthless claims and worked-out strikes, migrant Mexicans, homeless Indians and every variety of hobo, outlaw and drifter. With them he shared many a meal and campfire. It is possible he found them all more interesting and congenial companions than those who attended his sister-in-law's at-homes in Sierra Madre.

One Sunday morning Solon had callers. His landlords had come to find out about their unusual tenant who was in "Saturdays Only." Professor F. E. Perham was principal of the Santa Ana High School, and his wife, daughter of a whaling ship captain from Martha's Vineyard, was a woman of much perception; both had warm sympathies. A glance around the scantily-furnished room, now hung with miscellaneous art work, told them all they needed to know at the moment.

The following week Solon had another visitor.[11] A faculty member, the high school's botany teacher, needed someone to help with drawings to illustrate his lectures. Although plants and flowers were not Solon's specialty he offered his assistance.

After Daniel Reserve Wood had looked around enough, he asked, "Would you be interested in doing my portrait?"

The response was an enthusiastic affirmative.

"How much do you charge?"

The artist was surprised by the question, not having given such matters much thought.

What did Mr. Wood have in mind? he asked cautiously.

"Would five dollars be all right?"

There was quick assent. Then came the question that Solon was familiar with in his dealings with his friends in the mountains: "Do you have money?" He was able to answer with complete truth, "Not a cent." He may have been shocked to be handed three dollars, on account.

That night, we are told, Solon indulged himself. To his usual ration of oatmeal he added a handful of crackers and some potatoes, but he now had something more sustaining than cash — *hope*. Better, his future wife was to say, than cream on the oatmeal.

Dan Wood then brought two young ladies who wanted to be taught to paint, which gave the would-be teacher the nucleus of a class. The Perhams' interest sharpened. On investigation they found out about their tenant's recent past. Already acquainted with the Borglum Art Studio in neighboring Sierra Madre, they had no trouble guessing the whole story. With sympathies strongly aroused, they decided to make their tenant a member of the family. Their son Douglas let himself be moved out so that Solon could have his room to work in. The hospitable Perham home on the corner of West (now Broadway) and Washington in the city of Santa Ana thus became Solon's for a whole year. We owe to the son who gave up his room this glimpse of him: "My family thought a great deal of Solon, who had a most pleasing personality.[12] He could not say 'No' to anyone, and did plenty to pay his way."

Daniel Wood was more than a good friend. He and Solon became like brothers and discovered that they even shared the same birthday, though Dan was several years older. Solon never forgot the debt of gratitude he owed him.

At last Solon was able to take his next step. Aware of his need of more education, the only question was "Where?" This presented no real difficulty as the Cincinnati Art Academy was then at the height of its fame. A school, as Emma describes it, "in a museum where pupils breathe art from morning until night." Dramatically situated atop one of the hills of Eden Park, its isolation and intimacy made it ideal for Solon.

Bearing letters of introduction from Dan Wood and provided with funds from the sale of his work* and a railroad pass from his ever-generous and thoughtful brother Arnold, Solon arrived in Cincinnati in November 1895, a month after the term had begun.

Now in his twenty-seventh year, Solon looked considerably older than his classmates, with deeply-etched lines on his face and hair noticeably retreating from his forehead. At first, the renewed experience of city life filled him with nostalgia for plain and wood. The walls of his room seemed like those of a

---

* A sale of his work which was exhibited[13] in the YMCA building, and announced in the local paper, netted him some sixty dollars.

prison, his little window yielding only a glimpse of the sky. His yearning for the open spaces of the Plains became practically a sickness. The swarms of people he passed in the streets only made him lonelier; they were strangers with whom he could share nothing.

Work was for him the only cure. The bright lights of the city which caught the eye of this cowboy were those of the government mail stables, illuminating incessant activity through the night. On the corner of Main and Sycamore streets, not far from the Academy, they became, since it was habitual for Solon to get up early, a stopping point on the way to school. This enabled him to get in several hours of sketching before classes began.

What this meant to him, then and always, has been stated by his wife: "That companionship with his old four-footed friends was a great comfort to him. He studied every movement of their bodies, their form and action, and while he was studying them he became more and more in sympathy with them. He really knew them, and as always with animals, they returned his affection. Horses loved him and later, when he bought a farm in Connecticut, his horses and cows crowded him in the little paths as he took walks in our fields and woods. They would hear him coming from a long distance."

The onetime pupil of the Eakins School was not satisfied with smooth exteriors. What lay under the horse's hide was just as important. He needed to study muscles and sinews. So he gave himself special courses in anatomy, both of the horse and, spending many hours in the city morgue, of the human form. It was later stated that, had he wished, he could have received a diploma in anatomy from the medical school, where he also dissected the human figure.

One day the head of the sculpture department, Professor Louis T. Rebisso, received a note with an unusual request. A student asked the professor to come to his room to view a piece of work. Professor Rebisso ignored the request. Only on its renewal did he respond. When he saw the reason he exclaimed, "Borglum, if I had known[14] what you have here I would have come the first time you wrote." What he saw was a modelling, quite small, of a horse of the plains pawing the dead body of another.

The depiction was not the least in the romantic style. Another teacher might have derided or ignored it, but not Rebisso who was himself a discriminating artist. In fact, he was so pleased with what he saw that he submitted the work for the Academy's annual prize in sculpture. It had to be disqualified for not having been done in class, which Rebisso knew very well might happen, but its sculptor received a consolation prize of fifty dollars, with the promise of a scholarship.

Solon spent the summer vacation in Santa Ana, returning to the Perham's to again become one of the family. The summer was an active one. Douglas Perham tells of a day's excursion into the mountains with the entire family, picnicking at the Modjeska Ranch. Solon painted some sheep, while Doug watched. Other landscapes, among them "Clouds Over Black Mountain," were also painted that summer, together with "A Study of a Boy." These paintings along with four 12-inch circular intaglios — one for each member of the family — were given to the Perhams "in appreciation of their help and kindnesses." The output of that vacation included landscapes, portraits, several horses done at a nearby stable, a head of Silkwood, the famous trotter, and the statue of a buffalo which Dan Wood had cast into bronze. That summer, it seems, Solon tried his hand at everything.

On his return to school in the fall Solon stopped off in Omaha to see his family. His sister Harriet, then fourteen, later recalled a clay horse wrapped in a wet shroud, and rolled-up paintings. "I'll never forget Solon's visit," she said, "because that night I walked in my sleep and went straight to the dining room table where Solon had placed the statue, all wrapped up in a wet cloth. I touched it and shrieked, which woke me up in a fright!"

Harriet was to see Solon five years later in Paris, and again she would store up significant memories for the future. Although youngest in a large family, she stands out as its most observant member. Nothing escaped her. She was small, alert and liked by everyone.

The Academy's recognition of Solon's "Horse Pawing a Dead Horse" is a vital link in Solon Borglum's career. It provided the crucial test of whether ideas based on realistic portrayals of ranch life had artistic merit. The clear pronouncement, not only by Rebisso as head of the sculpture department, but by the Academy's other heads as well, gave him the encouragement he wanted and needed after his experience at Sierra Madre. The decisive switch to sculpture, not to be completed until he reached Paris, can be attributed to his second year in Cincinnati and accounts in part for the affection he always had for that school.

There was another indication of his new status. Professor Rebisso now had such esteem for Solon's work that he invited him to share his studio and live with the family. Solon accepted happily and to pay his way he tended the stove and did odd jobs for the family. Then he formed another intimate friendship, that with Dr. and Mrs. Allen, acquaintances of Dan Wood and the Perhams. It was of such a character that he spent most Sundays with them at their home.

At the end of his second year in Cincinnati, Solon had 17 pieces of sculpture in the Academy's Annual Exhibition. One of the local newspapers reviewed it in part as follows:

"It is generally felt[15] by the Art Academy management that Mr. Borglum's horses in sculpture in Professor Rebisso's department have constituted the strongest display ever made by a student in the school. Mr. Borglum's work is marked by absolute individuality. It has the freshness of the first strong artistic impulse of an enthusiast, imbedded in strong talent. It also possesses that germ of which our country's art is in such great need — the native spirit and national motive. Personally, Mr. Borglum impresses one much as does his work. He seems the very essence of will, and apparently whatever he conceives is destined to be realized in the sense of execution."

In conclusion the newspaper reported: "So much were visitors interested in Mr. Borglum's work that of the piece called 'Winter' twenty-four copies were sold."

The sales of this with other works enabled Solon to fulfill his long-cherished desire to go abroad and "take a look around." To stretch his money he worked his way over on a cattle boat. Having been awarded a full scholarship for the next year, Solon planned to return before Christmas.

"Seeking Shelter." Last known painting by Solon H. Borglum, 1897, unfinished. *Walter Russell.*

CHAPTER V

Why Paris?

The statement of fellow artists, quoted earlier,* refers to Solon's step of going to Paris as "a strange mixture of irony and dedication." [1] With their knowledge of both the man and the sculptor and student life in Paris, at that time, it continues "though in a sense in Paris he found himself, it might in a real sense be said that in Paris there was nothing else for him to find; . . . first, last and all the time, Solon Borglum was, and is, pure American." Solon's own statement to a reporter on his return to America confirms the idea: "I set out for Paris,[2] but when I got there I was suddenly dismayed. . . . I said to myself 'Why have I come?' and the whole time I stayed I struggled not to let my work lose its stamp of American life."

Why had he come? The question, a good one, provides the topic of this chapter. In spite of his remarks Solon's life taken as a whole does not support the idea that he put a low valuation on his Paris experience. Indeed the reverse is true. No experience could have taught him so much so quickly nor opened his eyes more effectually to what could be accomplished through sculpture. Sculpture

---

* See page 41. At the time of the posthumous publication of Borglum's book, SOUND CONSTRUCTION, dealing with his ideas about art, a committee was formed to assist in the difficult task of gathering together material, making necessary selections and issuing comments relating to his position among the artists, and his achievement as a sculptor. The Advisory Committee consisted of 18 prominent artists, among them: Herbert Adams, Robert I. Aitken, Paul W. Bartlett, George Grey Barnard, James Earle Fraser, E. H. Blashfield, Daniel Chester French, Anna Vaughan Hyatt, Hermon A. MacNeil, Frederick W. MacMonnies, Attilio Piccirilli.

was a comparatively new art form for Americans, the boundless possibilities of which would strike Solon with tremendous force as he wandered through the maze of Paris streets and squares and visited the many museums. In consequence his assertion that he did not touch brushes again[3] after reaching Paris can be accepted. He had much to learn; and who could better teach him than the French masters, at that time the best in the world? The experience could have been the most broadening of his life.

A true instinct brought Solon to Paris. A leading critic of the time who was a familiar figure on both sides of the Atlantic, Charles H. Caffin, is authority for the observation that "there is not a thought wave[4] in art that did not emanate from or finally reach Paris"; he called Paris "the world's clearing house of artistic currency."

A fresh vigor had come in the last generation or two to the ancient art of sculpture, producing a genuine renaissance, and it had happened in France. Inspired by renewed contact with nature, and by a more realistic if still romantic treatment of it, the smooth lines of neoclassicism typified by the Italian Canova and the Dane Thorwaldsen had given way to a style called the Beaux-Arts, which was a mixture of the new realism and the impressionism that was so fashionable in painting at the time. Among the initiators of this new style were the Frenchmen: François Rude (1784–1855), Jean Falguière (1831–1900), Jean Carpeaux (1827–1875), Henri Chapu (1833–1891), and the first and greatest of all animal sculptors, Antoine Louis Barye (1796–1875).

It is not irrelevant to consider at the outset what confronted Solon, the student, during his stay in Paris. Much of the early life of these French artists had its appeal for the former cowboy. Before becoming sculptors, Rude and Carpeaux had worked with their hands, the former as a coppersmith, the latter as a mason. Barye's concern with the anatomical perfection of his animals would impress a student who could, as was said of Solon, have qualified for a diploma in anatomy. As for natural drama, another leading French master, Emmanuel Frémiet (1824–1910), specially noted for his animal sculptures, did not hesitate on occasion to depict dramatically the savagery of nature; the ape in his "Gorilla and the Captive Woman" breathing defiance, grips his victim with one hand while with the other he clenches a rock to hurl at his attacker.

As a matter of record, Borglum has been compared to Barye, but chiefly, it will be noted, to emphasize the difference between the two artists. Caffin said of

Borglum's work: "In breadth of handling[5] and his knowledge of animal structure and movement we might compare him with Barye; only to find, however, that the latter far excels him in nobility of line and mass, and falls as far behind him in expression of sentiment."

A recent arrival among these French masters was Auguste Rodin (1840–1917), destined to be perhaps the greatest of them all. Though long considered a highly controversial figure, Americans were particularly questioning the greatness of that antithesis of classicism — as Mrs. Proske aptly put it,[6] approaching "the great master gingerly." Attempts have at times been made to include Solon as one coming under Rodin's wide influence. Thus Caffin in his appreciation of Solon's art[7] has this to say: "In its disregard of symmetrical composition, in the frequent appearances of passages left suggestively in the rough, and in the vivid naturalness that characterizes it, we may for a moment fancy that we detect the influence of Rodin." But Caffin is quick to note a marked difference between the two sculptors, saying that Borglum's work shows "none of the latter's feeling for subtlety of modeling and by comparison is crude; moreover the point of view of each is widely different." While Rodin's art is profoundly analytical and introspective, Borglum's is "spontaneous and instinctive, aiming to interpret in a vigorous *ensemble* the vivid impression of an objective fact." There is no record however of any personal contact between the two men.

Rodin's "Balzac" was a sensation of the Paris art world soon after Solon's arrival. It must have made a deep impression on Solon Borglum for he told the story[8] to one of his own students many years later to illustrate the possibilities inherent in abstract art. Solon had visited the Salon soon after reading a short life of Balzac at a nearby bookstall on the quais. One of the first works he saw there was Rodin's sculptured "Balzac" "with a heated and an argumentative crowd about it." To Solon, Balzac himself seemed there before him in that monolith of a figure with its defiant head. That, he told his young friend, was what he considered abstract work. "The truth, the soul of the subject were there and complete, without the insistence upon detail and petty fact. Balzac, the soul of Balzac, lived in this figure, while Balzac's collars and shirts and ties remained at home in the wardrobe where they belonged."

In the statement to the news reporter Solon conceded[9] that he could learn in Paris what he did not want to be, namely an American who went to Europe but became in the process a European, absorbing the mythology and the classicism "which in Europe are the true thing but which in America are not true." Solon had reason for the thought since many of his countrymen lingered on abroad preferring the pleasant congenial atmosphere found there to the cold indifference, if not outright hostility, which too often confronted the native artist in his homeland.

If we were to select one of his American predecessors as a spiritual ancestor it would be Henry Kirke Brown (1814–1886), who after four years in Italy returned home imbued with one idea — to make American art, American subjects, done in American style, his life's work. "All art," [10] Brown wrote on this theme, "to become of any national importance or interest, must grow out of the feelings and the habits of the people and we have no need of the symbols or conventionalities of other nations to express ourselves. Our country has a rich and beautiful history to illustrate . . . every American artist should endeavor to infuse into his works all the vitality and national policy in his power that when future generations shall look back upon his work they may see that he has expressed himself with truthfulness and honesty."

Solon Borglum could have used those exact words. What he did say was, "I wish I could tell you[11] how deep in me lies this American idea; how sacred to me is the ambition to make my work typically American, to have it express the democracy, the splendid youth, the crudeness too, if you will, of my native country. Such ambition in us all is the only basis of a great national life."

The substitution of Paris for Rome and Florence as a mecca for American artists — which has since been reversed — began 30 years before Solon came to Paris. Previously, with their neoclassical art, Horatio Greenough, Hiram Powers and Thomas Crawford, who preferred to live abroad, had dominated American sculpture. The substitution began in 1867 when Augustus Saint-Gaudens came to the French capital for the first time, gaining admittance to the exclusive and prestigious Ecole des Beaux-Arts. With this as the first of a noteworthy series of firsts for his countrymen, Saint-Gaudens' name and personality assume the utmost significance. Second, Saint-Gaudens made his own country his base of operations, which ended the preceding expatriation. Third, his first major work was done in Rome but with no trace of the Classic; it was an American subject — Hiawatha. In establishing this new direction for American artists, especially with his influence spanning most of the new era, he richly justified being called "Father of American Sculpture."

In his use of American subjects done with a new and "invigorating naturalism" Saint-Gaudens' statue of Admiral Farragut, unveiled in New York in 1881, is a milestone. Among his other "firsts", Saint-Gaudens applied the term abstract to one of his works. His depiction of "Silence" did not come under the influence of the neo-classic. The concept of "silence" is a universal one, belonging to no specific period, and Saint-Gaudens had adopted *le style libre*. This is a most important innovation and was to inspire many future sculptors, including Solon Borglum.

The presence of Augustus Saint-Gaudens in Paris attracted other artists, among them Frederick W. MacMonnies, his associate. MacMonnies became a favorite of the French, who honored him many times. His work was described as "daring, decorative,[12] inventive, exciting and prolific." He came to public attention in 1889 with a Diana, a classical subject treated in a non-classical manner. For his statue of Nathan Hale, erected in City Hall Park, New York City (1890), no likeness was to be found. The sculptor had to rely on his own imagination. He chose to depict the moment just before his execution when Nathan Hale spoke his defiant words, "I only regret I have but one life to lose for my country." In the creation of this work MacMonnies produced a statue about which this has been written: "The smooth surface of mid-century statuary[13] has been replaced by the lively textured ones typical of the Parisian school, and the entire image is endowed with a spiritual animation that was seldom obtained before the last quarter of the century. With the face alive with emotion and the hands betraying the helplessness of the bound man, the artist sought to carry his work beyond mere portraiture." Another of MacMonnies' works, his Bacchante, which scandalized Boston, revealed an uninhibited *joie de vivre*. A replica of it which attracted members of the American artist colony in Paris was presented by the French government to the Luxembourg Museum with the Legion of Honor for its creator — the first American piece of sculpture to be so honored (1893).

Other American artists who chose Paris over Rome include Bela L. Pratt, Hermon MacNeil and Alexander Phimister Proctor. Pratt (1867–1917), the son of a Norwich, Connecticut, lawyer and described as "one of the finest sculptors[14] in the Boston area during those years," first came to Paris in 1890, entered the Ecole des Beaux-Arts, worked in the ateliers of Chapu and Falguière, and was back again now, having in the meantime done work for the Columbian Exposition in Chicago. MacNeil (1866–1947), a Yankee from Massachusetts, had also come to Paris earlier (1888), studied with Chapu at the Académie Julian and with Falguière at the Ecole des Beaux-Arts and was considered a deft exponent of the new style. He too had worked on Indian figures, doing a full-size portrait of Black Pipe for the Chicago Exposition. His most popular work was his "Sun Vow," which he did in Paris receiving a silver medal at the Exposition Universelle in 1900. Proctor (1862–1950), like Solon Borglum, was a Westerner from Colorado where he had known the blizzard's bite and the loneliness of the snowbound cabin. He too, as a boy, enjoyed companionship with Indian children. Answering the call of art at 16, he had come to New York to study at the Art Students' League and the National Academy of Design. He had now come to Paris to study with Denys Puech.

There was Solon's special friend of the future, Cyrus E. Dallin (1861–1944), "The Sculptor of the Indians." Also of pioneer stock Dallin was born in Utah near Salt Lake City, son of a mining engineer. Like Borglum and Proctor, Dallin had Indian children as playmates and grew up to respect and sympathize with the Indian way of life. At age of 19, Dallin came first to Paris in 1888 as a pupil of Chapu at the Académie Julian, though he too like Solon absorbed no more than the techniques of his trade. From the first his heart and interest were directed toward immortalizing the old life of the West. The first of Dallin's four noted equestrian statues of Indians, "Signal of Peace," exhibited at the Columbian Exposition, showed his great understanding and profound sympathy with the red man's problem and dilemma in dealing with the whites. A charter member of the National Sculpture Society, Dallin returned to Paris the same year that Borglum arrived, and in the Salon of 1899 he showed the second of his Indian equestrians, "Medicine Man," again capturing the dignity, pathos and tragedy of the race. "Medicine Man" was a statue that gained praise from the sophisticated French critics, being awarded a medal and a place of honor at the Paris Exposition the following year. After returning home to take up residence in Boston Dallin continued to cultivate those subjects and interests.

Of other American artists who played a part in Solon's subsequent career, Daniel Chester French created "The Minute Man" familiar to all who remember World War One. He came to prominence at the Chicago Fair and was in Paris in 1900 for the unveiling of his "Washington," in time to commemorate both his nation's Independence Day and France's Bastille Day. Lorado Taft mixed sculpture with writing and lecturing throughout his life. His 'History of

American Sculpture', first published in 1903, was later brought up to date in a revised edition which remains an authority in the history of American Sculpture. He studied at the Ecole des Beaux-Arts, and was always well-liked and respected in the art world. James Earle Fraser, a younger man than Solon, was Saint-Gaudens' assistant during his student days in Paris. He had also joined the class of Falguière at the Beaux-Arts and exhibited at the Salon of 1898. Fraser, whose first contact with the plastic art came on his father's South Dakota Ranch, was a Minnesotan; thus he swells the list of sculptors of Western origin. He settled in the East and for many years was Solon's neighbor in nearby Westport, Connecticut. A builder of many important monuments, he is however best remembered for his rendering of the buffalo on the nickel and a group depicting the final defeat of the American Indian, "End of The Trail."

Beaux-Arts, the name of the style in which all these artists worked, including Solon, though in his case with reservations, proclaims its foreign origin, deriving its name from that famous Paris art school which was once so popular with Americans. The style is architectural in origin dating from the great days of the architects, Richard Morris Hunt, H. H. Richardson, and the firm of McKim, Mead and White — architects who made the designing of the magnificent mansions according to the taste and affluence of leaders of fashion principal monuments of the age. One can see but little difference between the work of the American adaptors and the French originators. If there is a subtle difference, it lies in spontaniety, greater freedom of expression, Americans being a little less hampered by tradition. The eye attuned to the cultural and political characteristics of the two societies becomes aware that there must be a difference, that there must be more inspiration to democracy. In American monuments one is brought a little closer to the people, in a physical sense they become touchable; witness the life-size Hans Christian Andersen done by George Lober and erected in New York City's Central Park. The companion of children, seated, book in hand, attracts boys and girls of all sizes who perch themselves on his lap, his arms or shoulders, as though he were truly there. It may be homely art but it captures attention because one thrills to a basic human appeal, gaining a sense of the oneness of humanity, which is after all only to be expected of a style that has crossed the Atlantic to make a home in the new world.

Perhaps, too, at long last Henry Kirke Brown's admonition to his fellow artists to stick to American subjects was bearing fruit.

Among Solon's early drawings is a street scene in Paris. It is inscribed, "Arrived Paris — July 1897." Optimistically Solon had established himself at the Hotel de la Haute Loire but his limited means soon brought about a change of residence, which is described by his future wife, Emma; "All the time[15] . . . in Paris, except the first days at the Hotel de la Haute Loire, he lived in a most primitive way, cooking his meals on the oil stove which had been his faithful companion. Soon he was rich enough to buy oatmeal in large quantity, it was easy to cook and the grocer store on Boulevard Montparnasse, almost around the corner, had it. One had to ask for Quaker Oats which is called something like *Kakair* for Quaker. Of course there was no cream or milk with it, but there was always as much as needed."

The hours not absorbed by visits to the famous museums, which he had haunted during his first weeks, he employed touring the city streets, studying the sculpture which decorated most of the parks. These excursions proved to be perplexing to a foreigner more accustomed to guiding his travels in the illimitable space on the Plains by the stars.

Toward the end of the summer, with his meager funds running low, Solon made what he thought would be a farewell visit to a favorite spot, Le Jardin des Plantes, the Paris zoo, to sketch lions. A. Phimister Proctor had the same thought; the two Americans met and introduced themselves. Interested in what the younger man was doing, Proctor invited him to his studio. Here Solon met Bela Pratt. On learning that Solon had no place in which to work, Pratt offered him what has been described as a woodshed and tool shop combined, doubtless large and roomy.

One day, Solon did more than pass a livery stable on Boulevard Raspail near his lodgings, he stopped and went in, with the inevitable result — the Cincinnati experience was repeated. The steel filing was once more drawn to its magnet! To talk with the cabbies Solon instinctively used the sign language he had learned in childhood to converse with his Indian friends. His pleasant manner did the rest. Once admitted to the stables, it did not take him long to make a discovery. Among his new friends in the stalls he recognized the unmistakable lines of the mustang. Buffalo Bill had recently completed a European tour and before sailing for home had sold off some of his ponies to defray expenses.

Now with a place to work and live subjects for models, his mind active with ideas, only one needful thing remained: Western equipment. He wrote his father. Presently two Western saddles were on their way to Paris, and Solon was on his way to fame.

The chance meeting that was to revolutionize Solon's Paris life is best described in a news article published in 1912. Three old friends were gathered in Bela Pratt's studio reminiscing about their participation in the Chicago World's Fair, the Columbian Exposition of 1893. Suddenly their host interrupted the flow of talk, "Say, boys, come out here[16] and take a peep at my back shed, I have something to show you." With that he led his friends, Augustus Saint-Gaudens and Frederick MacMonnies, out the back door to his toolshed where they discovered "a studio, bedroom and workshed combined, its occupant absorbed in modelling." Both men, we are told, were impressed by what they saw nearing completion.

The group, "Lassoing Wild Horses," [17] that became "a living, breathing thing" under the sculptor's hand, was far removed "from those classical subjects which often dominate the young American student living and working abroad." The lithe, tense figures of the cowboys, one of them sitting his horse erect, with an arm upraised in the act of throwing the lariat, the other clinging confidently to his struggling bronco, "epitomized the wild free life of the West and thrilled the beholder with a sense of primitive strength and power . . ."

Saint-Gaudens gave Borglum criticisms and introduced him to Emmanuel Frémiet. Frémiet quickly endorsed Saint-Gaudens' high opinion and advised Solon to stay in Paris for further study, with particular attention to techniques. Techniques include the making of armatures and durable plasters, in both of which skills Solon Borglum became notably proficient as recent castings of his work prove. We are afforded a glimpse of Solon doing what was customary in those days, hiring a cab and riding across town to fetch Frémiet whom he now looked upon as his *master* to view something he had done and to give him a criticism.

The change of plan delighted Solon, he wrote Joseph Henry Gest, director of the Cincinnati Art Academy, requesting transfer of his scholarship to Paris. Permission granted, he enrolled in Denys Puech's life class at the Académie Julian. Saint-Gaudens continued to watch his progress with more than ordinary interest. The two men, despite the disparity of age and experience, had an affinity that extended beyond their art. Each in his own way was something of a perfectionist.

"Lassoing Wild Horses." Salon, Paris, 1898, Place of Honor; Exposition Internacional, 1810–1910, Buenos Aires, silver medal. R. W. Norton Art Gallery, Shreveport, Louisiana; The Cowboy Hall of Fame, Oklahoma City, Oklahoma; The Detroit Institute of Arts, Detroit, Michigan. *Solon H. Borglum.*

The next few years were to be crucial for Solon, as they were crucial for his compatriots and for America. The Paris World's Fair, *L'Exposition Universelle,* and what it could mean to artists, was never far from the minds of any of them. Looking back to those years, one can see the Paris World's Fair at the turn of the century as an important link with the Columbian Exposition at Chicago, vital to the emergence of American sculpture. The importance of these world's fairs, which punctuate in turn the life of almost every Western center of culture and population, must here be emphasized. They played a conspicuous role in Solon's career, as they did in that of many artists on both sides of the Atlantic, and we shall have occasion in this book to mention them from time to time. It is difficult indeed to imagine the artist subsisting without these periods of stimulation to his art. They developed his talents; they enabled him to make comparisons with other artists; they gave him fresh ideas; they spread knowledge and appreciation of his unique gifts; they provided, not infrequently, the economic substance that enabled him to continue his craft. They appear essential to his very existence.

The Philadelphia Fair in 1876, marking the centennial of the nation's birth, has since come to be regarded as a landmark in American art history, providing the native artist with his first genuine impetus on American soil. Not because his work had any real part in the exhibit but because he was able for the first time to see what was being done abroad. It opened his eyes to the possibilities of sculpture as a decorative and practical art, giving reality to his aspiration. Similarly the Columbian Exposition of 1893, held in Chicago to celebrate the discovery of America, is a second landmark in the development of American art. For the first time America demonstrated to the world that there were now outstanding native sculptors who had been schooled abroad. Then it was that the Beaux-Arts style finally dominated the American scene. The establishment of the National Sculpture Society in the same year was a natural result of the gathering together of an imposing group of native American sculptors, giving status and standards to the "new art," attaining equality with painting and architecture it had previously lacked.

The plastic art became not only popular but lucrative. Captains of industry vied with politicians in decorating public buildings and parks with statues of noted men, lavishing commissions on their designers in a hitherto unheard-of way. Not since the Renaissance, noted Saint-Gaudens, himself often called "a Renaissance Man," had there been anything to compare with the assemblage of sculptors for the Columbian Exposition. For the first time in history American sculptors could look their European confrères in the face without feeling inferior. The new eminence of Americans became frequently visible in the parks and squares of Paris, where the equestrian monument of George Washington, erected in the Tuilleries Garden, was the work of Daniel Chester French and his collaborator E. C. Potter. It was shortly to be joined by Paul Bartlett's statue of Lafayette. Clearly the great Republic across the seas had come of age culturally, industrially and politically.

It says much about Solon Borglum's personality and single-minded dedication to his art that so little of the events of the time is visible in the records he left behind. The Dreyfus Affair was raging with all the fury of a civil war almost from the first day of his arrival; that prophetic voice of social reform, Emile Zola, went on trial soon afterward. But one would not know any of this from what Solon is reported to have said or written at the time; the story of his stay in Paris could be told without their mention. In the same way events in America left no visible impress. America might have a new President, William McKinley; the economic depression which paralyzed the nation in the nineties, spawning the Populist movement, could end; the Spanish American War could agitate the world's chanceries and newspaper offices; business could give the nation the highest tariff in history, all apparently without disturbing the even tenor of Solon's stern application to his art. And why should it be otherwise? Despite internal political upheavals Paris, the City of Light, the scars of 1870 erased, was the acknowledged cultural capital of the world, its glamor undiminished; its Eiffel Tower, built to demonstrate the use of steel in celebration of the centennial of the Revolution of 1789, still the highest edifice in the world. One can only conclude that Solon found the atmosphere so stimulating to his art and generally satisfying that nothing else claimed any part of his attention.

When he was allowed to use his scholarship in Paris it became necessary for him, a poor correspondent at best, to report his progress to his old school, the Cincinnati Art Academy. In a letter dated Washington's Birthday, February 22, 1898 his former teacher Louis Rebisso wrote: "Dear Friend Solon . . . I suppose M. Frémiet was over to look at your work. I saw the two photos you referred to in your letter, Miss Gray had them and I had the pleasure of a good look at them.

I am indeed much pleased with them and am waiting for the others which will
be taken before you are ready for casting. I am anxious to hear what M. Frémiet
has said in regard to your work. Don't fail to let me know. Have you entered in
the Academy or any other school? I have been asked the question — and I said
not to my knowledge . . . The war cloud seems to hang over the horizon at
present. Spain seems bent to try the U. S. . . ." He closed with the words
". . . will always be pleased to hear good things of you, from your faithful
friend, Louis T. Rebisso, Sr."

When the group "Lassoing Wild Horses" was finished it was sent to the
Salon, which accepted it and gave it a place of prominence. With it was also the
statuette of a little horse of the Plains, suffering in the cold, titled "Winter." His
Cincinnati friends were so pleased with Solon's rapid progress and success that
some twenty of them,* headed by Albert T. Goshorn, decided to purchase
"Winter" for the sum of $300, and present it to the Cincinnati Museum. Solon
received the money "a little at a time" because he had already gained the
reputation of being unable to keep money in his pocket. He had come perilously
close to losing the friendship of the Allens when they learned that the $60 they
had given him to be put aside "in case of an emergency" had landed in Gutzon's
pocket. Solon would be the last person in the world to think about emergencies
and he was as openhanded with money if some one was in need as he was frugal
in respect to his own physical wants. Alphaeus Cole, his studio mate, recalls how
quickly he fell for the sad tale of a marble cutter who came to the door with his
arm bandaged and unable, he said, to work because of his arm. Solon had no
money and borrowed a few francs from Cole promising to pay him back later,
which he did. But they never saw "the rogue" again.

Independent, proud and shy, Solon may have deliberately chosen the
solitary way in this teeming metropolis, but such stubborn independence could
have had the opposite result, attracting friends who knew that it would be hard
going to make it alone, especially for one of his sensitive nature. Following
Saint-Gaudens' lead he was included more and more frequently in the informal
gatherings that were so popular among Americans. Joanne Holbein, daughter of
Phimister Proctor,[18] tells of one of these gatherings at which grown men played

* Among them: W. W. Taylor; M. E. Ingals; D. H. Holmes; Alexander McDonald; L. B.
Harrison; J. A. Schmidlapp; J. G. Schmidlapp; Albert T. Goshorn.

games with lead soldiers, cannon and home-made gunpowder. How on one occasion they defeated the concierge is a story in itself, for Mrs. Proctor, herself an artist, had painted out the damage done the wallpaper when the bullets went astray! Like cowboys around a campfire they would swap stories and experiences with characteristic relish. Solon was among them, and Joanne recalls her parents' admiration for his work, ". . . and Dad was inclined to be very critical of other sculptors . . . I remember very well hearing both Mody (her mother) and Dad tell how much they loved him — and they used those words!"

After his debut at the Salon of 1898 and the recognition that followed, Solon acquired a large studio specially for the making of a life-size group of stampeding horses. He shared this studio on 16 rue Boissonnade with Alphaeus Cole who was studying painting in Paris. During this period Solon discovered or was discovered by the McIlwaines who became life-long friends. David McIlwaine, Albert Goshorn's cousin, was in Paris with his wife and two daughters, May and Isabel, all of whom were to play key roles in Solon's life in America. Thus Solon was no longer the friendless lonely Westerner he had been when he arrived in Paris.

In a sense Solon had arrived twice — once physically when he came to "look around" as a student, again as an artist. And the second "arrival" was to be far more important for his career: it gave him not only distinctiveness, which none would be able to take away from him, but provided the authentic Horatio Alger touch to his debut.

CHAPTER VI

A Paris Bride in Indian Country

"Solon is busy and in love, which is double occupation." [1] Lisa Borglum's remark sets the stage for this chapter.

Solon's marriage to Emma Vignal, a Frenchwoman, needs a word of explanation. It alarmed his family in Omaha and stunned, even angered, many of his friends and well-wishers. Why did he tie himself down at this crucial moment, and why to a foreigner? A foreigner was unlikely to have much in common with this pioneer from America's West, the very opposite of all that a sophisticated Parisienne would take for granted in a husband? The thought of what such a marriage would do to his career was painful.

Clement Barnhorn, soon to succeed Rebisso as head of the Cincinnati Art Academy's sculpture department, was responsible[2] for bringing Solon and Emma together, but he must be acquitted of any matrimonial intentions, if only because he was a confirmed bachelor. The Vignals were old friends. He knew that a newcomer, especially one as interesting as the Academy's star student, would be welcomed in their hospitable home. From Solon's standpoint Barnhorn sensed that some social life would be beneficial. He could scarcely do better than introduce him to a home such as the Vignal's where culture and religion intermingled. Pastor and Mme. Vignal's daughters were charming and gifted musicians in their early thirties with diplomas from the University of Paris, and years of sojourns in England. They had their own studio in the family's spacious home, where they entertained fellow artists, many of whom were Americans.

Jean Vignal was a Baptist minister with his own brand of pioneering. Years before on a visit to England he had come under the influence of American Baptist missionaries. A family account describes how on his return he went into the Pyranes, disturbed in faith, unsettled in mind. After several months of study and meditation he became a Protestant, possessed with the idea of being a missionary in Paris. His little church, the first Baptist church in Paris, was located on the rue de Lille, close to the Seine and its famous quais on the left bank. He remained its pastor until near the end of his long and dedicated life.

Pastor Vignal's family, with reason, regarded him as the symbol of all goodness, its devotion to him giving the home a special character. Nevertheless, a Calvinist of Calvinists, Pastor Vignal was perhaps too strict, for while his children adored him, they respectfully went their own way. Lydie, the Pastor's wife, provided the needed balance, being more secular in her tastes, with social interests that stemmed from her own family. She never forgot that she was a Letalle, the family's lineage and social status being enviable.

With the siege of Paris, starting in 1870, Jean Vignal stayed with his flock while Lydie bundled her three children off to England for the duration. Old family ties were renewed and new ones cemented which all together served the children well in later years. Their English was the fluent and correct speech of an educated person, with the addition of a delightful French accent.

Foreign visitors are usually quick to learn where they are welcome. Many of those who found their way into the Vignals' unusual home did so by attending services in the little church of the rue de Lille. Not infrequently the pastor found his modest income augmented by a paying guest from overseas. One of the features of the services was singing by Emma, accompanied on the organ by her sister Lucy. Emma possessed a rich contralto voice and Lucy was on her way to being a concert pianist. Emma was noted for her beauty and wisdom, Lucy for her wit and vivacity. They not only used their studio for lessons in voice, piano and French, they gave recitals and soirées. Besides Barnhorn, guests included artist Timothy Cole, his wife and their two sons, Alphaeus, who presently shared Solon's large studio at 16, rue Boissonnade, and Lucius, the one a painter, the other a violinist. John M. Synge, the Irish playwright, who was a visitor at that time, added another violin to the musical ensemble.

Barnhorn had difficulty making the actual introduction at the Salon. Solon himself would certainly be at the *vernissage* as "Lassoing Wild Horses" had been given a place of honor. He wanted the two Vignal sisters to meet him there, confident that they would each engage the other's interest. But the plan miscarried. Solon with his cup of happiness overflowing was not in the mood for making what he thought would be ordinary social acquaintances and kept at a safe distance. He took in the situation, however, liked what he saw, and next day asked for the introduction he had avoided, but it was to Emma that he was particularly attracted.

An excellent portrait of Emma Vignal by Alphaeus Cole still hangs in the Solon Borglum Studio in Silvermine. It attests to her rare good looks. Dark curls cluster above a prominent brow; the no less prominent nose can only be called patrician; features are regular, face is oval; a "mona lisa" smile plays around the lips. In addition, alert and studious, Emma could boast a superior education. In after years she would claim that she had gone as far academically as a Parisienne of that day could. Her knowledge of literature and music, and cultural matters in general, was so much above the average she could hold her own in any company. An early home had been close to the Faubourg St. Germain where she had had interesting neighbors. She recalled how François Coppée's "wonderful blue eyes" had shone in his dark Roman face, and she remembered Barbey d'Aurevilly, Alphonse Daudet, and other noted figures. Of all her qualities none equalled her sagacity. She was to use her erudition, not to "score off" or compete with her husband, but in effect to enhance him. At the same time she took great delight in reminding people that it was *her* native land that had discovered his genius.

First they went sightseeing, Barnhorn, Solon and two other Cincinnati art teachers in Paris for the first time, guided by Emma, who confessed that she too was seeing her city for the first time. "That spring," said Emma, "I learned about Paris, and I learned also what a good man Solon Borglum was."

In the summer the sisters visited England as usual. As Emma could not take her fox terrier she accepted Solon's offer to care for it. Upon her return, there began a whirlwind courtship. "The first week after my return Solon came twice to spend the evening. The next week more often. The next we were engaged, not knowing when we would have an income large enough to get married." She need not have worried! She was engaged to a man with an immense confidence in his own future.

They were married on December 10, 1898 — twelve days short of Solon's 30th birthday. Emma was 34.

Emma Vignal Borglum, 1899   Painted by Alphaeus Cole, Paris. *Walter Russell.*

An American newswriter gives the reason why Solon and Emma could not take an immediate honeymoon. Georgia Frazier, who covered the Paris Salons for her paper, was not impressed with most of the works on display, though the standard was higher than in the past. "The freaks are few in number and the poor work is less in evidence," she stated bluntly. There were no sensations; the leaders from America were not represented; and if they had arrived in Paris they were holding back for the coming exposition. There was nothing at all noteworthy in the so-called "New Salon," according to her view; many of the sculptors avoided it entirely, remaining loyal to the old Salon. But one piece in the Salon attracted her attention. It had been awarded the "Honorable Mention." She wrote: "Borglum the sculptor has a spirited group, "Wild Horses on the Edge of a Precipice," calling it "one of the best and most noticeable things in the sculpture gallery." Her article in *Art Education* was illustrated with a photograph of the group. We shall hear more of that group, under a different title, "Stampede of Wild Horses."

Six months after their marriage, June 15, 1899, Emma and Solon left on their deferred trip.

Solon's plan was to spend the summer in South Dakota, visiting the Sioux. He made the arrangements with Hackeliah Burt, missionary at Crow Creek (still known as Fort Thompson), through the friend of his ranching days, Bishop Hare. The needed funds were advanced by Emma's brother Paul, a rising French Army officer, graduate of the Ecole Polytechnique, who had just been appointed military attaché at the embassy in Washington.

The date set for their arrival among the Sioux was July 4th. There was a special reason for the selection of that date, for it was the day the United States government permitted them to foregather as in the past. Only on that singularly chosen occasion could the former lords of the prairie again wear their regalia, perform their tribal rituals, chant their familiar songs, and possibly forget their recent unhappy experiences. However, if an artist wanted to catch that moment before it vanished, he had to hurry for it was already passing. The new life of the reservation would soon be the only one the Sioux would be allowed to know.

The railroad failed the visitors. Instead of depositing Solon and Emma at the nearest rail point, Chamberlain, South Dakota, in time to catch the stage to

"Stampede of Wild Horses." Horses rearing before a precipice. Salon, Paris, 1898, Honorable Mention; Exposition Universelle, Paris, 1900; Cincinnati Art Academy.

Fort Thompson, it was already six p.m. on Independence Day and there were still thirty miles to go. They had missed the last stage.

The rest of their story is best told in the account Emma wrote for her family and friends. The translation reads as follows:

"My husband went everywhere to find a buggy and a driver, but all the horses had been used for the celebration and the sixty-mile round trip made a problem for the driver. We were hungry and we went to a hotel for our dinner, waiting for Providence to help us. Everyone in Chamberlain knew that we would pay any amount for a buggy and driver. As we were finishing our dinner, Providence presented itself to us in the form of a cowboy, a tall, thin man dressed in leather trousers, which I learned were called chaps, a black shirt, long hair, dirty face, and on top of that an enormous felt hat. The man answered to the name of Rattlesnake Jim. We asked him how long it would take to cover the distance to Crow Creek. 'Four hours would be sufficient,' he said, 'Indian ponies can stand a lot.' We began smiling again. It was seven o'clock and we accepted with joy. Only, the ponies were not in Chamberlain. Rattlesnake Jim had to go and get them. We waited two hours, until nine o'clock, with night falling. Just as we were starting, a man asked if he could go with us to Crow Creek. He looked respectable so we accepted him gladly; I was thankful because the appearance of our driver, who looked like a bandit, which did not seem to worry my husband, frightened me terribly. The night was dark and very cold. The innkeeper, a good soul, lent me an old horse blanket and a raincoat. And so we started on our trip in the midst of rockets and firecrackers celebrating the Fourth.

"I was astonished to notice that on such a dark night our man did not light any lantern. I could not see the road. My remarks started our companion laughing and the driver let out a kind of horselaugh with an oath. He never had a lantern. I could not see the road because there was no road. We simply followed the ruts which had been made by the wheels that had preceded ours for years. In some places they were a foot or more deep, but this attracted no one's attention but mine. In the few months we were on the Plains I became used to those roads. They were only bad when you had to get out of the rut."

Shifting to the present tense Emma continues. "We go up a steep hill, the horses are breathing hard. We arrive at the top, and I hope the poor beasts can rest a little. Illusion . . . The driver whips them with all his might. Then begins a crazy run. The buggy jumps to the right, then to the left, sometimes it jumps right out of the rut. Now we feel the road going down. Fortunately we cannot see the ravine, which is immediately to our right. A jolt, a little stronger one, and the back seat on which my husband and I are seated slips and we find ourselves tumbled on the floor in the middle of our sacks of provisions. Rattlesnake Jim stops his team and helps us to put back the seat. He advises us to be careful as one of the back wheels is very weak. I really believe that my husband is beginning to feel a little uneasy although he comes from the Far West. Then we continue . . .

"We are in a low place now and can hear the noise of the wheels and the horses' feet in the water. The rut has disappeared. Suddenly, the buggy stops, one of the horses is down. We all jump out. We are not in water but in mud. The poor beast struggles, making muffled sounds. My husband is afraid it is the death rattle. The driver swears some more, fearing the trip will cost him a lot. They unhitch. We are in the mud to the top of our boots. It is now midnight and we hope to be in Crow Creek soon. Sweet illusion! Rain is threatening. If we could revive the horse, perhaps we could continue on slowly. Rattlesnake Jim regrets he has no whiskey, a remedy he has used on his horse as well as on himself. We have none, but our companion has. The men force the horse's mouth open and pour in a pint. When the horse ceases groaning the three men lift him. He falls again, but the second time he walks a few steps, trembling all over. Our driver, an habitual drunkard who knows how to conceal his condition, has only a faint idea now of his direction. . . . It is a good thing the horses know the way, better able than their master to conduct us to where we are going."

After a few less hair-raising moments, they reach their destination at four a.m., just as the sky was paling. There they found their hosts, Mr. and Mrs. Burt, not expecting them, their wire having miscarried. No matter, the Burts were delighted to extend a welcome. Solon and Emma discovered to their joy that they had not missed the entire celebration, which was to continue another day. The sight that met their eyes when they arose was ample reward for the arduous journey. Emma counted no fewer than 600 tepees, stretched out in a wide circle over the plain. A wonderful sight such as few were privileged to see again.

The change in Solon was something Emma noticed at once, impressing her as much as anything that had happened since she had known him. He came alive in a way he had not done in Paris. This was his home. The life she saw was his. The Plains, even the mirages, were "his old friends." She spoke of the "unmitigated sun, with no trees, no shade," air so full of alkali the least gust made it electric. The whole atmosphere of the country was plainly his. Emma, who only "shriveled" in the dryness, so different from Paris, could scarcely in fact have entered into the adventure better if, like her husband, she had grown up in the West. Solon's pride in his French wife increased greatly in the next few weeks. For her the very novelty of the experience, its utter contrast with what she had known, left an indelible impression.

A highlight of that remarkable summer was an eleven-day trip with a young Indian couple across the trackless prairie in a springless wagon. Solon and Emma shared the wagon by day and the tepee at night with Long Feather and his wife. This was an experience the Paris bride would never forget, and even, at first, accepted with reluctance. Mrs. Burt, the missionary's wife, reassured her, explaining that there was no need for embarrassment. If anyone misbehaved or caused embarrassment it would be the ones who did not know Indian etiquette.

It was so hot in the daytime, wrote Emma, they roasted, and at night so cold they had to break the ice before they could wash their faces. When they tried to protect their meat by putting it on top of the wagon, the eagles got it; when they tried putting it under the wagon, the coyotes got it. By the time they reached Yankton, for the Episcopal convention led by Bishop Hare, their faces were so covered with dust they could hardly be distinguished from the Indians.

On the way Emma encountered a French farmer who was married to an Indian woman and had not seen a countryman of his for forty years. "What did she think of him being married to a 'savage'?" he wanted to know. Emma cautiously replied that "he could have done worse."

"Is there anything I can do for you?" he politely asked. "Yes," she said emphatically, "there is." She had forgotten to bring her pillow and had been given the horse's feedbag as a substitute. "It is not such a bad pillow at first, but since the horse eats the oats, there is at last no more pillow. Will you be kind enough," she asked the Frenchman, "to fill my bag with *HAY?*"

The ever-important thing to Emma was her husband's work. "That was booming," she stated. In those words she reveals her deep understanding of him and the secret of their successful marriage. Her faith in him never wavered.

So that he could start modeling at once, Solon had brought along a supply of plasterlene and had ordered a barrel of plaster to be sent from Chicago. The plaster arrived at Chamberlain, but a fire broke out in the storehouse before he could pick it up and it was ruined by the water used to extinguish the fire. Solon had to order a fresh supply, which would take weeks to arrive. In desperation he looked everywhere for clay which he could use as a substitute. He even scraped the bluffs along the Missouri, but in vain as the region was all sand!

Witnessing a performance of the Buffalo Dance was among their more memorable experiences. Women imitated the neighing of horses, men reenacted the actions of the chase, and the medicine men took the roles of the animals. The episode was stored, like others, in the crucible of Solon's mind, emerging four years later as "The Sioux Indian Buffalo Dance."

One night, Solon's and Emma's sleep was interrupted by a fearsome noise issuing from the next tepee, which reminded Emma of the hooting of owls. Their missionary host explained it was the announcement of the death of a child. An epidemic was raging at the time, and eleven times in the course of their stay Solon's assistance was sought to toll the chapel bell for the funeral services, then join the little procession of wailing mourners as it wound its way up the bluff to the cemetery where these Indian Christians buried their dead at sundown. The result, "Burial on the Plains," became one of his more striking pieces.

Much more than ideas for future works of art emerge from these incidents. Deep and abiding sympathy was recorded for a people whose way of life had been ravaged and destroyed by the coming of the white man. "One can hardly believe when one lives in the middle of this population so quiet, so polite, so dignified in its movements," Emma writes, "that they could have been as cruel as history tells us. One forgets, generally, to relate the bad treatment, the unjust acts, and the treacheries which whites used to supplant the Indians on American soil. The only cruel thing I found among the Sioux Indians was the treatment of their horses and their dogs."

Emma was deeply impressed on learning that an Indian father had ridden for five days to find and bring back to justice an erring son. She observed that the Indian did not drink hard liquor, only water. In three months she never saw, she states, a drunken Indian, save those made drunk by their friend of that hair-raising drive who turned out to be a bootlegger. Neither did the Indians she saw fight, nor use loud words in their quarrels. The long silences of the council she witnessed and described were like a Quaker meeting. Compared with the Indian, the white man seemed to her often noisy, loud-mouthed and ill-mannered.

The Prairie Sculptor. Solon H. Borglum, summer 1899, among the Sioux Indians.

On their departure, the Sioux, whom "my husband and I had learned to love," movingly revealed their feelings. "We had a large box made up for the collection of buckskin clothes, bonnets, bags, etc. which we had bought. We had to have another box for things we had tried unsuccessfully to buy which were given to us when we said goodbye." Their hearts were heavy when that moment came, for Solon and Emma knew that they probably would never see their Indian friends again.

Nowhere in her journal, it is pertinent to point out, does Emma draw the obvious contrast between her Paris, the acknowledged center of world culture, and that spot on the rim of civilization where her husband took her for their deferred honeymoon. That she no longer shared the common belief in the infinite superiority of one civilization over the other can be the only conclusion. She had learned in these few weeks to view things differently, even in cultural matters. The Paris of that era, her Paris, was not a perfect model of human behavior. That she could see clearly. In France the era of the Dreyfus Case and the persecution of Emile Zola with its convulsion of savagery and emotion ruled all French politics.

It would of course be far-fetched to suggest that Emma was like Gauguin, deliberately escaping from the savageries of civilization to find something identifiable as genuine culture. Everything she put down in her account, however, implies this. It is not far-fetched to say that Solon Borglum's concept of America, and the art based on it, had henceforth to include those friends of his from the Great Plains, friends, as he would point out in the years to come, who sent his children gifts at Christmastime, his dear friends for life. He must then have formed the resolve to use his art to uplift those first *original* Americans, as he liked to remind people who criticized his devotion to them. In that resolution he would now have the strong support of his wife. "These things," Emma wrote, "had a mysterious appeal for him, his love for the West's past and hope for its future were keeping a life of its own in his heart."

The change that Emma had perceived in her husband becomes evident in his work. What he had shown at the Salons of 1898 and 1899 could be described, to employ Caffin's phrase, as "spontaneous anecdotes." They were memories of his life on the frontier, his experiences as a cowboy and rancher. Solon himself could have been the cowboy engaged in lassoing a wild horse, or the stunt rider, the original "Rough Rider," mounting his bronco in unorthodox manner, drawing his right leg to the front over the pummel of the saddle. In a few years' time this bit of exhibitionism would play its part in the rodeo. The same calm and confident guiding of the horse away from the ominous rattle of the snake curled up of "On the Trail" could be of himself, less dramatic perhaps but no less revealing of an expert knowledge. (Solon always said that a snake would not go out of its way to hurt anyone.) But to these anecdotes was now added a quality that gives Solon Borglum that uniqueness which distinguishes his work from Remington's and Russell's, from in fact most of the artists classifiable as "cowboy artists," as well as from other sculptors of the day. It is this that renders his work different from the Beaux-Arts style from which it sprang. It is also the quality that makes it different today and gives a claim to permanence. Recent retrospective showings have produced such comments as "Borglum sculpture is spirited, alive, active, authentic";[3] "it refreshes the spirit, it is a thing of health"; "it depicts the unity of humanity and nature."[4] In other words, Borglum's sculpture today is not considered dated by these critics it still possesses the ability to gain new friends[5] and evoke fresh enthusiasm. It cannot be dismissed as either sentimental or too refined, too literal.

Solon Borglum's artistry was perhaps most in evidence in knowing exactly *when* to stop. One of his pupils wryly tells of the time when she ignored her teacher's advice to leave her figure alone, it was "just right." But she had to add a few finishing touches, and thereby ruined her work.[6] In vain she then tried to recapture its original "feeling."

Another way of putting the matter of what distinguishes Borglum's work from the Beaux-Arts style is that he understood supremely well what he called, for want of a better term, "the abstract." (We should not call it that today as we reserve the term for the wholly abstract.) Perhaps "essence" would be a better term to describe what the sculptor sought. Caffin spoke of the "unfinished passages"[7] in the work of the new sculptor, which suggests the same thing. For what concerned Solon was the underlying truth of the situation he was describing. He considered details unimportant. One is reminded of what Gutzon Borglum said of his brother at the time of Solon's death: "His creations met (Michelangelo's) stricture in that they might roll down a mountain side and the best of them remain."

An illustration can be taken from the work of that summer — "Burial on The Plains." Quite small, not over 16 inches in height, its meaning cannot be

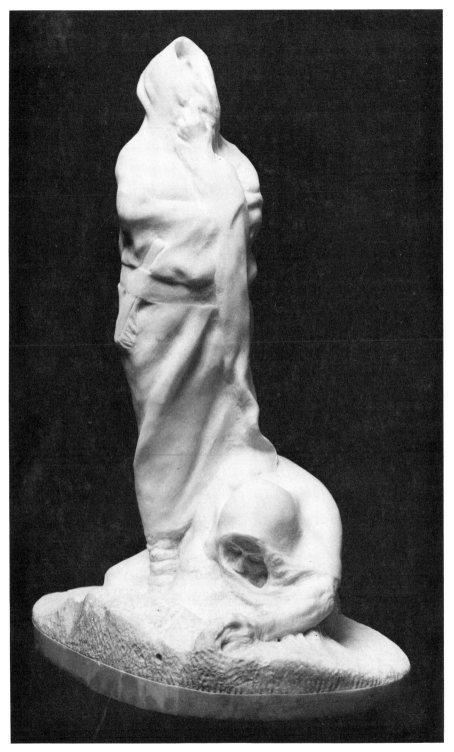

"Burial On The Plains." Marble, 1902. Height approx. 15½ in. (Sometimes called "Desolation.") *A. B. Bogart.*

taken in at a glance. Two women, both Indian Christians, are shown mourning over a slight mound of earth, the grave of a child. The standing figure is older and must be presumed to be the grandmother, who appears to be praying to the Great Spirit as her lips are parted and her head uplifted. The other, presumably the mother, is on her knees, cradling the little mound where her baby has been lain. The statue, embodying a drama often repeated that summer, caught the eye of the critic; Lorado Taft in his history speaks of "its mysterious emotional note, which has been touched by few indeed of our sculptors", possessing "a sentiment that might easily have been dissipated by a more insistent technique." It is even possible to consider this as having a deeper, more spiritual, concept of human grief than the famous statue, shortly to be seen by the Borglums, Augustus Saint-Gaudens' "Adams' Memorial" in Rock Creek.

"Bulls Fighting," another product of that summer, is to the casual eye just that, the title fits: two bulls are engaged in a death struggle, but examination shows that the bulls are different from one another. One is noticeably smaller and leaner, with long horns, whereas the other is larger, fatter, with shorter horns. The meaning? The artist is using the animals to depict the clash of civilizations, the primitive and the developed. The civilization that put beef on its cattle is the one that would triumph.

But it must not be thought that the reaction to Solon's sculpture was always favorable. Taft also wrote: "It cannot[8] be claimed that all Mr. Borglum's ideas are as artistic as these. He is not infallible in his intuitions; several of his groups show mistaken effort to depict rapid motion, and some are far from beautiful in line and composition. . . ."

The homeward trip was made by way of Omaha and Washington. In Omaha the visit was long enough to introduce Emma to her husband's family and to show the public the summer's work. An exhibition was held in the Hospé Auditorium. It consisted of two small sketches, each 16 inches high, a study of an Indian pony and five portrait busts of Indians, together with some of the mementoes which their new friends had showered upon them. The review in the local paper stressed the truthfulness of the work, especially the way the artist had caught the Indian spirit and idiom and imbued his work with them.

The loosening of ties in this once close-knit family had been evident for some time, the generation gap widening as the sons went their various ways. Dr.

Borglum had sent the saddles on Solon's request but the request itself could not have pleased the deeply concerned elder Borglum, who was coming to view his cowboy son as something of an enigma. Solon's independence and what he would himself have viewed as impracticality irked him. Solon's return to the life of the West, with only Indians as companions, must have increased his father's fears that his son was undermining the success that had just come to him in Paris. The anxiety is revealed in a letter Dr. Borglum wrote in response to Solon's request for biographical data. The doctor's own biography is evasive and incorrect. The advice he now gives his son[9] further betrays his feelings, underscoring a growing cleavage between them: "I send you here what you asked for, and that little is sufficient I think. The world, the mob, does not need to become acquainted with the particulars of our life. It is not their business and they don't care. In sending your biography you should leave out those sickening details about starvation, oatmeal, cowboy, etc. They give credit to nobody, nor sound any too well in print." . . .

In Washington, Solon called at the Department of Interior to convey the respects of the Sioux Chiefs as well as his own criticisms of the government for both the way the Indians were housed and the manner in which they received their allotted food.

Now for the first time Solon and Emma did a little conventional sight-seeing, visiting the White House, the Capitol. They saw Saint-Gaudens' "Adams' Memorial." Their friend's depiction of grief in the well-known work deeply impressed Emma. "It is so big," she said, "one can't give it a name; it is despair in all its horror; it is more than despair. The way it is placed adds to its effect. No statue has ever impressed me as did this one. One cannot forget it. It is great and terrible."

Shortly before the opening of the *Exposition Universelle* in 1900, the American jury for the sculpture exhibit came to Solon's studio, wishing to see if he had anything more to submit. Solon quickly replied that his life-size "Stampede of Wild Horses," which they had already requested, was available, and he was also sending a small "free standing" bronze buffalo. The committee of sculptors, Saint-Gaudens, MacMonnies, and Paul Bartlett, desiring fuller representation, asked about the group Solon was working on. He replied that he could not possibly finish it in time for the opening. "Finish it as soon as you

can," Saint-Gaudens said. "We will hold a place for it." Accordingly, a month or
so after the opening, this group, called then "The Scout," later renamed "On the
Border of White Man's Land," joined Solon's other works in the American
Pavilion. It depicted Black Eagle, one of Custer's favorite Indian scouts, peering
over a bluff to discover the plans of his hostile brothers, his pony standing by.

The *Exposition Universelle* was the highest point reached thus far in the story
of Franco-American relations; certainly, from the American standpoint, it was one
of the most exciting. Saint-Gaudens, acknowledged leader of his country whose
half French birth would not have been a handicap in France, carried off the chief
prizes, both at the Salon and the *Exposition*, with his "Puritan," his Boston "Shaw
Memorial" and the equestrian of Sherman, the statue that stands today in New
York at the corner of Fifth Avenue and 59th Street. Henry Adams, who was
present in Paris, expressed a common opinion that of all the American artists
Saint-Gaudens was the most sympathetic; which accounts for the fact that among
his many studio assistants and pupils Saint-Gaudens was not called "The Saint"
for no reason. Now his success was America's success. His countrymen besieged
him with congratulations. They sought to hug him, grasp his hand, anything to
show their appreciation of what he had done, for in addition to its artistry his
work was imbued with a lofty patriotism.

A notable absentee was John Quincy Adams Ward, perennial head of The
National Sculpture Society from its foundation. Where was, it could be asked,
that rival to Saint-Gaudens' claim of being "the father of American Sculpture"?
Born in Ohio, in 1830, of British stock, Ward's declared reason for not ever
following his fellows to Paris was that he feared, as he put it, his "sculptor's
manhood would be drawn from him" by what he found there. F. W. Ruckstull,
native of St. Louis and leader of the conservative element in sculpture, was
another notable stay-at-home.

France marked the occasion by building a new and special bridge across the
Seine, Pont Alexandre III, which reminded many that on the previous occasion of
playing host to the world, in celebration of the 100th anniversary of her great
Revolution of 1789, she had built the Eiffel Tower, still the highest structure in
the world.

Of the forty million people who flocked through the Porte Monumentale
on the Champs-Elysées that summer, it is safe to say that few could have missed

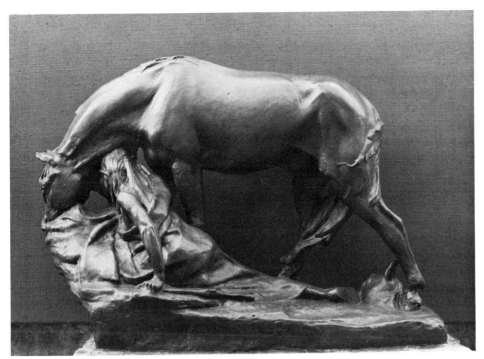

"On The Border of White Man's Land." Exposition Universelle, Paris, 1900, silver medal; The Metropolitan Museum of Art, New York City; Brookgreen Gardens, South Carolina. Height 20 in. *Metropolitan Museum.*

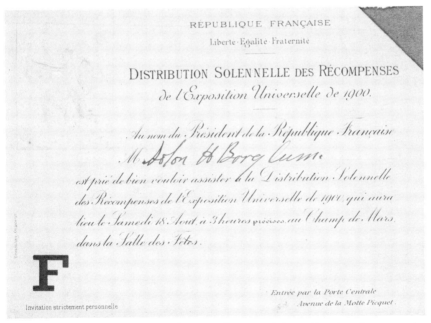

An actual invitation card entitled: Distribution Solennelle des Recompenses de l'Exposition Universelle, 1900.

the life-size group of horses, Solon's "Stampede of Wild Horses," which dominated the entrance of the United States Pavilion. Many would remember it for long afterward, with its late arriving companion, to be awarded a silver medal, and the little bronze "Buffalo," spelled "Bufflow," the recipient of a bronze medal. The critics awoke to the presence of a new sculptor, who was soon being called by the French, "Le Sculpteur de la Prairie."

Success piled upon success. In 1901 his own countrymen extended similar acknowledgment, awarding him a silver medal for his "remarkable success of 12 bronzes and marbles" at the Pan-American Exposition in Buffalo, rendered famous in history by the putting of T.R. into the White House through the assassination of President McKinley. 1901 saw Borglum's fellow artists invite him to join their newly-formed craft guild, The National Sculpture Society. Augustus Saint-Gaudens and Frederick MacMonnies were his sponsors.

In retrospect, the *Exposition Universelle* appears doubly an American triumph, the red American sharing the international stage with the white American. MacNeil won a silver medal for his "Sun Vow," and his "Moqui Runner" was praised by the critics; Proctor's "Indian Warrior" received a gold medal; Dallin got another for his "Medicine Man," and the Austrian government was reputedly chagrined because Philadelphia acquired "Medicine Man" for Fairmont Park. And as stated, Solon Borglum's "On The Border of White Man's Land" received a silver medal.

CHAPTER VII

New York

Solon had a quick answer for those who wanted to know the secret of his success: Hard work! And few artists have been carried farther by that means. Singleness of purpose and dedicated industry eliminated much that has complicated the lives of other artists. He had neither time, nor money, nor inclination for dissipation, or the Bohemian way of life associated with artists. But hard work can obviously be only half the explanation. One suspects the sculptor of evading the issue, if only because of his hearty aversion to being called a genius. Moreover, his total life history would not make sense if he had been only a talented hard-working artist, or even the genius he indignantly rejected. Nothing seems more surely to have aroused his temper than for flatterers to try to pin that particular label on him.

It is obvious that anyone striving so hard for excellence could not have been modest in regard to his work. Only to the non-artist world would that be Solon Borglum's attitude. Here he was governed by the same basic democracy which had marked his relations with his boys on the ranch, whom he refused to boss. The supreme aristocrat in all that pertained to his work, the complete democrat outside his studio, he lived simultaneously in two distinct worlds: great art and high ideals, ordinary people and everyday things.

If Solon had one quality which impressed his contemporaries in addition to artistic ability, it was charm. Clearly not deliberately cultivated to bring quick success, it was the genuine, spontaneous product of his nature, achieving without effort warm personal relationships built on mutual regard and affection.

Solon's life can be studied as a record of this kind of friendship. We can see

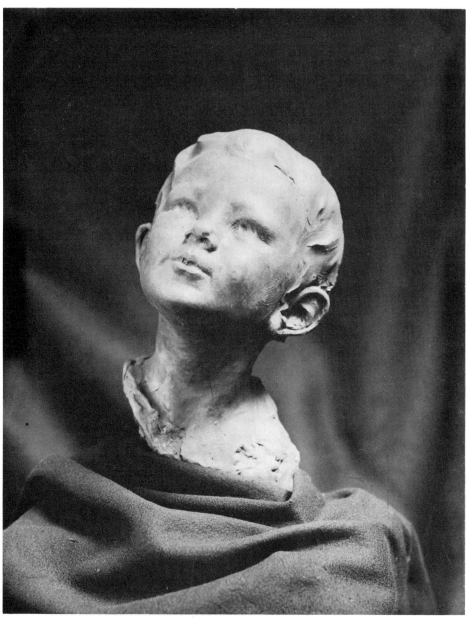

"Paul." Plaster, life-size bust that would later serve as a model for the marble. 1903. Later cast into bronze. *A. C. Bogart.*

him flourishing when surrounded by those who loved him for what he was, genuine, unselfish, without pretense or hypocrisy, perhaps suffering and vulnerable when denied this kind of sympathetic atmosphere. His searing experience at Sierra Madre comes to mind here. He responded to those around him who understood what he was striving for and, understanding, respected his courage and tenacity in adhering to his ideals. How often in his life these friends step in to aid at critical moments—the Perhams in Santa Ana, inviting him into their home; Daniel R. Wood, actively interested in his work; Louis T. Rebisso, providing another hospitable home; the Allens, alert to his need of money; Bela Pratt, responding to the need of a workroom. Illustrations can be multiplied. The chain of helpful friends stretched across the continent, and then across the Atlantic, and it would continue to lengthen when he returned to America and took up residence in New York and Connecticut. As the *Dictionary of American Biography* puts it: "Solon Borglum, wherever he went, had the advantage of a rare personal charm springing chiefly from native goodness, from his quick and abounding sympathy toward all life."

Marked changes had been made in Solon's life by this time. Lilli, the Borglums' first born, arrived May 1, 1900, to become a precocious charmer, adored by all. The new father startled his in-laws a second time by the proficiency he displayed in his latest role. With his large, square, sculptor's hands, so gentle, he handled the newborn baby with much greater confidence and skill than the inexperienced mother. Emma could proudly boast that a frontiersman was like that, fazed by nothing.

Emma did her best with Solon's French, which had utterly shocked her parents when they heard it, picked up as it was in a stable. She was highly amused some years later, when he was given work on the strength of his French. For his part, Solon once told a student he had needed only one word of her language to converse intelligibly with his fiancée—*ange!*

Whatever had been the extent of Solon's social life in his bachelor days, there is no doubt that he had an active and diversified life after marriage. He and Emma joined the American art colony, bringing old friends together with new.

When the *Exposition* reopened in the spring those who attended included members of Solon's family. Ida Borglum and Harriet, his sister, came from Omaha, while Gutzon and Lisa, with August, came over from London.

Even after a lapse of years Harriet would recall Solon's merry laugh as he guided her and her mother in a tour of the festival grounds, mixing edifying talks about art with the tour. During their visit he showed them the sights of Paris in a repeat of the happy sightseeing he and Emma had done several years before.

August Borglum astonished everybody by treating the Vignals to another example of American style, whirlwind courtship which by turns had shocked and delighted them when Solon won his bride. With his trunks already on their way to Berlin and intending to follow them for another year abroad, he never got farther than Paris. His fate was settled as soon as he laid eyes on Lucy, whom he courted, won and wed, all in a matter of weeks. Instead of going to Berlin he and Lucy, after a period of study in Paris, were on their way back to America to open a school of music in Omaha where, until the end of their lives they merged their talents in contributing substantially to making the developing city an important cultural center.

Following his marriage Solon's restlessness to return to his native land increased rapidly. His "look around" had now extended from a summer vacation to over four years. When he read that a boom in monumental sculpture, stimulated by the extraordinary success of American sculptors abroad, had actually started, he could hardly wait to obtain his share of commissions. In the next few years bronze monuments to heroes, of varied quality, were to be erected in nearly every American city and town across the land. It seemed that every sculptor wanted to have a hand in their creation.

With the approach of autumn, after the social whirl of the *Exposition* and the family reunion in Paris, Solon's return became urgent. Moreover, his New York foundry was not delivering his works as it should. One important bronze, intended for the Salon, had not arrived in time. When finally it did, the charges were so high Solon refused to accept it. He felt obliged to go alone to America, leaving Emma and Lilli with her parents.

Before he sailed, Solon and Emma took a few days off by themselves. They went to the Barbizon Colony, staying at the Maison Thormet. This was a most appropriate choice for a rebel against classical influence. Barbizon, the village near Fontainebleau, had been made forever famous by its association with J. F. Millet, Theodore Rousseau and Corot. Sentiments expressed by Millet and Rousseau obviously struck responsive chords in one who became an advocate of "the big line of direction in nature," one who was to say, "the most any artist can do is to live and work with nature." "For God's sake," wrote Rousseau, "let us try in our works to make a man breathe, a tree really live." Millet echoed the sentiment: "I try not to have things look as if chance had brought them together, but as if there were a necessary bond between them." These French artists had been unappreciated, poor and neglected most of their lives. But here is where the parallel ends. On the crest of a wave of success optimistic Solon is not likely to have had any qualms of doubt as he embarked upon the next phase of his career.

Barbizon was only a brief interlude, but long enough for Solon and Emma to savor a little of their life together and, while planning the future, to look back at their whirlwind courtship, their "imprudent" marriage. They must have thought much about their honeymoon experience in America, an extraordinary adventure for Emma. Solon could look with greatest pride at his *ange,* knowing that despite her delicate health and fastidious nature she had had the fortitude to take the trip with all its attendant hardships. Emma too was proud of herself. She was to recount her experiences many times, always fascinating her listeners. Her first words were an indirect rebuke. "My Paris friends," she would say, "thought I was going to a country where even in New York there were people still wearing paint and feathers." But thoughts of her future as an American wife must have been somewhat apprehensive, particularly at this point, for she was expecting a second child. She knew she lacked her sister's abundant energy. In comparison to Lucy, Emma was lethargic, her whole life a struggle with physical weakness.

Before leaving they spent a few days exploring the mysteriously beautiful forest of Fontainebleau, with its peculiar rock formations and peaks. One day Lilli took her nap under the "benevolent gaze of Millet" at the Millet-Rousseau Memorial. They returned to Paris while the Ile-de-France was exploding into color and completed Solon's preparations for departure. October 14, 1901, Emma wrote her sister in Omaha saying that Solon's trunk was in the dining room and that she was busy packing. She had several times been interrupted by reporters from American papers who wished to have the latest news of Solon's plans for his return to his native land. The separation would be short. She expected her husband to return for her soon and she was happy.

Not long after his arrival on American shores Borglum was described as a "quiet, unassuming,[1] decided man, simple in his habits, ready still for hardship, caring nothing for luxury" — a product of the frank, impulsive life of the Old West. Solon had not changed. The Paris experience had not vitally affected the

principles on which he organized his life, but marriage had made a change in his
outward appearance. The prematurely old face of a Cincinnati photograph, with
the marks of his "coarse bread" years so clearly evident, had disappeared. Thanks
to his wife's efforts, he was now neat and well dressed. But the man beneath the
clothes remained singularly well equipped for what lay ahead. He found himself
a room on East 14th Street around the corner from Fifth Avenue and got busy.

Walking first into the foundry where he had been having trouble, he found
it on the verge of bankruptcy. Since the intricacies of the law were not for him,
he could think of nothing better than to avail himself of Remington's
recommendation of another place. Solon had recently met Frederic Remington,
illustrator of the Old West with pen and brush, who himself had turned to
modeling. But a change of foundries meant a loss of precious time before sales of
bronzes could start and something Solon could hardly afford.

The breeze of monumental sculpture that had caught Solon's attention in
Paris had become a gale by the time he got home. He found that a competition,
the biggest thing of its kind yet seen — a monument of Ulysses S. Grant — was
just getting under way in Washington. It was not only to be the biggest in scope,
it carried the largest commission for the successful artist and had, therefore, the
longest list of competitors yet, no fewer than fifty-two. Among them was the new
arrival. This was Solon's great opportunity. He exerted himself to the utmost to
capture the commission. His enthusiasm accompanied by repeated reports of
work without rest concerned Emma, who wrote: "Dear boy, I hope you are
reasonable and take care of yourself, it would be better that the monument were
entirely smashed than you getting sick over it."

The U. S. Grant competition[2] is of interest as being the first known time
the two brothers competed as sculptors, but one senses that Solon, whatever may
have been true of Gutzon, never really stood a chance of winning.

Indeed the important commission, which was needed to bring his wife and
family to America, eluded Solon much longer than he had expected. He gave up
the idea of going back to pick up his family, though he still hoped that his
second child would be born in America. Instead, Paul was born in Paris at the
end of December.

As 1901 went into the new year and weeks slipped by, Emma's impatience
to end an increasingly uncomfortable situation with her parents and join her
husband became marked. With worry on that score already, there was also now

deep anxiety about her husband's welfare. Worried not only because of his overworking and financial recklessness, she also suspected that he had returned to an austerity diet. For the first time she became aware of one of his traits, that of showing the most confidence when things were at their worst. With his letters growing steadily less informative while their cheerfulness remained undiminished, her fears mounted. She had so much to worry about: "You know how I worry about your way of taking care of yourself. You deny yourself all the necessities of life and you don't hesitate to spend large sums on your sculpturing." And his important business letters? This was something she had been able to take care of when she was with him and she implored him now not to write them himself as people simply would not understand his variations of spelling, nor be able to decipher his handwriting. Later she would make a joke of this particular foible: "My husband says that it is a person with little imagination who cannot spell the same word in different ways." But this time was not yet and there was always the matter of money. Without money in the bank, she once confessed, "I feel as though I were near a precipice." It was a nearness that she must have felt constantly throughout her married life.

At last, "If it were not for the babies I don't believe I could stay . . . I would run for the ticket-office. The boat train leaves tonight to catch the *Lorraine*. Next Saturday I would be in New York . . . I am very happy the artists appreciate your work. You will have to get a big hat I am afraid. It makes me feel good as it means our being all happy together. I know how you miss us all and that dear little Paul that you have not seen yet."

Knowing the city fairly well by this time Solon had found a spot where an unemployed sculptor of ability and address could usually find work. Lorado Taft has immortalized[3] the Piccirilli marble-cutting business in uptown New York, describing how that Italian-born family led in New York "the life of a Florentine household of the Quattrocento." "The great dining room of the establishment is like an old-time refectory, where five stalwart sons with their wives and children gather round a kindly, keeneyed patriarch. In the large studios adjoining, much work is completed in marble for various American sculptors." Solon soon gained a corner for himself in that capacious establishment, and a place in the warm Latin hearts of those men, sharing the Piccirillis' generous board with its limitless quantities of spaghetti, crisp Italian bread and red wine.

The time of waiting for work was also used, characteristically, in working

for other sculptors, doing chiefly horses for those less skilled. It was anonymous
work of course, and not without its amusing side for one who had developed
considerable expertise in that field, as an anecdote illustrates. He was engaged in
modeling a horse for another sculptor when a visitor being shown around the
studio stopped to watch him work. Before leaving the visitor tapped Solon on the
shoulder: "Very good, young man, that could even be a Borglum horse." [4]
Naturally, however, such expedients were not what this artist had come home
for.

The year 1902 was rendered notable for Solon by the production of several
of his most interesting works, among them, "One in A Thousand" which for
many people has become a special favorite, no doubt made so by its superb
drama. It is recalled that when John La Farge saw this statue in an exhibit he was
covering for a New York paper he exclaimed that only an artist who was himself
"one in a thousand" could have done it.

One day, Solon received a letter from Saint-Gaudens,[5] who wrote from
Aspen, his home in New Hampshire, to tell him how pained he was at
Borglum's report of his experience since coming back to America: "That a man
of your talent should be in such a position while men of absolutely no talent and
less character have more than they can attend to is deplorable."

Saint-Gaudens said that the result of the Grant competition in Washington
had troubled him. "Before seeing the models I had great hopes for you but the
result proved what I have always maintained, that in the majority of cases
competitions are no good and are not the proper way of judging men's abilities.

"You certainly have done some remarkable things in your groups of
animals and for that reason should be entrusted with some serious work. Believe
me I shall do all in my power to help in that direction and if you can suggest any
way I will do so by writing letters, or anything else you please."

The St. Louis fair was approaching and he suggested that Solon write
F. W. Ruckstull,[6] native son and leader of the traditionalists who was then
director of sculpture for St. Louis. Saint Gaudens wished there were still room in
his studio but he already had more assistants than he needed. He ended by
strongly advising Solon not to enter any more competitions: "Yours is not the
temperament or talent for the brutality of such trials."

The suggestion of writing to the sculpture director for the St. Louis Fair
was an excellent one and paid off with a substantial advance which enabled Solon

"One In A Thousand." Bronze. Height 44 in. Cowboy and a champion kicker. George F. Harding Museum, Chicago, Illinois; Gertrude Vanderbilt Whitney Gallery of Western Art, Cody, Wyoming; New Britain Museum of American Art, New Britain, Conn. *E. Irving Blomstrann.*

to send for his family. In mid-summer of 1902, Emma, Lilli, and the new baby, Paul, arrived, complete with a French maid who represented the fulfillment of Solon's promise to his mother-in-law that he would never let her daughter be maidless. It was a promise, however, that was easier made than kept, for the damsel in question, although she had crossed the Atlantic first-class with Mrs. Borglum and the children, decamped the moment she set foot on American soil.

The Borglums began their American life in a Yonkers boardinghouse. They found domestic help six months later, and moved into an apartment closer to Solon's work on East 91st Street, Manhattan.

The years 1902–1903 were years of much joy, expectation, and fulfillment, tempered with great personal grief and certain anxieties. The rising young sculptor who, ten years before, had still been on a Nebraska ranch, had come a long way. He was now engaged upon works that could scarcely have been better suited to his temperament and talent, works that were to crown his long list of accomplishments in depicting life on the Great Plains and assure him his lasting position among American artists.

For the St. Louis World's Fair, he was given the theme that expressed the Fair itself, the story of Civilization as it moved westward into the wilderness. Four monumental groups were Solon Borglum's principal contribution to the Louisiana Purchase Exposition of 1904. The first, entitled "Buffalo Dance," depicted the Indian before the arrival of the white man. The second, "The Pioneer in A Storm," showed that arrival. The third, the establishment of the ranchman, "Cowboy at Rest." The fourth, "Steps Toward Civilization," depicted a converted chief directing his son to adopt the white man's learning. The last, which has disappeared except for several fragments, is noteworthy for the fact that the Indian chief holds a symbol of that learning in the form of a bound volume.

Borglum was now in *Who's Who*; a significant round-up of his career appeared in Lorado Taft's *History of American Sculpture*; and he was included in Charles H. Caffin's eleven *American Masters of Sculpture*, (the other ten being Saint-Gaudens, Barnard, French, MacMonnies, Bartlett, Adams, Niehaus, Warner, Brenner). Indeed, as was stated in St. Louis at the time of the World's Fair, Solon Borglum "may serenely look forward to the verdict of posterity, which

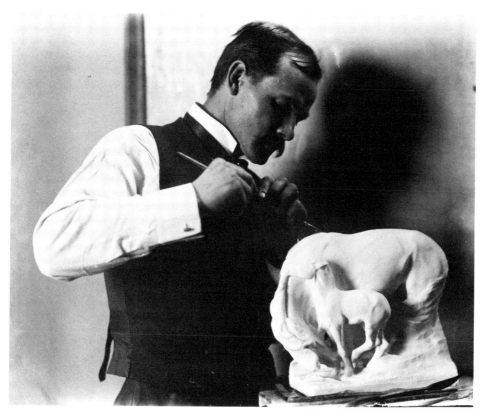

Solon Borglum carving "Snowdrift." 1902. Height approx. 11 in. Borglum had used as his model the bronze titled, "In The Wind, "also called "Snowdrift." *Gertrude Kasibier.*

undoubtedly will confirm the admiration of his contemporaries." * Were it not
for the simultaneous appearance of his brother Gutzon, now in New York,
claiming to be "Borglum the sculptor," Solon's skies could be called cloudless,
his future boundless.

To further describe Solon's mixed blessings, now that he was joined by his
family, he was immeasurably happy in his domestic life and naturally gratified by
his unsought publicity. Commissions which did not materialize baffled him.
Emma hit the nail on the head when she wrote a friend, "My husband is a rising
young sculptor which means articles in the magazines, medals, compliments, and
very little money."

Solon's one-man show at Keppel's Gallery was part of it all. On April 20,
1903, he exhibited no fewer than 32 bronzes, marbles and other sculptures.

But grief struck the following month when his precocious and frail Lilli,
conceived on the Plains, died at the age of three after a brief illness. The blow
was only mitigated by the birth of their second daughter, Monica, born on
December 9, for whom Mary Blanchard, missionary at the Crow Creek
Reservation, and Attilio Piccirilli stood as godparents.

The St. Louis World's Fair of 1904, or the Louisiana Purchase Exposition to
give it its official title, was designed to be in all respects the finest of its kind, and
it is doubtful if it has ever had its equal. The superlatives jump to the typewriter
almost as readily as they did to the pen of its chief promoter, the Hon. David R.
Francis, former governor of Missouri. Mr. Francis modestly called it "a marker of
the accomplishments and progress of man." It was truly the most beautiful, most
comprehensive, most spectacular, most festive fair yet held. The fair's organization had required six years. To promote it, Francis had made a whirlwind tour of
Europe, visiting all the principal capitals in 18 days, calling on the crowned heads
of Europe to participate, which they did. No fair has had a "fairer" setting. The
future Forest Park was transformed into an intricate maze of lagoons, drives,
gardens, fountains, buildings, cascades, hills, terraces — perfect for the statuary
planned to be the dominant feature.

Dedication was set for the actual Purchase date, April 30, 1903, with
exercises lasting three days. There was a military parade of 4000 Army Regulars
and 8000 National Guardsmen, reviewed in person by the President of the

* See References, p. 244, No. 9.

"The Sioux Indian Buffalo Dance." St. Louis Louisiana Purchase Exposition 1903. Intermediate size model used for the full scale monument. Bronze. Height approx. 3 ft. *E. Irving Blomstrann.*

"The Pioneer in A Storm." St. Louis, 1903. All the essential details have been sacrificed to emphasize the suffering the horse undergoes in a storm. Three foot intermediate size model. Bronze. *E. Irving Blomstrann.*

"A Step Toward Civilization." Sometimes called "Steps Toward Civilization." Fourth work done for St. Louis. The chief has thrown aside his bonnet and other effects of his culture and is directing his son to go forward and take up the culture of the white man, as he holds in his arm a symbol of the white man's learning.

United States. Both Theodore Roosevelt and his predecessor, Grover Cleveland, made dedicatory speeches. But the fair was not ready on the day set for the opening. Not until the following April was President Roosevelt able to perform the ceremony, which he did by pressing a golden key on his White House desk.

There were features aplenty to make the fair historic. Electricity came into its own. The fairgrounds at nightfall became a fairyland of light, surpassing even Paris, *la Ville Lumière*, so it was boasted. Attendance set records, 200,000 passing through the turnstiles on opening day. Even the weather did its part in the success, it being a cool summer.

Of the display of art intended to be the chief feature, Governor Francis spoke only the truth when he said, "At no previous exposition did art receive so much recognition and attention." If the Columbian Exposition in Chicago was recognized as having given a stimulus to American art, St. Louis was going to give it that much more of a boost. Indeed, if American culture had maintained the curve it was traveling in Governor Francis' fervent imagination, it would soon have hit the stratosphere! St. Louis was all set to establish a new standard most especially in sculpture. It would mark an epoch in world history as a thousand historical, monumental, allegorical, decorative groups, motifs and figures of every sort, turned the fairground into a sea of statuary. An Erie railroad roundhouse in Weehawken, New Jersey, was acquired for the mammoth operation of enlarging the many sculptors' works. Over a hundred craftsmen were employed on this one process alone.

On opening day, 1904, a seated figure of Thomas Jefferson appropriately presided over the entrance, while just beyond there stood a monument to the famous Purchase itself, both works designed by the Exposition's new chief of sculpture, Karl Bitter, Ruckstull having been removed. An apotheosis of the spirit of St. Louis, by Charles Niehaus, took shape in an imposing equestrian figure of Louis IX of France in full armor. On the Saint Louis Plaza were Solon's four groups, flanking the steps leading from the launch landing of the main lagoon.

Solon displayed more than his four large groups on the Saint Louis Plaza. In the Art Palace on top of the hill were nine additional bronzes, one of which, "Snowdrift," was awarded a gold medal.* [7]

---

* This small bronze statuette was first titled, "In The Wind." This is the only one cast into bronze and the marble of the same size, done after it, is called, "Snowdrift."

Solon's work attracted critical attention. Both Henry Bargy[8] of *L'Illustration*, Paris, and T. Johansen,[9] writing in Denmark's Art Magazine, *Kundst*, noted an advance in the sculptor's work, comparing it to groups seen in Paris earlier, which Bargy had called original and forceful, but violent. Bargy speaks of the "intense life" rendered in sculpture, when "he fights the clay between his hands and the animal he imagines between his knees," and the artist seems determined to "express the inexpressible." In St. Louis, he felt Solon's work had gained in harmony without loss of vigor. " 'The Lookout' (*Cowboy at Rest*) . . . possesses a tranquility, a simplicity and a truly classical purity of line, but it nonetheless evokes the silence, the atmosphere, the mystery of the endless prairie." The Frenchman called Borglum "the most typically American sculptor."

Johansen likewise preferred what he saw in St. Louis, declaring it to be more interesting, better art. He took note of the *virtuosity* of Borglum's talent, calling attention to those groups that elevated the vigorous and rough life of the cowboy, compared with the later work which revealed the maturity of the artist.

The arrival of this "most typically American sculptor" had not passed unnoticed at home. Among the first of the magazines to alert the public was *The Art Interchange*[10] in which an illustrated article appeared in 1901, followed by many others, including full page illustrated stories in the Sunday supplements across the country. The New York *Herald* carried a full page well-illustrated story, titled "A Sculptor of Cowboys" by Charles Caffin. The Denver *Times* reprinted most of the excellent story of Arthur Goodrich from Walter Hines Page's *World's Work*. And the Omaha *World-Herald* had proudly quoted Augustus Saint-Gaudens' prediction that Borglum, "once an Omaha boy," might become the leading sculptor in America.[11] These appreciations were followed by a *Century*[12] piece, in which Frank Sewell expressed his conviction about what Borglum's arrival meant for the nation: "In the production of young Borglum's chisel . . . was the free citizen of the Great West, whose vision is as broad as the prairie sky, whose muscle is as firm as his heart is tender, and whose eye looks straight for the truth."

Solon Borglum's St. Louis groups on the Saint Louis Plaza at the main launch landing.

"The Indian Love Chase." c 1903. 38 in. The youthful Sioux is often as fleet as the wind. Bronze. New Britain Museum of American Art, New Britain, Conn. *E. Irving Blomstrann.*

CHAPTER VIII

Monumental Work

In the panorama of Solon Borglum's career the groups executed for St. Louis represent a watershed. While these four groups, with the life-size "Stampede of Wild Horses," presented by the artist to the Cincinnati Art Museum, served to initiate him in the techniques of monumental sculpture, they also mark, in a general way, the summation and completion of his output as a portrayer of life on the Western Plains.

The sculptor was to undertake a new kind of creativity, that of working under the direction of a committee. What he had accomplished so far had been undirected. Even the St. Louis groups were no exception. Given the theme, the rest came out of his personal experience and inspiration. His works had been created in freedom, and one concludes that this was the case because of Saint-Gaudens' deep appreciation of what he had done, together with an expressed faith in his capabilities. Although Saint-Gaudens could not accept responsibility for directing the sculpture on account of his failing health, he was in the background, giving of his great talent, his invaluable international experience and infinite patience.

Thus the sculptor had so far been very much on his own. A monumental sculptor *per se,* however, must usually answer to a committee of people who may have little artistic knowledge but an infinite amount of authority. The sculptor must learn to take other people's ideas, adopt or adapt them, or give convincing reasons for rejecting them. He must be pliable, without losing his own integrity. Many a fine piece of work founders at this precise point. The sculptor must be a diplomat in behalf of his ideas and how they are to be presented. Solon had not succeeded with his concept for the Grant Memorial in the Nation's capital and, as a result, Saint-Gaudens had cautioned him[1] against entering competitions. Of course he did not know the mature man who would face the bruising criticisms of unsympathetic members of a committee, and emerge on top. He did not reckon with Solon's driving ambition, nor his stubborn nature, nor the infinite confidence he had in himself. Competitions were on the high road of every aspiring sculptor and really could not be avoided, nor would Solon have wanted to avoid them had it been possible. He had announced his intention by the very fact, almost immediately on landing from Paris, of entering the Grant competition. Had not that, after all, been the chief reason for his eagerness to get back to America? Monumental work was the "big-time" challenge.

Solon was thirty-six when a fresh opportunity arrived. In May 1905 he was commissioned to do the equestrian statue of General John B. Gordon, Confederate States Army, for Atlanta, Georgia.

The chief contender in the competition was Ruckstull, who was a formidable and popular sculptor and a veteran of that kind of contest with several Civil War generals to his credit. Solon did not take the archconservative Ruckstull lightly. But he still had the enthusiastic support of Saint-Gaudens, in this case more so than ever. In offering to help, Saint-Gaudens declared he had never felt greater willingness to testify regarding "the relative merits[2] of you and the sculptor you speak of."

Solon's winning design of a youthful military hero mounted on a spirited charger, full of action, nostrils dilated, received enthusiastic praise when the model was put on public display in the state capitol. The commission followed as a matter of course. It is at this point that Solon's troubles began, for second thoughts soon assailed those responsible for the project.

In the first place, it was to be no ordinary monument. Gordon was the hero *par excellence* of the whole state of Georgia and far beyond. He was the epitome of all that was cherished in the South during four terrible years of war, the Lost Cause itself, the people's freedom, their chivalry, their idealism. He was all this. Or, as it was to be expressed at the dedication, General John B. Gordon was their "Soul." How to express the inexpressible, to use Bargy's phrase, such was virtually the sculptor's assignment.

What then occurred in Atlanta illustrates one particular difficulty inherent

"The Twelfth of May." Winning model of competition for memorial monument to General John B. Gordon, Atlanta. 1905.

in any literal representation of public figures, that of determining the precise point in a hero's career which is to be depicted.

There was no question that Gordon had been one of the most authentic heroes of the Confederacy, vivid and colorful. His gallantry on a score of bloody fields had earned him the title of the *Chevalier Bayard* of the Southern Cause. The winning design had caught that dramatic moment, the "Twelfth of May" (1864) episode when, in the battle of Spotsylvania, he had "ordered" his commanding officer, none other than Robert E. Lee, to the rear for personal safety because of the particular danger of the charge. His cry had been taken up in the ranks of his regiment and had prevailed over Lee's desire to lead the charge himself. But that moment had come in youth, over forty years before, whereas Gordon had lived on to be seventy-two. In fact he had just died; but the last forty years of his long life had been spent as a civilian in the service of his people. He had served in the nation's capital for two terms as United States Senator and one term as Georgia's governor. At the time of his death he was generally considered to be a co-worker with General Lee in the reconstruction of the South. It was a point of concern, as regards a monument, that he was primarily remembered as a man of peace who traveled all over the United States, addressing vast audiences. His voice was known to thousands "eloquently defending[3] the South and proclaiming the greatness of our reunited country from Maine to Texas." These facts, together with the knowledge that the "boys in gray" who had known him as their youthful commander on the memorable Twelfth of May were becoming very few, decided the issue. Soon the boys would all be gone, but the great statue they were planning would live on to inspire new generations . . .

A new statue was ordered, one which would show the elder statesman with uncovered head, mounted and in uniform, reviewing the United Confederate Veterans as he had unfailingly done on the day of their annual reunions. This was how the citizens of Georgia wished to see their hero memorialized.

Being only a compromise, the solution led to fresh complications, involving the sculptor in all sorts of time-consuming problems unrelated to his art. With the committee's members often in conflict with one another a range of ideas and suggestions now besieged him.

No artist likes to scrap his work, least of all when it has just swept the field, but that is what Solon found himself forced to do. As photographs and snapshots arrived from relatives and friends of the general he was confronted with the figure of an elderly officer mounted on a quiet and most unmartial-looking animal. Further study confirmed the additional impression: the horse Solon had given the general resembled the horses of the West more than the blooded animals of the South.

At this point Solon's good friend Attilio Piccirilli presented him with a horse named Barrie that had just distinguished itself at Madison Square Garden. This solved his chief problem. But some Atlanta critics still felt the reins and the martingale were not right. The committee now seemed to comprise every notable in Georgia. With every one of them an expert, the floodgates of criticism were open wide. From the swish of the horse's tail to his bit and the kind of spurs worn by the general, there was argument on just about everything. At this point one recalls Adelaide Adams' classic remark, "Solon Borglum was an artist,[4] not a harness maker."

To cap it all, some wondered why the horse the general was riding was a *mare*. Was *that* usual? Solon replied that it was not only unusual, it was quite likely without precedent! But research had shown that the general had been partial to mares and that the general's mount depicted was the famous mare that had broken through Federal lines and been captured. Renamed "Marye," for the ridge, she became Gordon's horse for the rest of the war. The committee was satisfied.

When Georgia's Legislature elected "The Gordon Monument Commission" to replace the "John B. Gordon Monument Association," for lack of funds by the latter, the sculptor's work went into a new and decisive phase. The Commission appointed a committee of three, accompanied by Mrs. Burton Smith, one of the general's daughters, to go to Solon's studio in Mamaroneck and inspect the full-scale plaster monument. After a few minor changes it was enthusiastically approved. However, the committee decided that, before returning to Atlanta, it would "adjourn" to Solon's New York studio to have a look at the first model, the figure of the youthful Gordon on the Twelfth of May. Here the small group so captivated the committee it decided on the spot it wanted *that* one. With this it was the sculptor who balked, but he had only to give the committee his estimate of the cost for the decision to be reversed once again.

The day set for the unveiling in Atlanta, May 25, 1907, was an historic one for its citizenry, perhaps the greatest in its post-bellum history and certainly the one giving it the purest joy. Tragic memories were brought back, but the valiant

"General John B. Gordon." Finished monument before casting into bronze. 1906.

spirit of the man being honored was present. All that was most dear seemed knit together in this leader for forty years, John Brown Gordon. The *Constitution* reported that "in every window[5] on every floor, from the front entrance of the capitol back to the Hunter Street side, on the projecting ledges, were eager, expectant throngs. . . . Young men and boys perched up on the convenient telephone poles like so many blackbirds."

It was a great day for Solon, too, his work acclaimed, its success acknowledged. Even the military experts declared themselves satisfied. Solon's chief critic, the one he had found most difficult to satisfy, the general's other daughter, Mrs. C. O. Brown, was in ecstasy. She said a thrill went through her every time she saw her father's statue. Her note of appreciation to Solon ended with the words, "The genius which could so catch[6] the spirit of a man, not to mention the likeness of a man he never saw, this genius is inspiration straight from God."

It was a day of promise. With his pleasant manner and thanks to the success of his statue, Solon made a variety of friends, some of whom he would revisit from time to time. "Mont Rest," the Venable home near Stone Mountain not far from Atlanta, was frequently visited. An Atlanta newspaper[7] quoted Solon as saying the South's materials were "as rich as any in the world" and mentioned the sculptor's desire to do other subjects. Solon's interviewer wondered who would be the one to carve the epic of the Confederacy. Was she perhaps thinking of the artist she was interviewing?

It was a great day also for Emma, possibly the greatest since her arrival in America. Her husband's triumph had confirmed high hopes for the future. The way Solon and she were received was nearly overwhelming. She would never forget that special hospitality for which the South is famous. They were wined and dined, flattered and made much of, and Emma loved every bit of it. Her Gallic soul responded ardently, adding many more friends to those she already had on this side of the Atlantic.

Solon received a second commission which he executed at the same time as the one for Gordon. This was to design the Captain William O'Neill Memorial, which has come to be referred to as the "Rough Rider Monument." It was in the opposite corner of the South, in Prescott, Arizona. The contract was signed in April 1906.

An instructive contrast can be drawn between the two commissions, with an illuminating illustration of Solon's methods. The monuments could scarcely be more different in design, the one formal, the other quite the opposite. One was designed to meet a particular set of requirements; every line of the other revealed the spontaneous joy of creation. One was reposed, the other full of fire; one was dignified and elderly, the other a man in the early prime of life. The Prescott commission did not depend on the result of a competition. From the very first it was all Solon's.

William Owen O'Neill, known affectionately as "Bucky," had been mayor of Prescott and sheriff of Yavapai County. As captain of Troop A, First U.S. Volunteer Cavalry, he was killed in the charge on foot up San Juan Hill, Cuba. Just previously he had boasted that no Spanish bullet would be killing *him*. He had a reputation for devotion and gallantry and his returning countrymen wanted at once a suitable monument in commemoration. The idea caught on quickly. Following necessary legislation the chairman of the state committee arrived in New York in search of a sculptor. His mission was handicapped by the fact his funds were wholly inadequate for obtaining a name artist. Thanks to a tip given by Borglum's friend, Bernard Cunniff, a much-traveled mining engineer, Solon was put in touch with the chairman.

Cunniff had urged Solon to take the initiative and make himself available, but when Cunniff told him what the Arizonans had in mind Solon needed no urging. They wanted "a sculptural design which, within the limits of artistic necessity, should depart from the conventional, be essentially modern in treatment, and without exaggeration be typical of and embody the spirit of the West."

There is no reason to question the veracity of the following newspaper story, for it catches the spirit of the occasion.

A knock at the door,[8] and in walked Solon, who lost no time coming to the point of his unexpected call.

"Mr. Morrison, would you like to have your monument done by me?"

Mr. Morrison was too stunned for the moment to know what to reply. Recovering from his surprise he said, "Would we *like!* Would we like to have a cherished dream come true? There is nothing in the world we would like better. But we simply don't have the money to commission you, Mr. Borglum."

"How much do you have?"

"Ten thousand dollars."

"You shall have your monument."

With that Solon left, not bothering to go through the business routine though the usual contract was drawn up later.

The spirit that originated the "Rough Rider Monument" remained in the project to the end, giving it a uniquely colorful place in American history. If the legislators of Arizona were wanting with regard to the generosity of their appropriation, the ordinary citizen made up for it. A fund was established into which contributions flowed from cattle ranch, mining camp and pack train, in fact from just about everywhere. A monster pumpkin was raffled again and again. A cigar maker named a new brand "Bucky O'Neill," contributing all profits from its sale. Arizona copper companies proudly contributed the metal for the casting. Finally, a St. Louis hat maker brought out a Bucky O'Neill sombrero and Solon himself wore his for years, long after its elegance had departed.

Only patriotic fervor could have produced the following news report: "When all the dollars were gathered in they could have told a tale to inspire even the hand of Solon Borglum. But Borglum himself was part of the land and the time that had shaped Bucky O'Neill's genius, and drawn the men of the Rough Riders together to give their lives if need be for the freedom of a land and people far from their own Southwest. Solon Borglum worked in the same spirit. And out of these fused fires came the greatest equestrian statue in the United States — equaled only by one other in the world, it is said by critics of great sculpture — to stand on the plaza made beautiful by O'Neill's hands."

The artist himself was more reserved. If he felt that he had done a masterpiece he did not acknowledge it and is on record as saying merely, "I never worked for a better committee." But his happiness in his work can be gathered from what he added: "everything was left in my hands." This explains in part how he was able to create and successfully execute two major works in such a short time. Beyond this, he was inspired, knew what he wanted and could do it quickly.

Solon went from Atlanta to Prescott in time to direct the search for the kind of boulder he had specified for the monument's pedestal. The boulder had to be of a certain size, large and therefore heavy. Where could it be found and, when found, how could it be moved to the city hall plaza in one piece?

The perfect boulder was located on a hillside near the city. It was a

"Captain William Owen O'Neill." Finished plaster model, with young Paul Manship. 1906.

beautifully shaped and weathered rock, just the desired size and rounded in a way that would require a minimum of cutting to form the base. It weighed twenty-eight tons. In the spirit of the enterprise, a local contractor volunteered for the job of getting it down. The rock crashed down the hillside, breaking trees in its path but not itself. It reached the plaza square in triumph.

The question then arose of what had happened to the statue. When last heard from the big bronze had been crated and put on its way from the Roman Bronze Works in New York City. That was weeks earlier and nothing had been heard of it since. With the day set for its unveiling approaching, the freight manager of the railroad was appealed to. Mr. Drake dispatched a man to ride the rails until he found it. The man rode as far as Albuquerque before he found the "mislaid" Bucky, standing forgotten in the yards. Another delay came when the flatcar broke under its load. At length, just two days before the important date, the big bronze statue reached its destination and palpitations ceased.

The "Rough Rider Monument" was unveiled on July 3, 1907, the auspicious ninth anniversary of the famous charge. There were an opening parade, musical selections, a recitation by the California poet John McGroatry, the introduction of the sculptor, and many speeches, all topped off with a band concert by the 5th United States Cavalry, fireworks and a grand reception.

"Were you called upon⁹ to make a speech?" Solon was asked by a reporter.

"Yes," he acknowledged.

"And did you?"

"Well, I — bowed."

"Even at the painful recollection of being called upon to make a speech," the news account said, "the sculptor blushed like a schoolboy."

From the moment of unveiling, the "Rough Rider"-Bucky O'Neill Monument aroused enthusiasm. Some who saw it became lyrical. "I was the first to cheer," cried the poet McGroatry. "I could not have helped it had there been a law against doing so. My heart was in my throat and my soul elated with a thrill of admiration and joy."

"The way the statue grows on one is a perennial joy," wrote Bernard Cunniff. "We've stopped to look at it hundreds of times from every side. We have seen it in the rain and sunshine and in snow, at noon, at evening, at midnight under the moon; and my last trip to Prescott found us at five in the morning, still gazing out at the statue — and it's great in all moods, all times, all weather. We owe you much for the greatest pleasure we have every time we go to Prescott."

McGroatry and the governor of California noted how every muscle of the horse was firmly outlined and how the rider, one with his mount, turned smoothly as he reined him in. Governor Kibber likened it to a snapshot, catching horse and rider in the perfect split second. The New York art critic[10] Paul K. Thomas called it the greatest of Solon Borglum's many life dramas.

Another writer,[11] Selene Ayer Armstrong, quoted Emerson to the effect that no native son had yet arrived who with "tyrannous eye" perceived the value of America's "incomparable materials." She believed the lack had now been made good. She saw greatness stamped all over Solon Borglum's work, which she found "intensely American, intensely democratic," and an inspiring challenge to the shams, hypocrisies and insincerities creeping into American life. Different in its cleanness, simplicity and freedom, it was redolent of an era, she felt, where a man's worth was not reckoned in terms of possessions, but of what he *was*. Miss Armstrong's conclusion was notable: "To what measure of greatness [his art] will rise when the ego of the man becomes articulate it is interesting to speculate. He is in sculpture what Walt Whitman is in literature, a force as virile, as elemental and unselfconscious as wind or rain. To study his art sympathetically is to thrill to the rugged truth and beauty of primal things."

The acclaim became unanimous when the creator of the Rough Rider Monument received from the White House a letter of congratulations from the nation's top cowboy, America's Rough Rider himself:[12]

> "I like that statue of Bucky O'Neill very much. He was an absolutely fearless and daring man; and it seems to me you have caught his spirit exactly and made a thoroughly appropriate figure. For the bas-relief I suppose that the charge of the Rough Riders would be excellent.
>
>   With great regard, believe me,
>   Sincerely yours,
>   Theodore Roosevelt" *

---

* The fact that President Roosevelt, neither now nor at any later time, expressed pique or exhibited resentment over the artist's relegating him to the base of the statue suggests that along with his other great qualities T.R. had magnanimity.

With these two equestrians Solon was solidly in the realm of monumental sculpture, having achieved what had brought him back to America six years before. He had found a home in the country in which to bring up his children, and he now owned a high-raftered studio in which to work. Fortune, as they say, was smiling upon him indeed.

CHAPTER IX

Second "Borglum the Sculptor"

Lisa Borglum's astonishing outburst in Paris, "*What does Solon know about art? He is not an artist!*" provides a good starting point for investigating why Gutzon Borglum deserted his wife and a London career to become the second Borglum sculptor. Also, it is a clear indication of what is puzzling in the relations of the brothers. Lisa's exclamation, so heated as to be hysterical, so defiant of accepted opinion, suggests great fear amounting to dread of what Solon's emergence might do to her marriage, already in jeopardy. Lisa and Gutzon, teacher and pupil, with Solon the one-time cowboy, can be seen as principals in a drama whose first act takes place in Sierra Madre, where Solon's work is an affront to the conventional eyes of Lisa. In this drama, Act II occurs in Paris at the turn of the century when Solon, now an art student, is emerging as a rising young sculptor. Gutzon is visibly unhappy. Should he follow Lisa's teachings and remain under her influence, or should he take a new course born of the urgencies of his own nature? Lisa's outburst triggered his decision.

Instead of returning to Harlestone Villa in London, or occupying the new home in Paris on which he had just signed a three-year lease,[1] Gutzon went alone to America on the heels of his brother. Haunted by doubts of the Old World art which he had admired from childhood but to which he was now tied by his marriage, disappointed, so far, in his ambition to become a fashionable London painter, inspired by the freshness he had spotted in his brother's work, and attracted by the lucrative prospects that now existed for sculpture in America, Gutzon made a *volte face*.[2]

Gutzon Borglum as a young man.

Lisa explained his absence by saying that he had gone to America to see the latest in murals, having been promised a contract with the English Midland Railways for their hotel in Manchester. Before long, however, she learned that her husband was deeply engaged making models for the Ulysses S. Grant Monument[3] in the nation's capital.

The gathering tensions of the past years made Gutzon Borglum easy prey to the grave illness that overtook him in the late summer of 1902. Before he could get started on any new course he suffered a complete nervous breakdown together with a severe case of typhoid. Lisa crossed the Atlantic to be near him, but on doing so she came face to face with Mary Montgomery, Gutzon's future wife, whom he had met on shipboard. Gutzon's father and his brother Arnold joined them in New York. Upon recovering Gutzon spent several months with his family in Omaha convalescing.

At this point Lisa passes out of Gutzon's life. She returned to Europe in the vain hope that her husband would rejoin her. But at length she was forced to realize that her marriage had ended. She went back to California taking along her faithful servant, Jeanne, and a large collection of unsold canvases. In Sierra Madre and Los Angeles she picked up her old life, resuming her teaching.[4] At last she consented to a divorce.

The effects of this marriage on a man destined to write his name across the country and the world are worth pondering. The age gap is what focuses attention. Referred to by Gutzon himself when divorce proceedings began, he told his lawyer, "I am tired, tired and old. Ever since I was married at twenty-two, I have tried to live an older age and foregone my youth." [5] And it is underscored by his exclamation after the divorce was granted, "At last I can be young, I have my whole life ahead of me."

Now forty-one, Gutzon was a man who had suffered, but he was a man with sufficient courage and determination to retrieve his past. The coming of Mary Montgomery into his life had much to do with a renewed confidence. Born in Turkey, the daughter of missionary parents, a graduate of Wellesley, Mary received much of her education abroad. At the time of her meeting with Gutzon she was on her way back from taking her Ph.D. at the University of Berlin. As with Lisa, she brought to her future husband important connections, among whom was the writer Rupert Hughes who became a close friend.

In trying to penetrate the complexity of Gutzon's personality one suspects much of his aggressiveness — not equaled, nor even apparent in other members of the Borglum family — may have been a by-product of that first marriage. Lisa was one who knew how to make and use connections and recognized the importance of knowing the "right" people. That woman of the world who figures so prominently in Gutzon's early life, the redoubtable Jesse Benton Frémont, wife of General John C. Frémont, certainly knew the value of power and influence. With the death in 1902 of Mrs. Frémont and his separation from Lisa, Gutzon lost simultaneously the two dominant influences of his early life.

Dr. Borglum's prudent attention to his son's mental as well as his physical health contributed toward a swift recovery. Gutzon was back in New York before Christmas with his sister Harriet who acted as a companion and housekeeper.[6]

Remodeled by a leading firm of architects, Heins and La Farge, his studio at 166 East 38th Street was strategically located in mid-town Manhattan close to the two railroad terminals, Grand Central and Pennsylvania. Here he made his large panels for the British railway hotel in Manchester. When he was running behind schedule the English director suggested a second artist to expedite the work.[7] This drew the curt reply that Gutzon would not be interested in a collaboration, and if such were demanded, he would drop the contract. At last the great panels were completed and delivered and paid for. Now came the decision that so adversely affected Solon's career: Gutzon became a sculptor and never touched his brushes again in any significant way.

Gutzon discovered that his decision had its drawbacks, that although the name Borglum had a lot going for it, it was the other Borglum, not himself, that people were talking about.

It is not an impossible thought that Gutzon may have made his switch not realizing that Solon had established himself in an unassailable position. Gutzon had once before given his name to another artist, his teacher, thereby producing a humiliating pupillary position from which there was no easy escape. This interpretation of Gutzon's dilemma makes sense when studied in the light of the predicament that followed. The *volte face* was instinctive. It was an escape not carefully considered for there was Solon in his path. Solon, his only full brother, whom he had rescued from the ranch to put on his artistic course. Solon, generous and kind, but very stubborn. He would never give way. Particularly *now*, when he had sacrificed his painting career.

Sculpture was no new thing for Gutzon Borglum. From the first he had shown an interest in that form of art. He made a bust of Mrs. Jesse Frémont as early as 1889[8] and apparently she was very pleased with it. His first trip to Europe in 1890 led to a claim of personal friendship with Auguste Rodin in the days before either artist was recognized. He had been a student of Mercié at the Académie Julian.[9] He had made an interesting and lively group called "Apaches Pursued", which was exhibited at the Société Nationale des Beaux-Arts. In London, inspired by the Boer War, he made a study called "The Return of The Boer". However it should not be overlooked that Gutzon stated that while he had done some sculpture earlier he had concentrated on painting, "which had been most profitable, I had to live abroad and I had to live." [10] And in 1900, before seeing Solon's work in Paris, he spoke of his interest in painting as having "quite returned." [11]

These sculptures Gutzon brought along with him on his precipitate flight from Paris. Gutzon had done enough sculpture to support his claim of being a sculptor, but hardly a sculptor of the West as he claimed. Also, he was an impatient man, and his primary interest being in painting he had never mastered the techniques of building large scale works, especially the armatures. As a young art student in San Francisco he was criticized by his teacher[12] for being too hasty, always wishing to go on to something else without perfecting his work. The same applied at this point in relation to sculpture.

In New York Gutzon first exhibited at a National Sculpture Society show in 1902 at the Madison Square Garden, held in conjunction with the New York Florist Club. His work was well received, "Indians Pursued by U.S. Troops" (presumably the same work as "Apaches Pursued") being called a "stirring piece," and his rejected offering for the Grant competition seriously evaluated: "the whole group is full of character, both in general conception and in detail, and is so far removed from the usual manner of the equestrian statue as to deserve very serious study." [13]

Thirteen months later in Dec. 1903 Gutzon was elected to membership in the National Sculpture Society. By then he had successfully offered a collection of his sculptures to St. Louis for exhibition in the forthcoming fair. A short lived membership of the society ended in recrimination and angry resignation. Members were outraged by Gutzon's claim to being first of the brothers in the sculptural field, asking what about Solon? It appeared that being first mattered a great deal to him. If one recalls his pupillary status with Lisa it becomes comprehensible that he would claim Solon as *his* pupil. The laity, who had great difficulty distinguishing between the brothers, may have been impressed with the claim, but the effect on the profession was apt to be calamitous.[14]

For the immediate present however Gutzon's life was full of acute embarrassments and with the embarrassments came temptations. A stranger at the door of his studio inquiring if this was the studio of "Borglum the sculptor" would naturally receive an affirmative reply.[15] A story straight from a witness[16] fits here. Having gotten wind of the National Sculpture Society's intention to oust him for a breach of its code of ethics claiming a contract with the name Borglum on it which everyone knew was meant for Solon, he took the initiative by resigning.

The embarrassing situation was worsened by the fact that there had been an agreement to work in different fields in order to avoid confusion and to prevent a recurrence of the situation that produced the Sierra Madre clash. This is not generally known except within the family. Because of its reflection on Gutzon one is tempted to pass over this agreement, but it is a crucial link in the chain of events explaining why Solon so readily dropped painting for sculpture, following his success in Cincinnati, and why there was so much feeling among those aware of Solon's sacrifice. The brothers had seen each other when Solon passed through London on his way to Paris, and had made an agreement whereby Solon promised to drop painting forever, Gutzon on his part would devote himself exclusively to painting. That is, they would be artists, distinct in their individual fields.[17] Solon, as we have said, never touched his brushes after leaving London that summer of 1897; he may even have left them with Gutzon who was out of funds at the time. Nevertheless Gutzon's exhibits at the Société Nationale des Beaux-Arts, the "new" Salon, continued with the inclusion of sculpture, a fact that outraged Solon's French relatives besides leading to hot discussions in both families, many members of whom wondered why such an agreement had to be made in the first place.

The abortiveness of the agreement is reminiscent of Gutzon's impulsive offer to share his Sierra Madre studio with Solon, and the similarity leads one to speculate that it was Lisa, whose husband was described by one familiar with the situation as being "a tool in her hands to work whatever she sees fit to propose," who really killed the idea.

Gutzon on his decision to become a sculptor said he invited Solon to share his studio, an invitation that Solon declined. Gutzon may have provided one reason for Solon's refusal when in a letter to Dr. Guthrie, rector of Saint Mark's in-the-Bouwerie, New York, he stated, after Solon's death, "Upon his (Solon's) return from Europe.[18] . . . I offered him half my studio and a full share in money I secured, with the fullest retention of his individual position and his signing of all his own work." *Signing of all his own work!* "Shades of Sierra Madre," one can hear Solon exclaiming, "Won't my brother ever learn that he can't treat me as an appendage?"

The respect each had for the other's work reduces the suspicion that rivalry played a part in their careers. Instances of Gutzon's admiration of Solon's work have been given, to which one of his last published appraisals may be added: "Although the work[19] is the product of my brother's hand, I am forced to forget relationship and to say that the 'Bucky' O'Neill monument is a marvel. In my opinion it has no equal in this country — and so far as I know, it is unexcelled abroad." Much the same is true of Solon. An abstract piece such as Gutzon's concept of motherhood as a female Atlas won Solon's and Emma's admiration. And later when Emma had only the profoundest reason for distrusting her brother-in-law, she was never heard to disparage his abilities as a sculptor. The reverse is true. After Solon's death at the time of the Stone Mountain "blowup" Emma did not contribute to Gutzon's downfall as might have been expected, but is remembered as tearing up and destroying letters from his enemies,[20] who must surely have counted on her support. Solon and Emma may have feared Gutzon, but revenge and vindictiveness were no part of their natures.

Solon's problem was not that Gutzon was another successful sculptor. It was that he was — Gutzon. In that age there were many highly successful sculptors, with most of whom Solon was on terms of intimacy, respecting their work and on occasion competing, as a matter of course. For competition was not only the spirit of the age, it was the accepted thing. Happily there was enough work to go around. Gutzon may have been, as some thought, the greatest sculptor in the world. It would not have changed the situation. He and Solon collided, one soon discovers, *the moment Solon was unwilling to step aside.* And when that time came, the collision was severe, for do not the worst collisions occur between ships of equal tonnage?

Membership of the National Sculpture Society was a very brief affair. Gutzon was notified of his election in December (1903); a month later his name was in the headlines: "Gutzon Borglum calls[21] National Sculpture Society Exhibit a Disgrace;" and in April he resigned. The official version had it that Gutzon Borglum resigned after being called a liar by a member at a council meeting. The argument centered on who was Borglum the sculptor. Gutzon charged the society's respected president, John Quincy Adams Ward, with "insult and slander" and some of the members with "brutality." Being of a personal nature it was agreed to strike the incident from the record. Solon, by that time a council member, was asked to persuade his brother to change his mind. He failed and the resignation stuck.

The breach with the sculptors was momentous. Contention seemed to follow Gutzon now wherever he went. Within a few years he was resigning from another association whose vice-president he had become, The Association of American Painters and Sculptors, objecting to the way in which it chose its exhibits; "miserable works of favorites are surreptitiously invited." Here, as Gilbert Fite says, "he displayed insurgency among the insurgents." [22] He struck back savagely at the National Sculpture Society, terming it no more deserving of its lofty designation than the National Biscuit Company, and extended his indictment of artists to everything that could be labeled academic including the National Academy of Design.

The sculpture aimed at landing Gutzon in the field of Western art is titled "The Mares of Diomedes," but its history is still incomplete for today, in the company of many fine works of American artists, it resides in the storage basement of the Metropolitan Museum of Art. It was not always so, however. For long the group stood in the great entrance hall of the museum. "The Mares of Diomedes" was presented to the Metropolitan Museum by James Stillman, a wealthy New York banker, who is said to have paid $12,000 for it. The work was first shown in St. Louis where it attracted attention but did not win the Exposition's gold medal as claimed.* [23] The Mares was exhibited next at the Pennsylvania Academy of the Fine Arts and at the National Academy of Design, giving it a brief but distinguished career before going to the Metropolitan. Dramatic like most of Gutzon's work, the statue depicts five horses of the lean

---

* The gold medal was awarded to "The Return of the Boer," titled, "The Boer."

Gutzon Borglum, Sculptor. "Apaches Pursued by U. S. Troops." Inscribed "Exposition des beaux-arts 1901." R. W. Norton Art Gallery, Shreveport, Louisiana. Height 17½ in. *R. W. Norton Art Gallery.*

Gutzon Borglum, Sculptor. "Hercules Stampeding the Mares of Diomedes." 1904. Collection of R. W. Norton Art Gallery, Shreveport, Louisiana. Height 21 in.; Metropolitan Museum of Art, New York City. *R. W. Norton Art Gallery.*

bronco type in a frantic stampede, mouths open, ears flattened, nostrils flaring, eyes agonized by fright. On the back of the lead horse, perched with his hand holding onto his mane and legs clinging to the horse's flanks, is the naked figure of a man.

Willadene Price, one of Gutzon's biographers, throws some light on its origin; "Gutzon usually had a name for his statues[24] before he even started them, but he was ready to ship his statue to St. Louis and his group of horses was still unnamed." Gutzon, we are told, had got the idea from stories he had heard as a boy in the Middle West of the theft of range horses. He pictured an outlaw or an Indian leading a band of horses in a stampede, saying he took the clothes off the rider because they seemed cumbersome. "He was about to label the bronze 'Stampede' when a visitor in his studio, unaware of the theme used for the statue, remarked, 'What a magnificent portrayal of the horses of Diomedes!'

" 'You've just named the group,' said Gutzon. 'From now on they are the Mares of Diomedes.'

"Whether the rider," adds the writer, "is the fabled Diomedes, King of Thrace, about to be devoured by his own man-eating horses, or Hercules leading the horses after they destroyed Diomedes, is left to the viewer to decide."

Gutzon himself[25] is said to have settled the matter of title by saying that, although the horses had all the appearance of Western ponies, he liked the Hercules idea and adopted it "for the benefit of the great lay mind which always demanded a classical allusion in things it liked." But he also said the idea was to show the challenge of the individual against the brute force of nature.

In the Museum's catalogue, Albert TenEyck Gardner[26] wrote: "The classical title and the nude rider cannot disguise the fact that the real subject of this sculpture is a cowboy stampeding a herd of broncos. The allusion to Greek mythology was an afterthought that transformed a cowpoke into Hercules and his ponies into the mythical, flesh-eating mares of the Bistonian King Diomedes."

Just as Gutzon asked himself when viewing Solon's work in Paris, "*How* had he done it?" so now friends of Solon asked, "*Why* had he (Gutzon) done it?" Clement Barnhorn,[27] who had seen Solon's "Stampede of Wild Horses" exhibited in Paris at the Salon in 1899 and again in 1900 at the Exposition Universelle, was one who did; writing to an inquirer he said, "I always did feel that [The Mares of Diomedes] was Solon's introduction with an extension added." The two horses

added, Barnhorn compared to a city that put up a 10½ story building because of
jealousy for a neighbor that has erected a ten story building. Much the same
comparison could be made in relation to MacMonnies' "Horse Tamers," also
prominently displayed at the Exposition, which is a life-size group of rearing
horses, one bearing a nude rider. In studying these works, and others subsequent
to them like Proctor's monument to the Mustang in Austin, Texas, which
increased the number of horses to seven, no disparaging comparison of Gutzon's
"Mares" is intended. Rather, another possibility suggests itself: the determination
of the Second Borglum the Sculptor to prove his superiority in a field that the
First had made peculiarly his own.

A confusion that was rapidly becoming general is admirably exemplified by
what happened when the Century Company tried to find Solon in connection
with Frank Sewall's article, "A Sculptor of The Prairie," and ran into Gutzon
instead. Century editor Richard Watson Gilder had that experience in Europe
when Gutzon happened to be in London delivering his panels. It was repeated in
New York with the art editor, A. W. Drake. In the Gutzon Borglum papers at
the Library of Congress are two drafts of a letter, which prove Gutzon's
resourcefulness and his unwillingness to resolve a confusion by stating the
relevant facts. The date is March, 1904: "When you called," Gutzon wrote
Drake, "I did not think much about the confusion there exists since my brother
has come into the field. It is natural enough having studied with me and
following as he does the same kind of work I gave most of my attention to when
in the West." He made light of the confusion, blaming it on the newspapers who
"attribute my work to him and vice versa." But now it looked as though the
Century "had fallen into the same trap. When I met Mr. Gilder in London I saw
he was not sure whether I was the one." Deliberately evading the chance to
clarify the confusion, Gutzon continued: "The subject is naturally a delicate one
for me to press and I prefer therefore to leave it to chance — and I mean in the
confusion that exists now in New York." To Drake's suggestion of including
Gutzon with Solon in one article featuring Western art, Gutzon asked to be
excluded. "He is younger and while the noise and stir I have made has in a way
been a financial help to him it has great disadvantages . . . publicity in your
magazine will be a much greater help to him. . . ."

The coup which put Gutzon squarely on the sculptural map among topflight artists was his defeat of the eminent president of the National Sculpture Society, J. Q. A. Ward, for the honor of designing the Sheridan monument in the nation's capital. It also became a scoop for the press, which gave it a double benefit to Gutzon. Only a rare combination of abilities could have pulled off both feats. From now on this is the Gutzon Borglum history knows.

Gutzon, we are told, laid the groundwork of his coup with meticulous care. Determined not to have another rebuff like the one over the Grant, and still fuming over the disruption of his relations with his fellow artists, he now looked in the direction of Washington, D.C. Here he happened to have a long-standing friendship with the Herbert Wadsworths. It was a simple matter for him to arrange with Mrs. Wadsworth, a leading Washington hostess, a dinner party so that Gutzon might meet Mrs. Sheridan. The dinner party proved rewarding. The onetime protégé of Mrs. Frémont, at his most brilliant best in the society of ladies, sold himself as the one artist who could do her husband's statue. At the end of the evening Mrs. Sheridan is reputed to have said, "You seem to have such[28] a deep respect for men who have served their country that I am sure you will make a good statue of the General." She eagerly accepted the sculptor's invitation to her and her son, Lieut. Philip Sheridan, to visit his New York studio the next time they were in the city.

And so the American public learned that the longpending award was not going as expected to J. Q. A. Ward, creator of so many of the nation's equestrians and monuments, but to a newcomer, Gutzon Borglum. The announcement on July 31, 1907, was made by the Secretary of War, the Honorable William H. Taft, soon to be president of the United States.

This was a high point in Gutzon Borglum's career — and also sweet revenge. To have defeated, in single combat as it were, the doyen of the sculptors was a blow struck at the heart of the National Sculpture Society. But in the eyes of most of his fellow artists Gutzon henceforth was an unprincipled maverick who was exchanging their respect for the plaudits of the politicians and Washington society.

CHAPTER X

Collision

Gutzon Borglum, sculptor, was no longer a rumor. He was a fact. Thus, although the years 1904–1907 had been a period of fruition for Solon's early ambitions, culminating in the monumental sculpture he had come home to do, they were marked by the hard realization that once again he was in strong conflict with his brother, this time in sculpture. For this he could not hold Lisa responsible since she was no longer part of Gutzon's life. By his own words Gutzon proclaimed his successes: "I'm making a hell of a lot of money!" [1] No longer did he have to stand in the glow of Solon's fame. He was creating his own. He was writing his own script. One that would relegate Solon to whatever status he chose for him at that moment. Sometimes it would be pupil, and he the elder brother, the established artist of Western work. He could become sentimental referring to Solon as his "little brother" whom he loved more than any of the others. He quickly learned the cutting edge of these distinctions. When it did not impinge on his own position he could speak of him with great respect, and call attention to his achievement with studied praise.

Both the Borglum sculptors were fast workers, once they had their idea. Gutzon had his model of General Philip Sheridan ready to show when, by coincidence, another widow of a fighting man appeared on his sculptural horizon. To make the coincidence even more remarkable this one was the widow of a Sheridan lieutenant not only in the Civil War but on the Western Plains fighting the Indians — George Armstrong Custer. Custer had been in command of

Michigan's cavalry at Gettysburg; it was the state of Michigan that wanted to commemorate the man that had died at Little Big Horn. In a business letter to C. H. Davis Mrs. Custer announced the news. As it happened Davis had recently been instrumental in giving Gutzon Borglum a commission to do the John W. Mackay monument in Reno, Nevada. He and his brother Robert, editor of *Munsey's Magazine*, were great admirers of Gutzon whom they had recently discovered after twenty years' separation. They had been youthful companions of Gutzon's early L.A. days in California.

Davis grasped the opportunity to help his friend. He told Mrs. Custer that he considered Gutzon Borglum to be the peer of any sculptor living and unquestionably the greatest sculptor in America. To support his assertion he mentioned the bronze horses placed in the Metropolitan and the statue of John Mackay; and he suggested that Mrs. Custer might ask Mrs. Sheridan's opinion of Gutzon.[2]

Elizabeth Custer replied that she had seen the work of Mr. Borglum at the Paris Exposition and had been amazed at the fidelity with which Indians and their ponies were depicted. She said she had been interested ever since, cutting out the illustrations in the newspapers and keeping them. She said she would endeavor to see the bronze horses in the Metropolitan when she was in New York and hoped to have the pleasure of meeting Mr. Borglum. She adopted Mr. Davis' suggestion of writing to a friend of Mrs. Sheridan. She concluded by asking Davis to give her any thoughts he or Mr. Borglum might have for the statue.

The letter had to be telephoned to Gutzon who was out of town when it arrived. It was obvious that Mrs. Custer, like so many others, was mixed up over the Borglum sculptors, and Gutzon referred to that fact when answering Davis. Solon had an "exhibition" in Paris, work of the same character as his own,[3] and it was possible that she had in mind Solon's work. Of late years, however, he himself had given up the doing of Indians, leaving that particular field to Solon. He compared the equestrian of General Custer both in its importance and interest and general picturesqueness to General Sheridan's, which he suggested Mrs. Custer should see when she came to town. Gutzon added that he was not doing an old man thirty years after he won his laurels. It was scandalous, he said, the way America's generals were being represented as a lot of civilians in uniform, dressed for parade purposes.

Mrs. Custer came to Gutzon's studio and was enormously impressed by the Sheridan. She is quoted as remarking, "General Sheridan would be quite satisfied to sit on the horse through eternity." The sculptor had made the statue most dramatic by depicting the cavalry leader at the moment of reining in his horse after his historic ride from Winchester when he said to his defeated men after their Cedar Creek rout (October 19, 1864), "You will sleep in your tents tonight or you will sleep in Hell."

In fact Gutzon was quite confident of Elizabeth Custer's decision and he now wrote directly to her. He can be excused at that moment if he felt destiny itself was taking a hand in his affairs. But there was, right along, another sculptor in the running — Solon Borglum.[4]

Solon was still out West when these negotiations began, but his files show that he too had ardent supporters. The Harrison Granite Company, which had supplied him with the pedestal for his General Gordon Monument in Atlanta, was following an experimental practice of promoting clients when they heard of possible commissions. This appealed to many artists who did not like to promote their own work; it gave them an agent to scout the field on their behalf. This particular instance is the only time apparently that Solon was concerned in this way and it is clear that the granite company, as Solon later explained to Col. Briggs, had initiated the effort. Solon, however, was under no obligation to the company, or any member of it.

Following the conclusion of the O'Neill unveiling in Arizona and visits among friends in the Far West, Solon finally was home again. He was greeted with the news that the pending Custer commission was moving in his direction. George Simpson, Harrison's Detroit agent, wrote Col. Briggs: "I do not believe that there is a sculptor in the world who can give you a finer equestrian memorial than Mr. Borglum. . . . By birth, training and sentiment he is a son of the West. . . . I will quote what Charles H. Caffin says about him: 'His art is akin to great art; fresh in inspiration, large in feeling; poignant in repose, vigorous without exaggeration. Moreover, it is of American conditions and partakes of that large freedom whence it originated. It does not suffer by comparison with the grand art of foreign origin, such as that of Barye, but should be doubly appreciated by Americans, since in conception and manner it is a product of an infinitely larger environment and one that Americans of all others should most appreciate. . . .' " Referring to another client, Cass Gilbert, the architect, Simpson added, "I shall always remember your courtesy and kindness in the matter of the Gilbert Memorial with which I was connected . . ."

Simpson hinted that there might be a 'mix-up' between Solon and his brother. That information was immediately followed by more of the same from the company chairman: "Mr. Gutzon Borglum called up at 5.00 p.m. yesterday and stated he had no appointment with Mrs. Custer to-day; that he saw her about three weeks ago; there was no confusion in the matter, and that he had explained his brother's work to her. He repeated that there was no confusion in the matter and that he had no appointment with Mrs. Custer.

"The above is an exact notation made by Mr. Cottrell (who talked with Mr. Borglum) and laid on my desk.

"I judge from the foregoing that nevertheless, there must have been some misunderstanding somewhere that enabled her to get in touch with the wrong Borglum, and reading between the lines, I imagine that he will not go out of his way to promote his brother's interest."

Another letter exchanged between the head office and Simpson throws more light on the proceedings: "It seems that Mrs. Custer has Solon Borglum in mind. When I first called upon Father Crowley he wrote Mrs. Custer. Afterwards Mrs. Custer wrote him that she felt that Mr. Borglum, owing to his familiarity with Western life, was the one sculptor to do this work. I also understand that she may have gotten hold of Gutzon, thinking that he was Solon. Therefore please have Mr. Harrison and Mr. Borglum see Mrs. Custer at once and don't lose any time. . . ."

Unfortunately for Solon's chances in this situation, his studio was in transit to its new location in Silvermine. There was little to show of his work and there is no record of a visit to Silvermine at this point. Solon did meet Mrs. Custer. Apparently the result was to complete Mrs. Custer's confusion. In her effort to forget the Borglums she now began visiting other sculptors.

Early in December C. H. Davis made a strong effort to settle the matter and swing the commission in Gutzon's favor. He wrote to Mrs. Custer that he hoped she would not be misled by youthful enthusiasm where "knowledge, experience and good judgment" were of prime importance. "Borglum's brother," he explained, approached his work entirely from the commercial side, describing

Solon as being "hand-in-glove with a monument-building concern" whose efforts
were as far removed from Art as "the average manufacturer of stamped
silverware."

Whatever else the letter accomplished it did not dislodge the affectionate
memories Mrs. Custer had of Solon's work. Finally, she threw the entire
responsibility back to the committee and took refuge in a trip abroad.

On January 11 Gutzon, realizing that the commission was in fact now
going elsewhere, wrote Mrs. Custer withdrawing in his brother's favor. He
apologized for the overzealousness of his friends. He was appreciative of it all,
but work was piling up and he might not be able to do her statue should she
eventually decide in his favor. But there was Solon, whose work she so much
admired. "You have for the very best reasons the highest regard for my brother's
work." He stressed his own regard for Solon as an artist and as a person who
could "lend himself as readily" to the idea she had in mind for her statue as any
man she might select. It was a letter designed to allay any suspicion that might
have been aroused by the outrageous and denigrating statements made by his
friend.

The letter had the desired effect on Elizabeth Custer; "I do not know how
to reply to your beautiful letter about your brother. My heart was touched by
your expressions regarding him and it is most generous and brotherly to place his
merits before me. I find him, as you know, full of the poetry and the sentiment of
his work and so I have repeatedly written Col. Briggs. His pathos, the maternal
sentiment of some of his things, the fire of his O'Neill, the tenderness of his
stricken animals — everything appeals to me. . . ."

In February 1908 the Custer statue of the city of Monroe, Michigan, was
given to E. C. Potter, French's collaborator for some of his equestrians. So far as
Solon was concerned, the irony of the situation was heightened by the fact that
when Elizabeth Custer at last made her visit to Rocky Ranch she was thrilled
with the rustic barn structure and its many contents and became fast friends of
the Solon Borglums.

Gutzon Borglum's reputation as one who "would not go out of his way to
promote his brother's interest" could have come from reports of how he had
scooped other New York artists including Solon in the big contract for the
sculptural work of the Episcopal church being erected on Morningside Heights,

the Cathedral of Saint John the Divine. A matter of twenty full-size figures and some seventy-five lesser ones was a huge contract to be given to one man, especially for a sculptor still untried and relatively unknown as Gutzon was in 1905. Illumination of how he succeeded in capturing this extraordinary contract, getting it away at least from Solon, is supplied by the following.[5]

One day soon after the close of the St. Louis Fair, at a meeting in the vestry, the rector of New York's Grace Church, the Reverend William Reed Huntington, who was chairman of the sculpture committee of the new church, said to his parishioner Mrs. David McIlwaine, Solon's and Emma's intimate friend from Paris days, "We are going to give some work to your sculptor." He had had a long talk with Mr. Borglum, he said, in the course of which he had mentioned the St. Louis groups and Emma's receptions, to which he had been invited by the McIlwaines but which unfortunately he had been unable to attend. It was not until after the meeting when Mrs. McIlwaine was on the way home that it occurred to her it was strange this particular piece of good news had not been given to her by Solon himself, or by Emma. Her first reaction was to be vexed with her friends. But then the thought dawned: Was it Solon to whom her rector had talked, or could it have been Gutzon? She rushed over to her friends to learn the truth. When her suspicion was verified that it was Gutzon with whom Dr. Huntington had talked, it was too late; the contract for the entire work had already been given to Gutzon. The McIlwaines were stunned. David McIlwaine tried unsuccessfully to persuade Solon to let him make the whole deception public. "If ever you want the facts, I will give them," David said.

Another case of "mistaken identity"[6] occurred in Washington, D.C. The Pan-American Building was a deeply important development in the history of the capital. Solon's hopes of having a part in it had been raised to a peak when he arrived home from a conference with the architects, the firm of Cret and Kelsey, with a commission in his pocket to do two eagles, baldheaded and condor, which, placed over the entrance, would symbolize the two continents. There still had to be awarded two heroic symbolical figures representing North and South America to flank the entrance. When Kelsey wrote to say that Elihu Root, Secretary of State, had seen Solon's eagles and had been so impressed with them that he had said, "Borglum will make one of the large groups, at least," it looked as though another important contract was on the way. Solon and the other chosen artist, Isadore Konti, cast lots to see which of the two figures each would do, and Solon was delighted to draw North America.

But the jubilation was premature. At the luncheon meeting in New York, set for the signing of the final government contract with Director of the Budget John Barrett, who was also Director-General of the Pan-American Union, Solon was informed there had been a mistake. The contract was intended for Gutzon. No satisfactory explanation was offered. One is left with the impression that devious wire-pulling, politics, and the aid of Washington hostess Martha Blow Wadsworth proved too much for the stalwart Republican, Elihu Root.

Solon can be seen trying to cope with an impossible problem. He had tried various ways to deal with it. The way of escape, by flight — Sierra Madre. Of avoidance — the London pact to go separate ways. Again, the way of separation — refusal of Gutzon's alleged offer of a shared studio and profits in New York. The way of forbearance — the declination of the McIlwaines' offer to publicize the Cathedral incident. The pattern is unmistakable. Now there was to be a "new" Solon, though not so "new." The cowboy who had refused to give up his seat to a bully was still around.

The cloud that had been spreading so ominously across Solon's sunlit sky, the storm that had been brewing ever since the Sierra Madre trouble, the phenomenon that Solon could not cope with, the collision that had menaced their relations ever since Gutzon first appeared as a full-time sculptor on the American scene and entered the lists of monumental work determined to win — all came to a climax, with a grand medley of metaphor.

The spring of 1908 brought word that Nebraska was about to erect a statue of the man its state capital had been named for, Abraham Lincoln. At once the name Solon Borglum jumped to mind. Not only was he a beloved artist of international fame but as near being a native son as one not actually born in Nebraska could be.

On hearing about the project Solon immediately wrote his friend and native Nebraskan, James H. Canfield, Librarian at Columbia University, to express his strong interest. Shortly afterward, he heard from the chairman of the state committee himself. Mr. F. M. Hall, of the law firm of Hall, Woods and Pound, could scarcely have been more flattering. "I confess that I am entirely ignorant touching some features," Hall wrote. He was shortly going to Atlantic City and requested the sculptor to meet him there for a conference — that is, if convenient and if he had a desire to make a statue of Lincoln. He wanted to know if it was the customary and preferred procedure to have, say, two or three sculptors make competitive designs. How would a sculptor feel about this? In conclusion Hall wrote, "Mr. James M. Canfield, Librarian of Columbia University, has been kind enough to suggest your name, although I had your name on my list. I have remembered you most distinctly from your work at the St. Louis Exposition, and I have been greatly interested in many things that I have seen of yours although I do not remember having learned of any statue of Lincoln that you have ever made."

The goal of every aspiring sculptor of that era it seemed was to do a Lincoln. To bring out the full greatness of soul from that homely face and gaunt figure challenged whatever there was of greatness in the artist himself. Whether it was the challenge or the prestige involved, it was an artist's dream of dreams. Solon, himself a rough-hewn son of the soil, felt a more than ordinary affinity for the Railsplitter. "The Prairie Sculptor" and "The Prairie Statesman" would seem a likely and logical combination of artist and subject.

Weeks passed with no further word from Mr. Hall. When Solon heard that Hall had seen D. C. French, successor to Saint-Gaudens as dean of the sculptors, he could have been tempted to get in touch with him, for the Solon Borglum files contain the following letter from French to Hall: "My friend, Mr. Solon H. Borglum, has asked me to write you concerning his standing as a sculptor. I feel that it is entirely unnecessary to do so because his name and his work are well known, and he needs no praise from me. I have the greatest respect for his work, and should be glad to see him receive an important commission." And he sent the letter to Solon with a covering few lines, "There is no reason why you should not use my letter if you care to. I rather think they have given me up from their long silence." There is no indication that Solon used the letter, but it stands as a heartening proof of the sort of freemasonry among artists, particularly as the one who wrote it still had his own hopes for this commission and in the end received it.

Meanwhile many friends had endorsed Solon. In Omaha August and Lucy

Borglum saw members of the committee, among them Myron L. Learned, president of the influential Omaha Club. Learned was hopeful, assuring August that the whole committee was "more than friendly to Mr. Solon Borglum."

Among the committee members however was the U.S. Senator from Nebraska, who was something of a Lincoln expert. The Honorable Charles F. Manderson had been present at both the Gutzon unveilings in Washington, D.C., of the giant head of Lincoln in the Rotunda and the General Sheridan equestrian statue and had been impressed. It was with some trepidation that the August Borglums ventured forth to beard this formidable lion one Sunday afternoon. But the visit went off without a hitch. Lucy was asked to play and their hosts showed them their objets d'art. The General was particularly proud of his "Lincoln corner," where were prominently displayed familiar photographs of Gutzon's bust of Lincoln. Lucy reported to her sister that evidently Gutzon had made a great impression on the Senator. "We were very discreet, but when Mme. Manderson said to me, 'Solon is considered the better artist, isn't that so?' I told her what Remington had said and what Saint-Gaudens said to Elizabeth [Her sister-in-law who had known Saint-Gaudens in Paris]. Saint-Gaudens' letter was read by the General and apparently made a good impression." The Senator thanked the Borglums for coming. Lucy thought the visit justified.

There was an ominous conclusion to her letter. August had heard from Learned, who reported this from Chairman Hall (January 12, 1909): "A good many of Solon Borglum's friends have been pushing him for this commission and a good many of Gutzon Borglum's friends have been pushing him for the commission. I do not understand why two brothers should be in such strenuous competition for this commission." Hall suggested that no harm would be done if the matter were to be brought by General Manderson and Mr. Wattles before the committee.

It was the first intimation that Solon had that Gutzon was trying to get the commission.

Early in the new year Gutzon invited his brother to his studio. Gutzon, too, had been told of the ominous remark made by Hall, "I don't understand why two brothers are in such strenuous competition for this commission." From the conference emerged a sadly shaken Solon.

Much had happened recently to augment the second Borglum sculptor's ego. Gutzon had reached the pinnacle of his early career and was especially successful in top political circles in Washington, D.C. He had not only scored with his giant bust of Lincoln, just unveiled in the Capitol Rotunda, but with his Sheridan coup. Both had paid off tremendously. Gutzon would not have been at all willing to forego the advantage of "having done a Lincoln." He would not have heeded a plea, which surely was made by Solon, based on simple fair play, that it was now *his* turn, that *he* should have a chance to do a Lincoln. In fact this was so far from Gutzon's mind that the notion which came to dominate him was even then developing, that he alone was the true interpreter of the personality of Abraham Lincoln. There was not the slightest chance that Gutzon would have heeded a reminder that Nebraska was no longer his state, if it ever had been considered so. For years he had claimed to be a Californian.

Gutzon had set his sights on still other Lincoln targets. He was in fact about to do a statue for Newark, New Jersey. Another monument for the city of Cincinnati was in the offing, and he was already speaking of the pending commission for the greatest of them all, the National Memorial to be erected in Washington, D.C.

A simple record of the conference of Solon with his brother is contained in a rough draft of a letter to Canfield: "I also went to my brother's studio the other day at his invitation. We spoke about the Lincoln affair and I told him that Mr. Hall had thought it strange two brothers were fighting to get this work. . . . I was surprised that he thought so, too." Gutzon told Solon that he should withdraw in his favor, using the same reason other people use; he said "that I had never made a Lincoln, and that I did not know the real soul of that great man."

It was a rambling draft in which Solon takes up his own defense, emphasizing what the critics have said of his work, that he could and did bring out "the real soul of what I want to express, whether it has been the cowboy and Indians in the Western life, or General and Captain." Solon referred to the different subjects he had taken up which were not done in a sensational way, but in a way to "bring out the true character of our great men."

This incident stands as cruel proof that Gutzon could and did ride roughshod over Solon. A sorely troubled man can be seen taking the train back to South Norwalk, with the words, "You cannot do a Lincoln. You do not understand the soul of that great man," echoing in his ears.

To Solon's draft is attached a note to Emma who frequently wrote her husband's important letters. It tells its own story of that deeply troubled relationship: "Dear Emma . . . write this letter the best way you can, do not be antagonistic to Gutzon we cannot afford it."

So there was fear added to loss of confidence. What happened to this draft is not clear; the letter may never have been mailed for it is possible that Emma, looking squarely at the situation with a wisdom typically her own, advised Solon to trust his brother August, who was representing him in Omaha.

Whatever it was, a lull followed Hall's words to Learned, "I do not understand why two brothers should be in such competition with one another. . . ."

February and March passed without information reaching either Solon's or Gutzon's files. There is nothing to show the results of Gutzon's "lobbying for himself" and his visits to the Omaha *Bee*, which had done a particularly fine job in its handling of the Sheridan unveiling, a fact that Gutzon could be counted upon not to overlook. Whatever it was that transpired during these months, it was sufficient for the chairman of the committee to write a long letter, dated April 7, 1909, to Mr. C. Wright which shows a change of opinion as to the problem of the brothers:

"Replying to your letter of the 6th., I note what you say relative to the Lincoln statue and the connection of the Borglums with the enterprise. Let me suggest to you confidentially that you say to General Manderson the substance at least of what you have said to me in your letter. He has been rather friendly, I think, toward Gutzon Borglum because of the marble bust that he has recently made of Lincoln. I have suggested to General Manderson just what you suggest to me relative to Gutzon Borglum. He has been trying to land this commission in every possible way and that has made me suspicious and had a tendency to turn me against him . . ." General Manderson, on hearing from Gutzon, assured him that there had not been a meeting of the Committee having in charge the erection of the Lincoln statue at Lincoln, Nebraska. He told Gutzon that he was shortly to be in New York and would give himself "the pleasure of calling at your studio." Manderson then closed his letter with the ominous warning: ". . . a very decided effort" was being made in behalf of Solon, and the result of conflict between them was likely to be that "you would both be left in the cold."

I fear that should conflict come between your brother and yourself the result would be that you would both be left in the cold. These words were what caused two letters of withdrawal to be sent immediately to the chairman of the committee. Worded differently each tells its own story. The first from Solon:

Dear Sir:

I regret very much that it has been brought to my notice that the effort of my brother Gutzon and myself in trying to get the commission for the erection of the Lincoln statue is antagonistic and undignified for two brothers.

I wish to state positively that I never have caused any unjust personal feelings to be laid against my brother in a competition. This has been my principle towards him, or any other sculptor.

It was not long ago that a commission was given to me purely upon work *I had done.* The parties giving out the commission mentioned work my brother had done. I saw at once their mistake and refused to have any more to do with the commission until I had consulted my brother. I am very happy to say that he is now working on this commission.

I do not hesitate to remind you also that the first letter I wrote you was written with the full intention to help you get a sculptor for this work. I wrote it at the time when the Custer competition had just been given out. It was a great disappointment to me, because I had received encouraging letters from Mrs. Custer and through the committee expressing their approval of my works and the letter of introduction and one sent by my brother withdrawing from the competition. The work was eventually given to a Mr. Potter, who has always worked for D. C. French and was one of a number of names I had given to that committee.

If it is the desire of the committee to employ a sculptor of experience in making a statue of Lincoln or they feel at all embarrassed because two brothers are in this competition I gladly withdraw in favor of my brother.

Gutzon's letter was typewritten and he sent a copy to his brother:

May 3d 1909.

Dear Mr. Hall:

I have just received a letter from Nebraska stating "a very decided effort is being made on behalf of your brother Solon" and expressing "fear should there be a conflict" between Solon and myself "we would both be left in the cold."

I do not remember exactly what I said to you in Lincoln, but I did ask you some questions bearing upon the chances of your giving the work to my brother — I asked that before I discussed the matter with you. I do not remember your exact reply — you told me quite definitely that his work had not been of the kind that permitted seriously considering him in the making of the figure of Lincoln.

My purpose in asking you that question was none other than to inform you that if you were seriously considering my brother I should withdraw; and my recollection is that I said as much.

The letter that I received this morning comes from such unquestioned authority that I cannot help but feel that I am either in somebody's way, or the fact that Nebraska has *two brothers* who are sculptors, may be used to throw the work elsewhere.

I want to say, Mr. Hall, that I refused the Custer Equestrian because I would not permit the world to say that my brother and myself had struggled for it — and don't wish it said that you would have been glad to give one of the Borglums a monument for Nebraska but that they struggled against each other for it. That shall never be said.

My brother was my pupil, and as a sculptor is not outranked in American Art by enough men to use up the fingers of a single hand — and if he can give the kind of statue you want, or the people of Nebraska want — I believe the people of Nebraska ought to have it.

In conclusion permit me to say the conditions I learn of existing — whether real or political — are sufficient to destroy my interest in this monument. You will therefore greatly oblige me if you will withdraw *any* consideration of my name in connection with this monument . . .

Solon did not allow Gutzon's statement that he had turned down the Custer monument to pass unchallenged. He replied:

Dear Gutzon:

It seems that the last few days you and I have had about the same information from the west, which ended in the same thought. Sunday I wrote to Mr. Hall withdrawing from the competition.

There is one thing in your letter to Mr. Hall I do not understand. You say you refused the Custer Equestrian. I did not know that the work had been offered to you. If so, the letters from Col. Briggs and Mrs. Custer to me are entirely misleading. I knew that you had withdrawn from the competition recommending me very highly, and I had so informed Mr. Hall, and why Mr. Potter got this statue.

Affectionately yours,

/s/ Solon

Gutzon's statement, "My brother was my pupil," was far and away the most damaging. Pupil implies, is a corollary to, master, and what public body, concerned as much with prestige as with art, would prefer a pupil over a master, especially over a "master" that had those resounding successes in the National Capitol? From now on this became part of Gutzon's technique.

Solon was never given another chance to "do a Lincoln."

The award went to French.

In announcing the award the press also reported a luncheon meeting in Lincoln at which Gutzon, guest of the governor of Nebraska, used the occasion to vent his feelings. An angry sculptor charged Hall's committee with misconduct. Although he was not at the moment on speaking terms with Solon, Gutzon chose to speak for him, charging the committee with not examining the brothers' work, visiting their studios, or discussing the matter with them, and denied flatly that either he or Solon had withdrawn because of their competition.

At that luncheon July 8, 1909, Gutzon stated emphatically that he was about to commence construction of an $80,000 Lincoln memorial in Washington, D.C., adding that he would much rather have had the one in Lincoln, Nebraska. But he was wrong in his optimism. Neither that nor the one he was also counting on most, the Cincinnati monument, came to him. The Cincinnati Lincoln went to George Grey Barnard and the National in Washington went, as all the world should know, to Daniel Chester French — so that one result of the clash of two brothers was to send a distinguished artist on his path to greater renown. These were all bitter blows to the *amour propre* of this ambitious man, and Gutzon reflected them in his usual way, with a blast at the opposition — at Cincinnati, however, not at the expense of a brother but of a brother artist, George Grey Barnard.

The episode makes a significant point in the understanding of Gutzon Borglum: Gutzon may have treated his brother no differently from other artists who got in his way.

CHAPTER XI

The Finding of "Rocky Ranch"

A whirlwind reception with a Western flavor had marked Solon's visit to Prescott for the unveiling of his O'Neill Monument, complementing all that had taken place in the opposite corner of the South, only a few weeks earlier. Reunited with old friends and introduced to new ones, showered with gifts such as Navaho rugs, pottery and silver, he had had a glorious time. Before turning eastward he had visited Dan and Lucy Wood, now living in San José, and another friend of his old California days, Charles F. Lummis, Southwest Society secretary of the Archeological Institute of America. Then he turned his face homeward.

But home was no longer New York City. The death of little Lilli convinced the parents that the only place to raise children was in the country. As the first step to a permanent home in that direction they rented a frame house in Mamaroneck, a mile from the "village." Solon used the barn, a block away, for his studio. The homecoming of August, 1907, which Emma described as one of "great rejoicing," was to Silvermine, Connecticut. They began the move there before leaving for Atlanta.

The months following the St. Louis Fair and prior to the trip south were an eventful time for Solon. His four heroic groups went on from St. Louis to another World's Fair, the Lewis and Clark Centennial of 1905 in Oregon. A bust of Major William Clark, commissioned by the city of Portland and described as "a speaking likeness," led to Solon's election to one of the city's leading clubs, The Portland Commercial Club, "in token of its appreciation[1] of the superb artistic ability of Solon H. Borglum" and "as a partial expression of its deep appreciation of his work now adorning its home."

It was about this time that he received one of his last letters from the sculptor to whom he owed so much, Augustus Saint-Gaudens, stricken with the cancer that at last was to take his life. It included a final appraisal of Solon's work, "expressed with[2] a depth and sentiment which is unsurpassed."

In the Spring of 1905 Solon was asked to serve as a juror for the award of the Edmund Stewardson Prize by the managing director of the Pennsylvania Academy of The Fine Arts, Harrison C. Morris. This marked the beginning of a lifelong service of this kind to his profession. It contributed toward the establishment of a camaraderie among his fellow sculptors that engendered respect, as was recently recalled by the late Leo Friedlander who spoke of his "broad approach"[3] in judging the work of students and of his "unvarying kindness."

Now began a free give-and-take among those already established and those on their way to success. Solon served on the Council of the National Sculpture Society in one capacity or another during these years, in fact he was an active member of that fraternity of artists until the end of his life and in no small way contributed toward its distinction. Not by nature a man to enjoy formalities, and never an office-seeker, he responded warmly to the interest and respect of his colleagues. With his dislike of adulation, hatred of lionizing, and growing suspicion of publicity, he craved the honest exchange of ideas. With the establishment of the home in Silvermine came also the establishment of a colony of artists, which would call itself the Knockers' Club, in which objective criticism of each other's work, even among mature artists, was recognized as essential for growth. Solon was its founder and a vigorous leader of the often heated discussions that centered in the merits and weaknesses of the Beaux-Arts style.

On the home scene, things were going equally well. Emma's domestic problems had vanished the day "the incomparable Mrs. B" had slipped into their lives, bringing along her small boy, Carl, several enormous trunks, and a most willing, understanding, and dependable nature. For some seven or eight years she cared for the family as if her own; what was no less important, her presence freed the undomestic Emma for her happiest role.

Wherever artists are, friends and admirers gather. It was as natural now for

Emma to accept her position among sculptors as it had been in Paris among writers and musicians. "They are all alike, these artists!" Emma declared. She was at home in this atmosphere and she delighted in it. She used to refer to her "American" vocabulary which was the conversation of the studio and included many new words which she was at a complete loss as to how to translate when she returned to France. It was her double life. The first record of a reception and exhibition of Solon's work is that of one given in the studio that Solon shared with Alphaeus Cole in Paris. In New York this custom continued as friends gathered from time to time in Solon's studio at 30 East 14th Street. Here Solon was in command, his direct, unsophisticated, colorful, and often earthy speech balancing well with Emma's impeccable English, the English she had learned in England in her youth, but flavored with the charming accent from her native land. If Solon surprised people occasionally with his blunt speech, however, Emma could do the same. The kind of woman who liked to "call a spade a spade," Madame Borglum was loved and envied by many and respected by all. She had a knack for bringing interesting friends from Paris and New York together and when numbers required, she held her receptions in the home of friends of many years standing, the Dexter Ashleys at 346 Lexington Avenue.

In the autumn[4] of 1905 Solon took his family to Europe. For him it was a business trip as he wanted to see the latest in the way of equestrians. Emma had the opportunity of learning the craft of jewelry-making, in which she became so artistically proficient that she would exhibit her work along with the other Silvermine artists.

On their return, the studio activity gathered force, with new models and studio helpers appearing. A homeless Scot, described by Emma as a soldier of fortune who had fought in the Spanish-American war but never saved enough money to return home, became Solon's model for the Rough Rider Monument. About this time, Miller, Solon's elder brother, and his wife paid them a long visit which Solon took advantage of by having Miller pose for the first modelings of General Gordon.

In the Spring of 1905, twenty-year-old Paul Manship came to him as a studio helper, fresh from Minnesota. He stayed until October, 1907, when he went on to the Pennsylvania Academy of the Fine Arts, then to Rome, and so launched himself on a highly successful career.

Of those first days Paul Manship wrote[5] Monica: "I had little or no practical experience in sculpture. Solon 'employed' me because he liked me for my enthusiasm and earnestness. I lived with the family and he allowed me to be of such use about the studio as my meager equipment permitted. . . . I worked at anatomy while with your father. . . . The Bucky O'Neill equestrian came along about this time and watching your father work on the heroic-sized clay model taught me the application of the lessons in anatomy."

Paul met his future wife at the Borglums. In his own words: "very important to me was the visit to your mother of a young lady, Isabel McIlwaine," his letter continues. "I married her six years later after I had had a chance to establish myself. Isabel's father and mother had lived in Paris about the turn of the century and there had known and liked Solon, the art student. And so I owe my happy married life to your father and mother."

"While at Mamaroneck," writes Paul, "your father encouraged me to do practically as I pleased and I worked arduously at art. I remember making a group of horses pulling a sand scoop. I cast that piece in plaster and it was accepted by the National Academy of Design's exhibition, much to my joy, and I think to your father's satisfaction . . . About that time your mother helped me with French as I tried translation from a book on "L'Anatomie Comparative des Animaux Domestiques . . ."

The search for a permanent home in the country went on throughout the summer of 1906. Most fine Saturdays found Solon harnessing up the horse Attilio Piccirilli had given him to serve as a model for the General Gordon equestrian and sallying forth upon his quest. His precise requirements were simple: a large building for himself, with lots of room for the important work he was planning to do, and a small, very small, house for the undomestic Emma. Both were essentials.

Farther and farther eastward the search went on until, the summer over, the effort was rewarded.

When Solon crossed into Connecticut and came to Fairfield County's long high ridges, fertile valleys with open fields, he knew his quest was on the verge of success. This kind of land appealed to him.

One Saturday he was given some promising addresses and returned home in high spirits. Next week, he told Emma, they would surely find what they wanted. Saturday morning dawned clear and bright, a perfect fall day. From Mamaroneck

Emma and Paul Manship went part way by trolley to save the horse. They were met in Stamford by Solon and, all getting into the buggy, which made a tight squeeze, they took the Ponus Ridge Road to New Canaan. Emma agreed with her husband's appraisal of the countryside. It was enchanting, the very spot where she too wanted to settle.

At New Canaan they were given the address of a farm in Wilton township, just across the Silvermine River to the east. By now the beautiful light of morning had become dark and threatening. On passing an old farmer, "long and lanky, with a pail in each hand," they asked if he thought it was going to rain.

"Oh, no," he replied, looking at the sky, "It's an Irish storm, lots of wind but no rain." With a good laugh they pressed on.

Daylight was already fading when they reached the farm in question. They had just crossed a narrow wooden bridge over the Silvermine River and had climbed a steep, rocky hill beyond, on foot to spare the horse. At the top they paused to catch their breath, and were immediately fascinated by what lay before them: a slight dip in the road, then another hill, not as steep as the first; to the left were trees, to the right a sloping meadow, and at the top, to one side of the road, a large gray barn and a small, very small, white house just beyond, protected by a pair of tall pines and a grove of maples. A quick look revealed some open fields and a vegetable garden. Later they would find a brook running through the woods, an orchard and sixteen acres of hay fields; in all nearly forty-five acres.

The house, since it was small enough to be Emma's "dream house," received only a casual appraisal. The center of attention for the men, and for Emma too, was the weathered haybarn which was raftered, high and roomy. A large open utility shed was attached to the east and at a slightly lower level a carriage shed extended to the south. The structure's foundations, built into a slope, served as a stable and root cellar of easy access. Another shed housed farm equipment. For the first time in years Solon was looking at enough space.

Both knew this was the place. Emma laughed as she told how they had not even gone into the house. It was getting late and they were far from home. Excited, they drove back to New Canaan, handed "good Mr. Green" a dollar bill to bind the deal and made their way homeward rejoicing. Emma wrote in her journal, "Farm fever was already in our veins. Solon adored it. He called it 'Rocky Ranch'." To one who knows Connecticut landscapes and knows about Solon, the

The little house and the big barn on a hilltop: the future Rocky Ranch.

explanation of the property's alliterative new name is obvious. "Except for chickens," Emma continued, "we never raised anything but rocks. We always kept a warm feeling in our hearts for Mr. Green who brought us and our dear Rocky Ranch together."

CHAPTER XII

Silvermine:
"A Measure of Heaven"

The transformation that took place at Rocky Ranch is described by the New York art critic, Paul K. Thomas, who traversed the same dirt roads, arriving at the identical destination that had been Solon's just two years before: "A delightful drive[1] back into rolling country from the Connecticut village of New Canaan brings you to an old farm house on a hilltop. There is a barn near the house, and under the eaves of the barn is built a large skylight. This together with a small equestrian statue of a cowboy on a rearing, lanky Western horse set up in front of the barn, justify the suspicion that farming is not the sole occupation of the proprietor. The model of a group of fighting stallions is mounted on a heap of stones in the pasture opposite. . . . It is the studio of one of our foremost sculptors, Solon Borglum, certainly the chief interpreter in form of the poetry and drama of the life of the Western plains — of cowboys, bronchos, Indians, bad-men and buffaloes."

By the autumn of 1908, when Thomas investigated Solon's "hide-out" in the country, the first of 13 Annual Exhibitions had already been held in his new studio. It was an exhibition of work by artists "summering in and about Silver Mine, Conn."

Silvermine — originally two words, Silver Mine — the name has the sound of music. But the community, 45 miles from New York, does not have, and never had so far as this writer has been able to learn, any silver mine, although

Solon Borglum standing in front of his studio at Rocky Ranch. c. 1908. Bucky O'Neill statue on right.

This snapshot taken from the south shows the work areas where casting was often done and where the forge was kept. The carriage doors on the south wing were usually swung open when the weather permitted.

some defiantly claim that there had been several. The name derives from the Silvermine River, hardly more than a stream in many places, that makes its way, dropping over rocks and dams, through steeply wooded slopes, to join the Norwalk River before emptying into Long Island Sound.

Officially speaking, Silvermine does not exist. Long ago postal authorities swept it and its post office out of existence, even as a mailing address. As a community it is divided among the three Fairfield County townships of Norwalk, New Canaan and Wilton. Together these form an irregular triangle, Silvermine being roughly in the middle, though I venture to think that the true heartbeat of the early Silvermine was more closely related to New Canaan two miles distant, than to the other two.

The Silvermine River is the community's chief boundary dividing New Canaan and Wilton. To the east and west the community includes the ridges that band the valley, but hardly goes beyond. To the south and the north the land is the same, but if you venture too far in either direction the "feel" is gone. You are no longer in Silvermine.

Being a geographic anomaly, Silvermine's actual boundaries are nonexistent while its avowed boundaries are amorphous, determined only by the rustic charm of the land whose heart and lifeblood are the poetic, winding stretch of the little river. But for those who are fortunate enough to be Silvermine's inhabitants, boundaries are of no importance. In their minds and hearts the community is an entity.

The cultural story of Silvermine as an artist colony began soon after Solon and Emma moved into their "farmhouse on a hilltop." Until then it was a wholly rural community marked by the remnants of once thriving industries. A century earlier there were sundry mills—some accounts say as many as eleven—along the few miles of river supplying among them a rich assortment of products, from fur caps to cornmeal and ships' timbers. When the Borglums arrived the active mills still numbered three or four. Just below Rocky Ranch, Révillon Frères operated a tanning factory and spools and knobs were being turned across the dam, a half mile downstream, where today stands the Silvermine Tavern, then a private residence. Most of the uniquely beautiful Mill Road, which becomes River Road when it crosses the town line from New Canaan to Norwalk, was little more than a logging trail giving access to the mills. A short stretch of the original

road, King's Highway, which it paralleled on the opposite side of the river, still
exists — a charming remnant of other days.

One last most historic survivor of these industries was still active a few
years ago, a sawmill dating from 1709. It was operated almost until the last by its
long-time owner, Fred Buttery, and was swept away by the great flood of 1956.
The recurring whine of the saw, constant reminder of its existence, was a familiar
sound at Rocky Ranch. It was not only the community's most picturesque and
cherished feature, surely one of the most-painted motifs in the country, but
contributed much to the State, supplying, for instance, the timbers for a long
stretch of posts and rails for the pioneer of delightful motor roads, the Merritt
Parkway.

Beyond Buttery's sawmill, on the same side of the road and nearly as close
to the river's edge, the local blacksmith produced sounds that were also a part of
the valley's familiar music when the Borglums arrived.

Only a few of the houses were prerevolutionary, with the classic
architectural lines of the period as well as other claims to historic distinction.
Most were simple, unpretentious small frame houses like those scattered
throughout New England. There was a Methodist-Episcopal village church, a
small schoolhouse, a diminutive cemetery. John Guthrie and his son, Sid, ran the
village store. The Davis brothers, Sturgis and Hiram, were the principal farmers.
All close to the heart of Silvermine. Sturgis and Hi Davis were almost too slight
in appearance to be taken for farmers, but they were strong and worked their land
with a fine team of horses and a yoke of oxen which Solon modeled, casting into
sand cement and placing them on a large rock west of the studio, where their
unmistakable outline can still be seen.

No one could have been more anxious not to mar or destroy this rustic charm
than Solon. It would have been instinctive with him to have a close relationship
with all those families who were now his neighbors. Nor, unlike others who
have made the same transition, would he have experienced any difficulty. It was
natural and easy for him to win the affection and esteem of these New
Englanders as it had been with his more scattered neighbors on the plains of
Nebraska, for they recognized that, though art might be his occupation, he was
kindred to all who worked with their hands. Besides, Solon's personal ethics
fitted the ideology of the Connecticut Yankees as a glove to the hand. Being

what he was, his speech earthy, his heart warm, his spirit gay, he soon was as clearly a part of the early community as it itself became integrated into his own life and that of the newcomers. When he founded "The Silvermine Neighbors" it expressed in an extraordinarily complete way his own personality, including both the New Yorkers, the term loosely applied to new arrivals, and the villagers. No castes were permitted to develop. Solon saw to it, sometimes in a high-handed way, that both elements were represented in the decision-making. This was what gave the developing community its peculiar and particular tone.

Addison T. Millar stands out as a name among the first arrivals. He was a prominent artist, having made a reputation with paintings and engravings of the Mediterranean, Algiers being his favorite subject. Solon had met Millar in New York and they had become fast friends. Soon the sculptor persuaded the painter to come to Silvermine for the summer. Solon not only found him a beautiful piece of land along the river but helped him with the construction of what may have been the first ranch-type house in New England.

The Brinleys appeared in 1909, Gordon later famous for her Chaucerian renderings, Putnam, her husband, a rising young muralist. They had just returned from over a year in Paris and were longing for the country. In this mood they encountered Mrs. Charles H. Caffin, the art critic's wife, who said, "I know a place called Silvermine. Solon Borglum lives there. It is a lovely countryside. Would you consider sharing a house and expenses if I could find a place for rent?" Mr. Buttery had just the place for them, not far from his mill.

The Gruelles, friends of the Millars', were among the first arrivals. There were Richard and his wife and two sons, Justin and John, all of whom painted with varying talent and success. John Gruelle gained fame and fortune not with his art but as the originator of the *Raggedy Ann* series of drawings and stories.

Major artistic substance came to the colony when Hamilton Hamilton arrived from Pasadena, bringing with him his wife and twin daughters. Hamilton became the colony's recognized "dean," revered for being at that time the only one to hold the coveted N.A., and greatly beloved besides. His daughter Helen was a fine landscape painter in this community of talent while Marguerite and their mother were lively and entertaining hostesses at the annual exhibitions in the Borglum studio, which almost immediately became a feature of the colony. Marguerite recalls that it was Francis Green, agent for the sale of Rocky Ranch to Solon, who had told her mother that Borglum the sculptor lived in Silvermine.

Howard Hildebrandt and Henry Salem Hubbell, later joined by Bernhard Gutmann, gave the colony a trio of distinguished portrait painters of national prominence. Hildebrandt's portrait of Solon was painted for the National Academy of Design, where it became part of its permanent collection.

A handsome and lively couple joined the colony when the Cassels became summer residents. John Cassel, the New York *Evening World's* editorial cartoonist, was a fellow Nebraskan with whom Solon could relive his early days in the West. The two spent many an evening together spinning yarns, to the delight of any who listened in. The Cassels bought one of the genuine old houses along Mill Road. It had once been a tavern and John could point to marks on the boards of its basement walls where accounts had been kept. The house contained many of its original furnishings. Ernest Shackelton was a perennial summer visitor and exhibitor. His close friend and neighbor, Frank T. Hutchens, painter and world traveler, bought and remodeled one of the old mills on Perry Avenue, below and across the road from the Tavern, decorating it with wrought-iron artifacts picked up in his travels. Across the road from him Charles Reiffel, landscapist, joined the group. Others included George Picknell and Dorothy Randolph Byard, both of whom Emma had known during their student days in Paris, and Fred Yohn, well-known illustrator of the day. Of the younger men, the painter Carl Schmitt took lessons with Solon during the early years while camping nearby with his brother Robert. Together the Schmitt brothers built the house on the steep Borglum Hill overlooking the Silvermine River. When Carl married Gertrude Lord, this couple became and remained for many years the Borglum family's closest neighbors. Cliff Meek's wrought iron forge, long a leading craft of the village, was established during these years and his random recollections in the local newspapers have made engaging contributions to local history.

Austin W. Lord, dean of Columbia University's School of Architecture, bought the land next to Rocky Ranch and charmingly enlarged the standard farmer's house that went with it. Lord was succeeded at Columbia by another summer colonist, William A. Boring, who bought the classic old house situated on the hill above Guthrie's store, later purchased by Richardson Wright, the gardening expert, editor of *House and Garden*. Boring then designed and built himself a spacious home in what was an open plain high above the village, the present home of *Saturday Review-World* editor, Norman Cousins.

One of the Group's fixed rules was to confine membership to Silverminers, but at least four painters from outside the ill-defined bounds found their way in: Henry Thompson, sensitive impressionist who resided over the hills in what is now Wilton Center, Herbert Bishop and Augustus Daggy of Norwalk, and Ed Ashe of Westport, all four esteemed artists and good friends.

A flat open space across the river from the John Cassels was known as "Indian Plain" because an Indian was said to have kept a toehold there until only a few years before. One summer W. W. Matthews, a free-lance writer, brought an old ice wagon to the spot and camped in it for a season. He wrote and published the following description of the community he found:

"Our special neighborhood[2] has its literary circles; there are poets and publishers, novelists and art critics. But the pride of our hearts, our own particular joy, is the group of artists who meet every week in the studio-barn of a famous sculptor to compare notes and urge each other on in their delightful work. These are 'The Knockers,' a frank and fearless folk who live the simple life up here between earth and sky, and will one day make these Connecticut hills immortal, a veritable New England Barbizon."

Besides The Knockers' meetings on Sunday mornings for closed discussions, the group gave annual exhibitions of work done during the year. These were held for ten days at the end of August, and always in the same place, the studio-barn of Solon Borglum. Each year they grew more popular, with visitors from New York and points in New England, attracting such crowds that Solon was forced to open his large hayfields across the road to accommodate the ever-increasing number of cars and carriages. "Cars from all over[3] lined the roads to your father's studio," recently wrote painter Ed Ashe's daughter, Dorothy A. Thompson, ". . . the big critics came from New York. . . . The men were all representative of the time, and although they were not abstractionists nor cubists, nor social problem painters, I doubt if they could be classed as academic."

The Knockers' Club quickly gave way to the name by which it was most widely known, The Silvermine Group of Artists. One of the many articles describing this group was published in *The Christian Science Monitor*: "However vague[4] and undefined as a geographical locality the place called Silvermine, Connecticut may be, there is nothing undefined or vague about the Silvermine Group of Artists. This group is a very definite thing, simply organized, with its

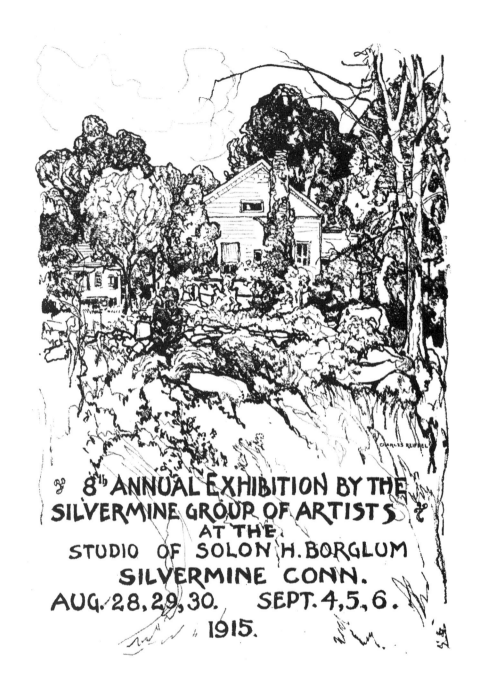

8th ANNUAL EXHIBITION BY THE
SILVERMINE GROUP OF ARTISTS
AT THE
STUDIO OF SOLON H. BORGLUM
SILVERMINE CONN.
AUG. 28, 29, 30.   SEPT. 4, 5, 6.
1915.

purpose clearly stated, holding weekly meetings, admitting to membership only professional artists, and requiring for admission of new members a unanimous vote, maintaining independence, needing no patronage nor asking any. Its weekly meetings held in the hill top studio of Solon Borglum, the sculptor, are not for relaxation. On the contrary, the member who brings his work to these meetings, as all members are privileged to do, knows that he is sure of frank and competent criticism, which while it may not augment self-esteem it is very likely to result in self-improvement. . . . There is therefore no lack of good pictures for the jury to select from when the time comes for the annual exhibition . . ."

An event that deeply shocked the village and demonstrated its closeness was the sudden and tragic deaths in 1913 of Addison T. Millar, Mrs. Millar, and John Guthrie's daughter Jessie, who happened to be riding with them. Driving one of the few automobiles in the village, Millar picked up Jessie on their way back from Norwalk to save her a streetcar ride and walk home. At a guarded crossing, due to some confusion on the part of Millar, the car was struck by a train on the Danbury branch and all but Dorothy, the Millar's daughter, were killed.

Dorothy, critically injured in the wreck, was left virtually penniless, inheriting nothing but the rambling shag-bark cottage by the river. Offers of help nearly swamped Solon, who became Dorothy's guardian. He was criticized severely when he announced that he was not going to sell the cottage. He had what proved to be a better idea, renting the cottage for a small annual amount, with the proviso that each tenant make some substantial improvement. This arrangement appealed to the Clarence Kings, who became tenants of the Millar property. In this way the little cottage received its first plumbing and eventually was so improved, since it never lacked a tenant, that in time Dorothy's inheritance became quite substantial. Solon's practice, King recalls, was never to write a lease, his theory being that if the landlord stood by his word the tenant would do the same.

Any description of Silvermine must include one who was extremely prominent in its life and activities, though not an artist, and who indeed lived beyond its undefined bounds, Harry B. Thayer. President of the Bell Telephone system, Thayer was in no wise prevented nor disqualified by his lofty position in the social and business world from being a vital member of the community. This could have been largely due to the close friendship he struck up with its founder. Thayer had come to New Canaan several years before the Borglums, buying a large tract of land up Valley Road and with it one of the many disused mills. He enlarged the mill, converting part into a comfortable house and the rest into what today might be described as a "fun house" suitable for the giving of all kinds of parties. This could have been one tie that brought the two men together, for each had an ingrained love of fun, and one of the traits that Silvermine brought out most strongly in Solon was this love of fun. Between Thayer's rustic mill and Borglum's studio-barn, there was ample room for all the fancy dress parties, Boy Scout minstrels, and whatever kind of frolic happened to appeal to these two grown men's fancy. All that was necessary was for the idea to catch fire and spread. Some of the parties that followed were riots.

One in particular was never forgotten. Whipped up at the last moment, like most stunts, but unlike any other, Solon the chief sponsor announced at the time of departure, to his bewildered and acutely embarrassed wife that he could not go. She would have to make his excuses for his inexplicable absence. But once Emma left Solon got very busy. And soon a masked bandit rode into view with his victim, whom he proceeded to string up to a nearby tree in true vigilante style. The party was made! Solon was in his element.

Nothing would be easier than to write sentimentally and nostalgically about those days. They were wonderful, everybody having so much fun at the drop of a hat, Solon's old "Rough Rider" hat, usually. One might even be a little incredulous, but they are documented. When and where else would you find people, presumably in their right minds, gathering at a moment's notice to plan a midnight search through the woods for a symbolic North Pole? Yet this is the way the Silvermine Group of Artists celebrated Admiral Peary's feat! They never stopped talking about it as one of their craziest and most successful frolics.

Explaining the community's success is much easier. Affluence did not count. The community was compact, self-contained, mostly uniform in economic status, and intimate; still sufficiently undistracted by outside activities for its members to know each other well, see each other frequently, pass the word of get-togethers from one to another, excluding no one. A "happy colony of gifted folk," as it was frequently described.

The tall gaunt figure of the poet Bliss Carman was often seen tramping the dusty roads between New Canaan and Silvermine. One of his poems entitled A Measure of Heaven reads:[5]

> Heaven is no larger than Connecticut;
> No larger than Fairfield County; no, no larger

A twinkle in his eye. Solon H. Borglum. *Library of Congress.*

Than the little valley of the Silvermine
The white sun visits, and the wandering showers.
   For there is room enough for spring's return,
   For lilac evenings and the rising moon,
And time enough for autumn's idle days,
   When soul is ripe for immortality.
And then when winter comes with smouldering dusk
   To kindle rosy flames upon the hearth,
   And hang its starry belt upon the night,
   One firelit room is large enough for heaven —
   For all we know of wisdom and of love,
And eternal welfare of the heart.

Solon and his friends knew what he meant. They would have echoed his sentiment and doubtless did, many times.

Rocky Ranch was a joy for both Solon and Emma but not in the same way. For Solon it spelled fulfillment. All that he craved was contained within its simple frame buildings and the stone walls that bounded its acres, an adequate workshop, domestic peace, closeness to nature, solitude, tranquillity, beauty in his surroundings, and a good place for the raising of his family. He undoubtedly shared John Burrough's belief in the superiority of the country over the city for civilized living.

Emma, the city-bred woman, the Parisian, saw it differently. Although she spoke of "our dear Rocky Ranch" and "good Mr. Green," the instrument that had brought "the farm and us together," she missed New York life, the large receptions that she gave with such skill, that she so much enjoyed. She hated giving up her more elaborate clothes for country things and the period furniture that she had brought from France, so unsuitable for country living. But her adjustment was speedy. She became an avid and expert bargain hunter at country auctions. She could spot a genuine antique ahead of others and gradually the house was filled with what she considered appropriate furniture.

Only when Rocky Ranch became a year-round home instead of a summer place, and she had to prepare for winter as well as summer residence, did her courage at first fail her. When daylight shortened, birds started south, and city friends came one by one to say goodbye, leaving her for company only a few distant neighbors, often inaccessible in winter, her anguish was acute. As snowflakes began to fall and the children danced with joy, her heart sank. At the moment of complete desperation, Solon would bundle her off to New York, where they kept a permanent *pied-à-terre* in the home of the Ashleys on Lexington Avenue. A few weeks later, she would return completely refreshed, revived and able to sing the songs he loved to hear. That was in the early days, before the community was established, before summer homes were winterized, before neighbors moved nearer, when life in the country grew less primitive. In later years Emma came to enjoy the year-round life almost as much as her husband.

She had specified "a small house" to reduce the risk if she had to take care of it herself, but occasionally Solon's absence required her to take charge of the entire farm. It consisted of no more than a cow, a horse, a few pigs and chickens, the hay fields and orchard, the inevitable vegetable garden, with a hired man to help. But even so, when that happened, the complaint of the city-bred wife could be heard. Once she confided to her sister Lucy that she was tired of "stroking the cow and disposing of unwanted kittens."

Emma's province was the flower garden and here, armed with Peter Henderson's illustrated catalogue with its alluring pictures, she outdid her neighbors. She became a charter member of the Garden Club of America and was a frequent prizewinner.

Solon's studio revealed the man. The bareness of the barn was relieved when the entire interior had been paneled and stained. Ample light entered from a skylight in the ceiling and a large north window, eight feet by twelve. Even though there were no other windows, it was only necessary to open the large barn doors, as was often done in summer, for the place to become a part of the outdoors that Emma had transformed through her love of flowers. A lawn and lilacs, a dancing fountain, and a three-foot model of the "Rough Rider" Monument standing on a pediment of rocks in a bed of iris, combined with Emma's wide perennial borders to lend new enchantment to what had previously been a New England farm of no particular charm or character. Solon added a modeling of his faithful Dalmatian, first in plaster, then in limestone, to stand guard at the door.

Bareness was still the dominant feature of the interior for that was the way the sculptor wanted it. A handsome buffalo skin hung for many years on the south wall, companion to a skull which perched below one of the great beams that reached across the room. On the shelves along the walls Solon placed some of his small plaster models and fragments. There were a few paintings of friends, including one of his own early sketches of horses galloping across a plain. For the rest, there were the subjects on which he was working, shrouded figures on movable pedestals so they could be placed to one side or wheeled into the shed on exhibition days. The large open shed housed three three-foot models of work done for the St. Louis Fair and the many other plasters of completed works.

Inside, Solon's study was littered with books. There were a flattop piano that had been converted into a desk, and a few favorite chairs. One was a Windsor that periodically collapsed, though never when Solon was in it for he knew where to 'put his weight. Although his favorite chair, it finally had to be put away in the loft. Solon then bought himself an authentic antique, a fine Windsor rocker, paying, when Emma's back was turned, the exorbitant price at that time of seventy-five dollars.

Solon built the fireplace for the study. It was as artistic on the outside as it was inside. He placed projecting flat stones at intervals, explaining to the children that Santa would be able to climb up more easily. Unfortunately the fireplace smoked, which brought advice from all who were willing to endure the smoke for the sake of conversing with the unusual man who built it.

Solon sometimes spoke of building a stone studio at the top of his hayfields across the road. The view from there was extraordinary, visible for many years before the encroaching woods cut it off as the area ceased to be cultivated. From the church spires of New Canaan to the west one could see all the way to the silver ribbon of the Sound and the misty outline of Long Island to the south.

The artist's daily routine was simple: up and at work with the sun, long before Emma stirred. About three he would knock off for the day, and tea would be served sometimes in the studio, often under the pine trees in front of the house. Lively conversation, punctuated by bursts of laughter, then became the order of the day. Though Sunday afternoon was their recognized "at home" day, neighbors often dropped in at teatime or for an evening chat after dinner.

Occasional breaks in the routine would come when shipments of marble or stone arrived for the sculptor. These involved the neighbors, for the hill that Rocky Ranch topped was rough, stony and steep. In the days before road

Emma Borglum and the team. (She was not as secure as she appears to be, but she made a valiant effort to learn.) 1907. Rocky Ranch.

The west end of the studio showing the alcove which was Solon's study. The entire studio has been cleared for an exhibition of the Silvermine Group of Artists. Paintings are hung at the other end of the building and in the south wing.

engineering and town maintenance or such vehicles as school buses, roads were taken care of by their chief users. This was Solon Borglum's road, and he took care of it, but in his own fashion, leaving it alone save at that one time in the year when exhibitions were held in his studio. Then several men armed with picks and shovels would try to smooth out the worst spots. If the bridge's planks rattled ominously there was a pocketful of nails to tighten them down. New boards, if needed, would be donated by Fred Buttery. In the winter snows the hired man would hitch up the horse to the homemade plow and clear the way to the schoolhouse and the church which the Borglum children attended.

The result did not impress those with fine cars. The more prudent chose to add a mile to the journey, approaching the studio from another direction. Even high-powered cars, such as they were then, had difficulties with the hill. A heavy Mack truck once tried to deliver a six-ton slab of limestone to the Borglum studio. Solon anticipated problems for he and a group of helpers were on hand for its arrival. When the truck faltered near the top and began to slide back, large rocks were swiftly placed behind the wheels. Solon dispatched a messenger to Sturgis Davis, who quickly brought his team of work horses. Hitched to the Mack, they inched their way up and over the hill. Great was the applause of the assembled spectators and helpers as they triumphantly followed the truck up the hill and into the driveway at Rocky Ranch.

"Use what you have"[6] was a favorite expression of Solon's frequently heard by his pupils, and an expression of his personality. There was almost nothing that Solon was unable to improvise, such as the iron chandelier he put together from the rim of an old wheel when he needed more light in his studio for an evening party. To study his homemade tools is to be convinced not only of his ingenuity and strength but the correctness of his belief that an artist should be able to make his own tools to suit his needs.

He bought some fine redwood to carve into panels for his fireplace. At Fred Buttery's mill he spotted an enormous oak log, several times too big for the saw and discarded for that reason. A little persuasion, perhaps a "deal" for which he was well known, and it was Solon's. But it still had to be carted up the hill, sawed in half, and the halves brought into the studio. Paul, his son, who helped in the operation, said it was a "big job." Even with a two-man saw "it took forever," but out of these massive pieces of wood came the carved "Blizzard," some two feet high, and bases for the sculptor's "Napoleon" and the busts of his children.

"Use what you have" was more than a teacher's platitude, it was his own motto.

When it came to bringing in the hay Solon had a way of impressing all members of the household for work in the fields, even visitors. Good-natured Bertha, of solid Bohemian stock, was not exempt from this service and she worked as happily around the farm as she did in the kitchen, where her homemade bread was famous among friends of the family. Mildred Nash Bly, student helper for many years, recalled with deep nostalgia how she felt about those days, how she too was put to work pitching hay.

"My years as apprentice[7] to your father," she wrote to Monica, "with all the happy associations with your mother and you and Paul will always be treasured memories. There was such a variety of interesting activities at Rocky Ranch besides the wonderful things being achieved within the Studio. I used to help in the hayfields along with the rest of the family. Sharpening and tempering the cutting tools was so enjoyable, watching the color in the steel reach just the right point before plunging it into the cold water, and so many other things I was taught to do."

Storytelling, for a brief Children's Hour in his life, was one of the new facets of Solon's personality that Silvermine revealed. Early life on the Plains provided an inexhaustible source of entertainment. The storyteller needed only to embroider his recollections to put together a bloodcurdling tale. Solon's storytelling faculty did not stop there, however, and an item of minor history can here be recorded. A once nationally famous character named "Twee Deedle" originated in Solon Borglum's woods.*

Twee Deedle was an elf who lived in a gnarled apple tree not far from the brook that passed through the farm. He was a remarkable little creature with a wonderful ability to make himself invisible whenever he wished. This happened when skeptics were around or when somebody made a noise like breaking a twig. The strange thing was, his seven-year-old daughter said, that her father was right!

---

* A fact which is not in the entertaining account of Raggedy Ann to be found in *Landmarks of New Canaan* (New Canaan Historical Society, 1951, pp. 321–326).

And, stranger still, she and her friends only saw Twee Deedle when her father was with them. One day Monica brought along her playmate Marcella, who had just become her nearest neighbor below the hill. The first time, Marcella saw nothing, heard only a rustle and squeak, but the next time she really *did* see Twee Deedle, and ran all the way home in great excitement to tell her parents.

The next morning Marcella's father, John Gruelle, illustrator and cartoonist, dropped around to see if Solon would have any objection to his submitting Twee Deedle as his own idea for a competition. It happened that the *Herald* at that moment was looking for a replacement for *Buster Brown*, having unsuccessfully tried *Little Nemo*. Solon had no objection and Twee Deedle, in Johnny Gruelle's hands, won the contest and a large money prize. For years the strange life and antics of the little elf, born in the mind and heart of Solon Borglum amid the woods of Rocky Ranch, delighted children of all ages in scores of syndicated columns across America.

With his children growing older Solon showed his interest in youth as a troop leader of the Boy Scouts. It was then genuine pioneering since the movement had only just begun in England and crossed the Atlantic. Solon saw in it a solution to a neighbor's problem, a widow with a large family of boys, two of whom were about the same age as his own son Paul. The troop Solon organized and led was built around these lads. And there are still those who enjoy recalling how he did it, his devotion, his playfulness, coupled with a deadly seriousness, which resulted in the maximum satisfaction and fun for all.

This was the side most typical of the man who possessed a knack for getting the most pleasure out of very simple things. His way of dropping in of a Sunday morning for breakfast is just another example of his neighborliness. He had a long list of close friends whose homes were open to him in this way, the Wardwells, the Borings, the Cassels, the Kings, the Thayers, the Butterys and many others.

He was a lover of good talk and he did not shrink from an argument. He had no use at all for a man who did not air his ideas and stand up for them. From the fierceness of some of his arguments he gained for himself a reputation as a fighter. Topics that aroused Solon (being a staunch Republican) usually centered on politics, or were associated with his chosen profession. In the area of rapid changes, pre-World War I days, Solon was known to be pulling away from the Beaux-Arts style, which still held captive many of his friends.

Solon's widow recalled his whistling, which was never cheerier than when the going was rough. His nephew, George Borglum, speaks today of the peculiar "timbre" of his voice which he clearly remembers. His sister, Harriet, wrote of his gentleness, one who would never hurt anyone.

Solon Borglum left as his legacy from his life in Silvermine two monuments of himself. One was his sculpture, unforgettable evocations in bronze and marble of the poetry and drama of human existence. The other was the community of which he was founder and for a time its unchallenged leader. It has been said that an institution is only the lengthened shadow of one man. That appears true of the early Silvermine as it relates to Solon Borglum.

CHAPTER XIII

The Mature Man

Solon Borglum once wrote: "During my whole life I have stood in awe of but two things — God, and learning." This statement can be found in an article by him, published in a 1909 issue of the *Independent*. He was frequently with Simon Newcomb (1835–1909), the astronomer and mathematician, making a bust in the last days of his life. The article describing his impressions of Newcomb goes on to say he had not previously come into close professional contact with a man whose lifelong habit had been "silent, profound thought."

In the quietness of his Rocky Ranch studio Solon became a great reader, and it may be that his father, who had once diagnosed this son of his as a possible Sanskrit scholar, was not really wrong, only off in his timing and making insufficient allowance for his son's independent nature.

"God and Learning" were now about to move from the study to the studio.

"I have often been asked what is the great backbone of success. It is work and work and work." The insistence on effort is typical of the man. He was a Puritan in the value he attached to work, but he was quick to add that along with it must go warm human qualities, "a great brotherly character."

Now he put his capacity for work to maximum use, rising at dawn, to do a major part of his day's work before Emma got out of bed, a frequently repeated claim which Emma never disputed, but which drew a friendly laugh from all.

History was Solon's favorite reading in these Silvermine years. His view of civilized man's beginnings was deeply colored by the idealistic concepts and the philosophy of the age in which he lived. He accepted the optimistic, contemporary belief in Progress. For him the hand of God was visible at every point in man's upward march, whose end result would be freedom. He thought of his nation at the start of the Twentieth Century as the culmination of a series of events from the crossing of the Atlantic, through the Renaissance, the Reformation, the Enlightenment, Romanticism, Realism, to contemporary idealism. All spelled for him the progressive deliverance of people from the bondage of fear, superstition and despotism. "God," he wrote, "always has the men ready to start a great movement when the time comes." They had often been completely unknown men, for the great movements originated, he believed, like the rivers. Their source can be traced "to the foot of the mountain, up the slope of the mountain, but then is lost in the heart of some beetling crag." His was a faith that could produce great art, as well as great living.

The man that emerges from the Silvermine years is the man who is remembered today, the mature man[1] "who took as his goal to be among the Olympians," the man "who stands alone," challenging the critic, whose "great privilege" of comparison becomes of little use in "placing" Solon Borglum. The writer of the foregoing, Robert Alexander Horwood, who had personally known the sculptor as teacher, concludes that Solon Borglum's last works, during these years, were "those of a mature master."

Frémiet's observation that Solon Borglum was happy because he had something on his mind, provides a clue to a greater maturity developing in the artist. He was happy not *when* he had something on his mind, but *because* he had something on his mind, an ideal becoming a fixed concept. Frémiet's terse analysis bears reflection. Solon Borglum worked with both his heart and his mind, as it is normal, particularly for an artist, to "feel" and to "think." However, since the purpose of art is to communicate feeling, or emotion, to others, its cause needed to be understood, analyzed, intellectualized in rational form and visualized. The process is simple but specific, that of converting what the mind's eye now sees clearly to the composition of matter which communicates "feeling" to the heart of the viewer. Solon rose to a level above self-pity, the resentments and frustrations that defeat the many. He was happy because he was thinking of something else.

As one comes to understand Solon and the home he founded it is clear that a price must have been paid for his periodic clashes with Gutzon, actual or threatening. Emma knew that her husband's whistling became loudest with the increase of his problems but he would always make light of them. How far they affected his health remains a question. He had periodic headaches, which may have been covered in what his physician father wrote him: "You are very intense in your work.[2] Take rest, recreation and diversity when you can." Although Dr. Borglum does not link Solon's health to his relations with his brother, there could be a very real connection.

When Emma joined her husband in 1902 in New York she discovered he had become a chain smoker. Dr. Borglum had warned her that Solon should not smoke — "Cigarettes are coffin nails for Solon." Smoking was no problem for Emma to cure in Solon. She merely joined him and that put an end to it! But the headaches persisted and Emma learned that there was nothing to do but accept them. Any loving attention seemed to annoy him. He would shut himself away from the family and struggle with his pain alone.

It is a sufficiently grim fact that for the space of at least three years no large monumental works came Solon's way despite his efforts to get them.

One of his failures caused an indignant admirer, Henry Irving Dodge, to write him, "As soon as I get back to town I am going to take off my coat and you and I will begin a campaign for the Exploitation of Borglum." Another came when Minnesota planned a monument for Governor John A. Johnson and Solon was invited along with other sculptors to enter the competiiton. He did so, submitting photographs of his work, but his entry was late. A friend wrote as follows: "Mr. Weiss returned from a meeting of the executive committee and I saw him and he greatly regretted the fact that they had nothing more of your work, and as he is unacquainted with you he could not venture too far in his recommendation," then added, "Your brother was very much represented by photos *et cetera*."

That these setbacks left their mark is revealed by entries in a small worn notebook: "You worked hard up to the last minute for this work. You lost it. Be happy that you were honest in it. Take this up as though it were the easiest thing you ever did, but," he added, "put the same effort into it as though it were the most difficult."

Friends sympathized with his plight. Dan Wood wrote Emma from California that he felt that Solon had had more than his share of misfortune. But Solon himself, while naturally disappointed at the turn of events, would not have been discouraged. There were, after all, compensations. For it is only in slack times when there are no commissions that the true artist creates freely, unhampered by the tyranny of committees and time schedules. Emma, the perceptive wife, recalled the productivity of 1902. It would be the same story now.

Two uncommissioned works date from this period. One depicts George Washington as a young colonial officer of 21 starting out on his first independent command in 1753 to warn the French to withdraw from the forks of the Ohio. The other is of Napoleon at Moscow. Very different, with the former dynamic, stressing movement, and the latter essentially static in concept, they have this one thing in common; neither military hero is shown at any high point in his career. Rather the reverse, as though the artist wanted to depict a popular hero at his least popular point. But more can be read into the sculptures. George Washington had been given by Governor Dinwiddie an impossible task, and he failed. (His dilemma was the theme of a notable TV drama performed on July 1, 1973.) Napoleon was not depicted in any of his many victories but at the time of his worst defeat, with his armies caught in the snows of Russia. Quite apart however from the natural preference of the artist, any artist, to take the unconventional approach, it is not fanciful to suppose that in his conception of his two statues Solon was himself wrestling with the problem of failure and defeat. But if he were, the titles he subsequently chose were more suggestive of his own resilient philosophy: "Pushing Ahead", "The Command of God." Also, he may have realized that Washington did not fail, in the wider view of history. The idea of "Pushing Ahead" could, indeed, be Solon's own. Solon believed that his work, as he once put it, would "speak for itself." Meanwhile, he would just — "push ahead" himself.

Of "The Command of God" it was later written; "here is the universal significance³ of the work; latent in the marble breathes the baffled spirit of man, his ambition arrested by the hidden voice of God, Whom in his vain might he had defied." The marble group is now in the George Harding Museum, Chicago, and bronze casts of its model are in the National Collection of Fine Arts, Washington, D.C. and The New Britain Museum of American Art, New Britain, Connecticut. "Pushing Ahead, Washington 1753" was first exhibited at the National Academy of Design, drawing a warm letter from William Goodyear,

An illustrated card: "To Solon Borglum who discovered me. I send my Xmas Greetings. . . . Mr. Twee Deedle."

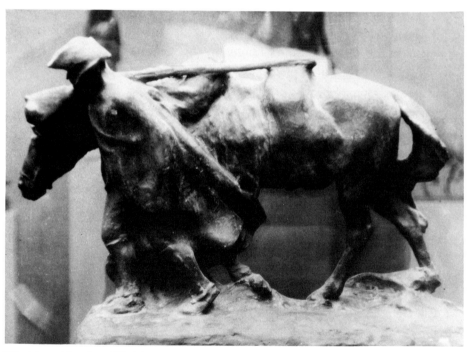

"Pushing Ahead — Washington 1753." The young Colonial officer facing the brutal winds and snow of a disastrous enterprise. National Art Gallery, Ottawa, Canada; State University of Iowa.

Director of the Brooklyn Museum (then known as the Institute of Arts and Sciences): "It seems to me very much the finest thing in the entire sculpture exhibition, and I hope you will not mind my saying so." From there it joined the first representative American art collection to be sent abroad since the Paris *Exposition Universelle*, ten years before, to the *International Exposition of Art and History* held in Rome in 1911. It was finally purchased in 1913 by the Canadian Government[4] for the National Gallery in Ottawa. Another cast was exhibited at the Panama-Pacific World's Fair and eventually purchased by the University of Iowa.

Relative to this group can be found evidence of the artist's developing prejudice toward publicity in a letter written him by Peyton Boswell, art critic of The New York *Herald*. Boswell chides Solon for being so brusque, telling him in such an off-hand way that he has sold his "Washington, 1753" to the Canadian Government. If Solon will send him a photograph of the bronze, writes Boswell, with details surrounding its creation, he will then have a good story for the *Herald*.[5]

Solon's "Pioneer, A Reverie" for the Panama-Pacific World's Fair, held in San Francisco in 1915, was of a totally anonymous character. It did not depict hardship, as did his earlier "Pioneer in a Storm," but an ancient man, erect and dignified, holding in his hands the symbols of his past, an axe and a rifle. The second part of the title, "A Reverie," explains the meaning of the symbols traced on the horse's surcoat, which is a buffalo skin. This pioneer is dreaming over his progress across the Plains. Not accidentally, the rider is mounted, not on a mustang or a bronco, but a heavy horse of the Northwest, a stately animal that, together with its rider, was equal in all respects to Europe's medieval knight in armor. In place of the ancient heraldry appear symbols of the opening of the West, buffalo robe, stockade and cross, with the faint outline of a log cabin. It is significant that the sculptor, himself a one-time pioneer, omitted a pick which suggests the miner, he who takes from the earth and does not give back.

Solon's "Pioneer" caused a flurry of comment,[6] for this was a "think" piece, a little deeper than most. Secretary of the Interior Lane opening the Fair had referred to the vanquished Indian, as James Earle Fraser's nearby "End of the Trail" represented him, coupling that idea with Solon's group depicting the victorious march of the white man. These groups became the most talked about pieces of sculpture at the Fair. After its close they were removed to Mooney Park,

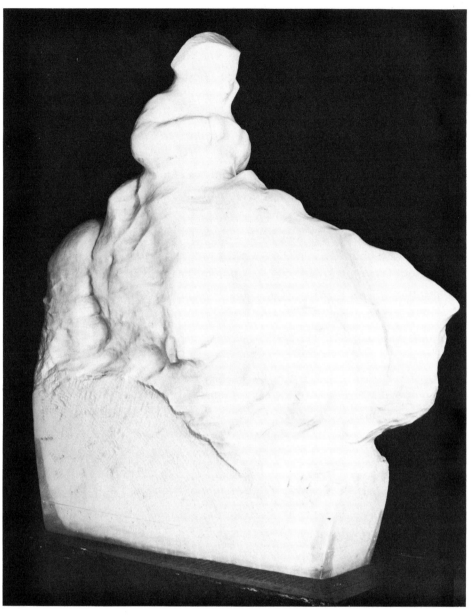

"The Command of God — The Defeat of Napoleon at Moscow." Marble. George F. Harding Museum, Chicago, Illinois. *George F. Harding Museum.*

"The Command of God — The Defeat of Napoleon at Moscow." This bronze was cast from the plaster model. Height approx. 28 in. National Collection of Fine Arts, Smithsonian Institution, Washington, D.C.; New Britain Museum of American Art, New Britain, Conn. *Walter Russell.*

"The American Pioneer, A Reverie." The San Francisco Panama-Pacific Exposition, 1915. After the fair closed this group was dismantled, brought to Mooney Grove Park, Visalia, California, where it was joined by Fraser's "End of the Trail." Now in process of being restored.

Visalia, Tulare County, California, where Solon's can still be seen in spite of many years exposure to the elements.

A contemporary description has a place here:

> "History of a later period,[7] nearer to the heart of Westerners, is embodied in Solon Borglum's lusty and venerable Pioneer. This impressive equestrian stands on the Avenue of Palms at the entrance to the Court of Flowers. It is interesting to note that, in this rugged and commanding figure, fineness, dignity and nobility are emphasized as well as the more customary endurance and hardihood conventionally associated with the character. On the leather trappings of the old Pioneer horse, the tepee, the canoe and other symbols of Indian life are marked. The sculptor is himself the son of pioneers and has treated this subject with sincerity and affectionate insight. The Pioneer has been greatly appreciated and has received special notice in a number of addresses delivered by distinguished guests of the Exposition. Its veracity is attested by the fact that resemblance to several famous pioneers has been imagined in it by their admirers."

The rugged statue of the Honorable Jacob Leisler was a dominating figure in the Borglum studio for many months. Few people know of, or care about, the legendary colonial governor of New York, Jacob Leisler, yet he was a very real and historically interesting man. He was as much maligned as he was later honored. Having been hastily executed for treason, following a premature rebellion at the time of the "Glorious Revolution," his name was exonerated within a few months on the extent of his loyalty being established, though disgrace lingered into history.

Jacob Leisler was born in Germany of French parentage. He was directly responsible for the successful transportation and settling of many French Huguenots in America. They settled along the windy shores of eastern New York, where they founded New Rochelle, calling it after their own La Rochelle, across the Atlantic on the coast of France. Following the Revocation of the Edict of Nantes in 1685, Catholic France had returned to its savage persecution of the Protestants. Leisler first purchased six thousand acres from John Pell. He later added more land purchased from the Indians which he then offered to the Huguenot refugees. It is interesting to read that, though they had a small chapel in which to worship, it was necessary for these devout Huguenots to travel, as they often did, 23 miles each way to take communion in the larger church in New York. Many covered this distance on foot as a matter of course.

June 25, 1913 was the occasion of the 225th anniversary of the landing of these first French settlers at New Rochelle on the rocky Bonnefoi Point which juts into the waters of Long Island Sound. Elaborate plans had been made for this celebration, including parades, speeches, the unveiling of the Leisler monument by Mrs. Montgomery Schuyler, a descendant of Leisler, assisted by Solon's son Paul in scout uniform. Fireworks followed and finally, winding up the occasion, a water pageant represented the arrival and landing of the Huguenots in 1688.

Solon had been commissioned to build this monument by the Daughters of the Revolution.* But he was given very little to go by, nothing to indicate what sort of man he was depicting, not even his size. Solon studied early records in the city archives before planning the statue, which he decided would portray a powerful man. The statue was erected at the entrance to Huguenot Park on the exact spot where the Huguenots had first gathered. One sees the wide, flowing cape of the period blowing freely in the breeze, but this early patriot of Huguenot parentage, his hand and elbow braced against a rugged stick, stands firm. The Huguenot conviction and his unshakable determination are stamped on every feature of his face.

Borglum's conception of the first Governor of New York takes its place beside two other noted works done without benefit of a likeness of any kind to guide the sculptor, Saint-Gaudens' "Puritan," and MacMonnies' "Nathan Hale." The sculptor of Leisler modeled features to denote a man of European, rather than Anglo-Saxon, origin.

Solon's long season of small orders came to an end in 1913. He had made some four or five bas-reliefs and nearly a dozen busts which included the one of Simon Newcomb and that of the last mayor of Brooklyn, before Brooklyn was incorporated into the city of New York, Charles Schieren. The reception that greeted the Schieren bronze on its arrival in the Brooklyn Museum in 1909 is typified by the comment of a fellow artist, Otto Walter Beck, who said that it "ranks among the best works done by American sculptors." This was a friend's expression of confidence for he knew that Solon's fortunes were at the time at a

---

* Not to be confused with the D.A.R. — Daughters of the American Revolution.

Jacob Leisler Memorial Monument. Erected in New Rochelle, New York in 1913. *E. Irving Blomstrann.*

low ebb. It appeared that Caffin's remark was all too true: "Were this gentleman a Frenchman,[8] the public would rank him with Barye. But he is an American and I wonder how many, or rather how few, Americans know of the existence of this genius?"

Friends had urged a return to the land that had discovered him, arguing that, despite the strong native quality of his work, Solon was better known in France than at home. Solon rejected the subtle suggestion, saying, "Let the artist be enough of a pioneer, let him love America enough to stay here and create an atmosphere. Someone must build interest in and love for art right here. . . . as for this everlasting talk of atmosphere," he added, "it is a habit among us to overvalue surroundings and externals. We must love our work so well that we could do it anywhere."

This was the moment of his life when it would have been easy for him to yield to the pressure of art dealers who wished him to provide them with more "Westerns." His small bronzes had been selling well and would continue to do so if only he would make more to feed the ready market. Solon went to great pains trying to articulate his feelings about leaving the field of Western subjects. He did not consider his work better, he said, but he was involving himself in another kind of artistic concept, the creation of pieces that represented a more highly developed abstraction, or allegory, in contrast to most of his earlier works, which in the main were anecdotes from life on the Plains. Nor did he put a low valuation on his Westerns. He limited their production in bronze to less than a dozen of any one model, including several that were 'unique,' believing, as artists did at that time, that it would cheapen the work to produce it in large numbers. Emma recalled in later years that he had originally planned to cast these small works in pairs, changing certain features in the wax, when at the foundry. Pressure of work forced him to abandon the idea.

When Solon was in Paris enjoying his first success, it was said that Borglum horses were all of the same Western type. Did this imply that the former cowboy could do no other? His reply to this criticism was his "Dancing Horse." This was a famous Lippizaner from the *Nouveau Cirque*, performing in Paris at that time. The Austrian equestrienne, Reza Rens, had promised to pose for Solon, but was suddenly called back to Austria, though Solon did get his Lippizaner. "Dancing Horse" is as unlike the Western mustang as Solon's first known drawing of a heavy, bemuscled dray horse in Los Angeles, while the lusty and venerable Pioneer rider's horse is reminiscent of the Spanish Appaloosa breed.

Solon disliked any kind of stereotype. The mere fact that "cowboys and Indians" were becoming American stereotypes would have been sufficient reason for abandoning them. There again, it is important to make distinctions. Solon Borglum's Indians were never stereotypes. They were Indians the sculptor had known.

The "Borglum Horse" idea, for a short time familiar to the artists' world, might have been used to give economic security to the artist's family but this would not have been in accordance with Solon's nature. In other words, to use his own phrase, he had to "move on."

Solon made a portrait bas-relief of Major-General Joseph Anthony Mower for Vicksburg National Park in Mississippi, which Architect Mundie of Chicago called the best thing in the Park. An invitation from the War Department to bid on commissions to do colossal busts of other Civil War generals for the Park followed. Solon's bid on the first was so low the official in Washington was understandably reluctant to accept it and wrote Solon to that effect. Solon's reply was: "It does not make any difference what I receive for my work, I always do the best I know how."

Solon's low bid had been made possible by an off-season "special" from his foundry. By the time he had cut through the reams of red tape that encased this government contract, however, the offer at the foundry had expired. Solon found himself out of pocket on the commission, but he went ahead, making five generals' heads in all, and all Confederates: Giles A. Smith, William S. Smith, Edward D. Tracy, John Gregg and Francis J. Herron. The colossal head of General Gregg greets the visitor as he enters the park.

Solon was asked to design a monument for two old friends that would be different from the general run of cemetery memorials. They were former Mayor Charles Schieren and Mrs. Schieren, who had died the same day within a few hours of each other. The thought of the simultaneous ending of two lives, both of which had been so long and honorably intertwined in service to humanity, inspired him. The result was a kneeling figure depicting the spirit of Death, which stands out distinctively from the forest of marble urns and angels that usually adorn cemeteries. He employed as beautiful a female model as he could find, with head bowed and arms outstretched to touch with gentle fingers the covers of two large, closed volumes, which symbolized the fullness of their years. There was much studio discussion of the question as to whether he should drape the figure. In the end, the lovely figure was shrouded because death comes cloaked in mystery, and Solon was a realist.

Solon's only other and earlier sculptural cemetery work was a small bas-relief, depicting a camp site with an outline of tents. The figure of a soldier lies in the foreground, answering his call for "Taps," above him, the symbolical figure of the angel of death.

Another bas-relief, a memorial to the educator Truman Jay Backus of the Packer Institute, Brooklyn, was placed above the large mantel in the library to "keep fresh in the minds? of the student body the memory of a man who for twenty-five years acted as the head of the Institute and whose tireless efforts . . . placed it on the high plane in the educational world it now occupies." It should be no surprise to learn that Solon here employed an Indian figure in a "beautiful piece of work," his idea being "to symbolize the development of Long Island from the era of the Indian up to the present day, when conditions are so changed by education."

Lynchburg, Virginia, has two identical bronze figures, done in 1911, of a distinguished local citizen, George Morgan Jones, who is represented in uniform for having served in the cause of the South. However much some have tried to make him out as a general, he must remain "Private Jones," which he was. Jones was also an educator who gave freely of time and money toward the establishment of Randolph-Macon College, in front of which this under life-size statue was erected. The second stands in front of the Jones Memorial Library.

Solon's attitude toward that milestone event, the Armory Show of 1913, was typical of the man. The Show is credited with changing the course of American Art, giving approval to the "avant-garde." The Silvermine Group of Artists became a natural forum for discussion; a healthy outpouring of the personal convictions of mature men normally stirs emotions, and there were arguments and angry retorts. Viewing the event after sixty years, one feels that Solon's interest was problematical. What had at first appeared to be an "American Show" claimed his active attention and support. Members of the Silvermine Group, notably D. Putnam Brinley, were very much involved. But when the Show

"Dancing Horse." Height approx. 17 in. A famous horse of the Nouveau Cirque, Paris, 1900.

"General John Gregg." Texas. 1914. This bust at the entrance to the Vicksburg National Military Park, Mississippi, is one of five colossal busts by Solon Borglum in the Park. *Phil Kovinick.*

suddenly exploded into a sensational demonstration of largely foreign art, Cubism, Abstractionism, and the like, when the most talked-about painting became "A Nude Descending a Stairway," Solon's interest and support waned. Although Black, Starr and Frost had sent a collection of five of his "Westerns" he turned his back on the show and threw his energy, with fresh zeal, into creating his own expression of what he considered true art.

During these years Solon's book, "Sound Construction," took shape. When it was published ten years later, Edgar J. Hesselein, reviewing it in *The New York Times Book Review*, ended with the words: "It is a book[10] that will stand with the journals and treatises of the greatest masters of the past; one that will show the thoughtfulness and intellectual force of one of the great masters of the present."

No artist of his day so fully illustrated in sculpture the poetry of life on the Plains as Solon Borglum had known it. Since he very seldom repeated himself his own conclusion was inevitable. Just as St. Louis had surpassed Omaha's Trans-Mississippi Exposition of 1898 in giving expression to the importance of Western culture, so Borglum's four monumental groups at St. Louis expressed his conclusions about the place of the West in American history, and his many small bronzes, marbles and plasters, widely exhibited and photographed, made his name and work familiar wherever art was studied. But the shift of interest was visible even in these days of small orders. It can be spotted in one of Borglum's St. Louis groups, with the chief directing his son to enlarge his horizons and learn of the white man's culture.

CHAPTER XIV

"A Man Who Stands Alone"

Solon went overseas in 1918, leaving behind him "The Heavens" and two figures which count as a single work, "Aspiration" and "Inspiration." All three are striking with a special loftiness of conception.

One's first thought about "The Heavens," a small cast of which is now in the National Collection of Fine Arts in Washington, could relate the work to the sublime words of the Genesis story, "And it was as God said." "Aspiration," hardly less powerful, is no less profound in its many implications. Both embody the strongest convictions of this American artist. Both are expressions of a deep religious sense.

Solon's brother August, who saw a lot of him during the last ten years of his life, referred to this sense of a creative design in life and the philosophy by which he lived: [1] "Outward it was difficult to know how much spirituality there was in Solon . . . but he had a philosophy of his own which was far-reaching in its effect not only in himself but affecting all those around him." "When he commenced to expound his theories on the works he was creating," August continued, "I would sit and listen with admiration at the bigness and broadness of his conceptions."

Solon Borglum was not, as his brother said, a religious man in any formal way. He did not belong, as stated at the outset of this work, to a particular church body, though still at heart, as Emma made clear, a member of Bishop Hare's mission church in South Dakota. Yet of all America's top artists, he could have been the one most profoundly imbued with a sense of religion. When he said he stood in awe of only God and learning, it is clear he was using far from empty words, whose full significance comes into view only as one contemplates the sculptor's last works. Solon's influence on his wife, who had rebelled against the extreme Calvinism of her Paris home, was profound. It is interesting to note how many of Solon's friends were church people, Bishop Hare and Dr. Guthrie, to name but two, not to mention his own father and father-in-law.

Certainly, too, the concept of the American Indian which Solon put into "Aspiration" and "Inspiration" was basically spiritual in nature rather than historical. It does not deny the Indian's cruelty and cunning. That the sculptor recognized the historicity of the other view is shown in the article, published in 1910, in which he spoke of the American pioneer as having to contend with "a cruel and cunning enemy all about him"[2] and therefore needing to possess courage and shrewdness, "otherwise his journey westward would be short."

The firmament itself is represented in the design of "The Heavens." A figure emerges out of space, strong, erect, magnificent in its physical perfection. Planets lie at his feet. He is half turned, looking behind as if to see the work of his hands. One fist is clenched and partially concealed, the other is upraised and bent, palm open, facing downward, fingers together. Symbolism and abstraction, according to the artist's definition, aimed at creating an impression of deliberate purpose, determined will and immense discipline.

Solon must have liked erect figures, else he would not have used them so often. The Indian representing "Aspiration" is erect. The American Pioneer is erect. The standing figure in "Burial on the Plains" is erect. The figure in "The Heavens" is erect. Rectitude was a basic attitude of the sculptor's concept of human life and physique.

In studying the life of the man together with his art during these Silvermine years, his work takes the form of an extension of his life, an enlargement of life itself into artistic achievement — from the study, that is, to the studio.

Some three years after Solon bought his Connecticut home Gutzon announced that he had purchased a tract of land in nearby Stamford, also in Connecticut. The two hundred acres comprising lovely hills and dales he called "Borgland." He was now married to Mary Montgomery. A woman of unusual

"The Heavens." On the back of this photograph was the date in Solon's handwriting: November 25, 1915. Clay. This picture shows the main part of the studio, cleared of all furniture, paintings and decorations. It was later cast into plaster at Rocky Ranch, delivered in 1919, and has since disappeared.

Detail of "The Heavens." Bronze. This photograph was taken of the intermediate size model for the heroic group. The National Collection of Fine Arts, Smithsonian Institution, Washington, D.C.; New Britain Museum of American Art, New Britain, Conn. *Stan Benham*

intellect and imagination, from now on Mary Borglum made Gutzon Borglum her business. To her must be given the credit for whatever stability existed in the mercurial life of her husband.

The move marked a rapprochement with Solon. The brothers were now often seen together. Gutzon's large black Lincoln would travel the narrow dirt roads of Silvermine, up the steep Borglum hill and into the drive at Rocky Ranch. Solon's children came to know their uncle and aunt. Mary Borglum's retiring and gentle ways belied the strength of her character, which Emma respected.

Solon and Emma responded to the changed relationship in different ways. No seeming trace of resentment for what had occurred in the past prevented Solon from welcoming his brother into his home. (It is interesting to discover that during these Silvermine years Solon was known to wear a small gold stickpin in his tie, the three "See no evil, hear no evil, speak no evil" monkeys with their hands over their eyes, their ears and their mouths.) With eyes twinkling Gutzon and Solon laughed happily together, and presently Solon was describing his personal ambitions, his hopes for the dawning of an American art that would supersede anything that had been known in history. It would be completely original and distinctive. Solon and Gutzon were dreaming again.

True to her nature, Emma retained some of her reservations. She rejoiced at the birth of Mary's child knowing what this would mean to Gutzon, who had longed for a family of his own. But a new concern is revealed in a few words written to Solon from Paris in 1914 when visiting her father. She regrets that Solon takes fourteen-year-old Paul to Gutzon so often. "I don't want him to be like Gutzon. I want him to be like you."

In the late fall of 1913 an imaginative and lucrative commission brought the brothers together in a form of collaboration, reminiscent of earlier hopes and dreams. It was a tremendous scheme offering unlimited opportunity for artists of vision; and money, too often a limiting factor, was here of no consequence. It was even left to the artists to decide the materials in which they would work.

Archer M. Huntington, well-known philanthropist, historian, poet and writer, was deeply involved in the work and objectives of the American Geographical Society, of which he was president. The empty plaza at the entrance to the Society on Audubon Terrace, Broadway at 155th Street, must have aroused his imagination with its rare possibilities each time he crossed it. Perhaps to screen off the city around him, he visualized an extensive grille, behind which would be erected sculptured figures depicting subjects that had come to his mind: "The Earth," "The Heavens," "The Waters," "Man."

Gutzon Borglum had recently done some work for the Numismatic Society, another of Huntington's interests, and it was possibly because of this association that Huntington discussed the project with him, offering the commission to him. However, the great scope of the project was clearly and quickly evident, influencing them to call in other artists. The sculptors selected were Solon, Chester Beach and Charles R. Harley, all men who would doubtless work harmoniously under the leadership of Gutzon, who was named chairman. All agreed that this was an opportunity to advance the beauty and cultural status of the city of New York.

The first formal gathering of the four sculptors took place in Gutzon's New York studio on December 23, 1913, when the contracts were signed. That it was a project demanding teamwork among the artists is shown in the following paragraphs:

"For the purpose of executing[3] this work to the best of our separate ability, and to the advantage of the work as a whole, we jointly agree to divide the remuneration connected with this work into four equal parts, sharing like and like to help each other to collaborate, and to at all times aid each other in carrying out the work as one general plan, and each to make at once one or more sketches of the entire scheme, embodying the motives suggested in the agreement with Mr. Huntington, a sketch model of which is to be ready by March 1, 1914, and to be made one half inch to the foot.

"We further agree, that at our meeting on March 1st we shall adopt a general plan and apportion the four parts of the work equally. It is of course understood that each man shall maintain his individuality and is expected to bring to the general work, free and untrammeled expressions of his thoughts upon the subject treated, and the four sculptors shall at all times work in unison for the general uplift of the work.

"We further agree to complete all work apportioned to us under this agreement within three (3) years from date, and agree to begin at once the sketch models of the subjects allotted to us March 1, 1914, and thereafter, and in all ways comply with the agreement entered into with Mr. Huntington."

When the sculptors met again to judge each other's work and make the selections for the various subjects, Solon's figure depicting "The Heavens" was chosen for him to develop. Chester Beach's model, another standing figure, was chosen as a companion figure to Solon's. Little is known of the nature of the other two works, which were never apparently enlarged beyond the first small figure.

Solon moved rapidly toward the finish. June 1915, when the Rocky Ranch studio was a hive of activity, saw the completion of the casting of the intermediate forty-inch model into plaster, and by November 25 of the same year he was able to photograph the full-size figure, showing its virtual completion. By the first of the new year he was in touch with Chester Beach, whose work was not quite as advanced as his, but who was anxious to have a look at Solon's: "I think we should get together[4] on the exact base size, however, and now also is the time, if you are ready, to look over each other's work about whatever details may appear wrong."

On July 7, 1916, Gutzon wrote Mr. Huntington, giving him a round-up of Solon's and Chester Beach's work. All was ready, but he said it was agreed to hold all over until the following March. There is no mention of his or Charles Harley's figures. A letter to Solon from Archer Huntington dated May 28, 1917, throws a little light on the impending fate of the project. Again no mention of Gutzon's or Charles Harley's figures. Huntington regrets that he was unable to make the trip to Rocky Ranch to view the statue. "That it is a splendid work I have no doubt, because it is yours. For the present it is obvious that nothing can be done, and probably not before the end of the war . . . I understand that both you and Mr. Chester Beach would prefer not to cast the statues until you know their position in relation to the proposed arch, which is certainly wise."

From time to time the chairman continued to report to Huntington on the progress of the work, his actual words in December 1916 being "the artists are all happily engaged on the project." But the impending entrance of America into the war forced an interruption intended only to be temporary, until bronze again became available for casting. The interruption, however, proved permanent. The project was never carried out, but was swept aside in Gutzon's life by an even larger one. Once again there was a parting of the ways for Solon and Gutzon. This time permanently.

Solon learned to his amazement that the chairman of the great project had taken his family and gone to Atlanta to live. His second child was born there.

Solon Borglum in his study with Mike, c. 1916. *Keystone View Co. Inc.*

Stone Mountain had come to occupy Gutzon's attention to such an extent that he had little time for anything else, clearly no time for the execution of his "portion" of the Geographic project. To share and share alike had lost its charm, if indeed it had ever held any for Gutzon Borglum. He was not one to work well with others. Nor was his artistic forte known to be in the field of ideas. Gutzon's gifts lay rather in the field of portraiture. It was evident that it was easier for him to visualize the mounted figures of General Lee, Jackson and Davis, with a large supporting army trailing off into the distance, than to fasten his creative attention on such nebulous subjects as "The Heavens," "The Waters," "The Earth" and "Man." He was devoting his attention, and Solon was also, for Solon, too, had an interest in Stone Mountain, to fund-raising lectures, it being a project that involved superlatives both in size and money — a mountain instead of a city courtyard, with money running into millions instead of some fifty thousand dollars shared among four sculptors.

The Huntington commission came to Solon at the time when he was most prepared to become involved in this kind of creative work. During these Silvermine years he was, as we have seen, formulating his ideas for a book which was to point up this characteristic about the meaning of American art. The project was well suited to one of his philosophic, imaginative cast, and Solon entered into it with the zest reminiscent of the enthusiasm he showed over the "Bucky" O'Neill. His scale model together with his suggestions in detail provide insight into his deepest thoughts:

"We are a scientific and religious people and the mythology and superstitious beliefs of the nations which have long passed should not be allowed to enter here." Consequently "there must be no copying of the works of classical antiquity." He conceded that the greatest works of sculpture had been created by the artists of antiquity, but that was not the point now. "These works do not comprise the highest thought today, and we will not succeed in making works of art as great as theirs by borrowing from them." This was becoming a favorite theme and echoes of it will be increasingly heard.

"The whole grille is to be modeled with great elaboration of historical epochs, beginning with the earliest history and coming down to the Fifteenth Century.

"The mass of the grille on the right represents the Old World: flat, as the people believed it was; the Ocean with the Serpent of Superstition, fish, mermaids, winding in and out among the sea foliage. Across the whole center will be modeled the greatest occupation of the different nations — War.

"The first column on the right is to be embellished with great movers in earliest history: Queen Tyi of the Eighteenth Dynasty; Abraham, Joseph or Jacob. The first circle: Moses and Christ. The second circle: Apostles, philosophers, explorers. These are great movers, and they had freedom to build monuments of higher thoughts.

"The second column is to show not only the great trials of social life during these periods, but the bondage and despotism of the people.

"The third column, next to the gate, will have figures representing the breaking away from all of this — the great uplift and progressive movement of the Fifteenth Century.

"The gate is the Ocean, the passageway into the New World, and is to be decorated with the fish and foliage of the sea.

"The grille on the left shows the New World as it was seen when the Spanish discovered it, and flat as the people thought it was, the whole lower half being the sea with a mass of decoration of fish and natural sea-growth. In the center, the war and hunting life of primitive man. He has no tradition to give us. The top is decorated with clouds and birds.

"The top of the whole grille is surmounted by the gods of all periods. To make this grille, which is intended to shut off all the old beliefs, we must exhaust mythology by entwining it all through, like a network. By doing this we will enclose ourselves so that we, or no other sculptor, will put out any works of art that retrograde to the old ideals in the court.

"The whole grille will be modeled flat on both sides, and on one side repeating the other, except the circles and columns which will be embellished with characters who have advanced civilization to the Fifteenth Century."

For the four themes within the court Solon phrased his conceptions thus:

Man: "Not the great physical force he is supposed to be, but what he is now — a great spiritual or mental force, always searching upwards and onwards. This figure I propose to place on the axis to the entrance to the Geographic Building."

The Earth: "My conception is entirely centered in a planet, whirling through space, and as a female figure, gathering, warming and bringing to life the drifting atoms which cling to her body."

The Water: "My conception is entirely the thought that it assembles itself into large bodies, such as the ocean and seas, and then goes out again purified to sustain life."

The Heavens: "What we feel strongly now — not a place where a lot of gods are hidden, but a great physical force and one supreme power and guidance, hidden in an endless blue."

The idea of a great physical force led the sculptor to a false start. As his first model he chose an ex-prizefighter who personified muscle and sinew, nothing more. Out of this preliminary study, however, came the general pose, but the small figure was never enlarged. What the artist was really trying to depict was the power of mind and will. A most difficult pose developed, requiring of the model perfect balance. Behind the raised arm with open fist and fingers together, suggesting the Biblical idea of Creation, can be discovered the closed fist of discipline and determination. The sculptor found his final model among his Silvermine neighbors, George Fry, remembered even today by old Silverminers who recall him as he walked along the roads, bound for the Borglum studio.

For many years "The Heavens" in its various stages of development dominated Solon Borglum's studio. Why was this ambitious project of Huntington's, on which the philanthropist had spent thousands and on which so much dedicated work and planning had been done, not completed?

So far as Solon Borglum was concerned, there is this eloquent tribute: After saying in a letter to Monica that his and Solon's were the only two statues to be completed, Chester Beach added, "Solon Borglum was a great man, admired by all his fellow artists; it is too bad this project could not have gone through and one more of his fine works been put into permanent bronze." *

A friendship that ended only with the life of Solon Borglum[5] began in the Christmas season, 1916.

William Norman Guthrie, Episcopal rector of Saint Mark's in-the-Bouwerie in Manhattan from 1911 to 1937, can today be regarded as a forgotten figure, but only because our memories are short. He was a valiant pioneer in a continuing

---

* This situation has now been partially rectified by the limited casting of two small bronzes. One is part of the collection at The National Collection of Fine Arts, Smithsonian Institution, Washington D.C. and the other forms part of the Solon H. Borglum Collection in The New Britain Museum of American Art.

revolution that is still very much with us, revolution in the Church and the relation of the Church to society.

Today Guthrie's attempt to knock down old walls of tradition and abolish ancient taboos seems relatively innocuous, compared with contemporary trends. It is hard to believe that so much dust was stirred up by such a restrained program.

When Guthrie came to Saint Mark's it was already a derelict parish in a run-down neighborhood where danger lurked around every corner. Its location at 10th Street and Second Avenue discouraged anyone with conventional ideas of the role of a parish priest. These did not describe the intentions of William Norman Guthrie however. Dr. Guthrie's program was moderate enough, merely conceived in a way, as he put it, to attract to the parish members who, while they possibly continued their financial support, never darkened the doors of their church. As an educator and writer, steeped in the cultural history of the Christian Church, Guthrie's thought was to achieve his program primarily by cultural means, "aiming to make our old church a place for reverent experiments in promoting the free life of the spirit and involving its relation to art and letters." He would endeavor to clean up and make safe the surrounding neighborhood by acquiring real estate with the idea that inexpensive homes would thus be available for artists to become involved in his venture of faith and worship. One of the first signs of success was the spruced-up appearance, a colorful "old world look" that slowly crept along neighboring streets.

Nor did his "experiments," at least by today's standards, ever cease being "reverent." Nevertheless they deeply offended conservatives of that day who could not find it in themselves to accept the drawing of a curtain across the altar, when it was accompanied by the introduction of drama and dance into the rest of the sanctuary. Traditionalists were of the opinion that this was sacrilege and denounced the man responsible as a "radical." As time went on their opposition became so merciless that Guthrie ended his ministry under a cloud, at odds with his bishop, and this writer believes, greatly maligned.

Guthrie's dynamic personality could have contributed to this result. Meekness and restraint were not conspicuous among his virtues, nor was he the kind of Christian who suffers equably either fools or Philistines, nor did he always distinguish between them. He was a born fighter, and like many fighters, something of an autocrat whose "democracy" on occasion could wear extremely thin. He believed that cultural advance had sometimes to be engineered, if not imposed, one way or another. As he wrote his new friend Solon, "The day of enlightened despots is over. We have only self-advertising plutocrats left and they are an inferior lot when compared with Lorenzo the Magnificent or with Phidias, the Athenian Tammany Boss." Guthrie's chosen substitute was a little devious "scheming."

Guthrie had flashing black eyes and large bushy, black eyebrows which made him look Mephistophelean in comparison with the conventional shepherd and his manner was characterized by a vehemence seldom heard from the pulpit. Such a man inevitably makes enemies more readily than friends, especially when he is as sound in his positions as William Norman Guthrie usually was, and able to support them with as much erudition.

Dr. Guthrie was definitely and genuinely a man ahead of his time. He admitted the indictment himself: "I suppose you know," he wrote Solon, "I am not winsome, but by a combination of bludgeoning and stroking the dog, pulling his tail and throwing him tidbits, one gets nearly anything one wants in this world."

It all began when the sculptor received an inquiry from the architect of Saint Mark's, Edward Tilton, asking if he would be interested in undertaking an idea of the rector's for two figures of Indians representing attitudes of aspiration and inspiration, to be placed on each side of the church portal.

At first glance, which is probably all it received from too many people, it was a fanciful idea that only made sense when considered in the light of the church's unique history. It then made a great deal of sense. Saint Mark's occupied the oldest piece of consecrated ground on the entire island of Manhattan. Its name, "in-the-Bouwerie" is the clue, "Bouwerie" (bowery) meaning "farm" in the old Dutch of the 17th century. Before the English took over, Peter Stuyvesant, governor of New York — then New Amsterdam — had his farm two miles outside the walls of the settlement. As this was too far for the people there to come to church, especially because of the threat of Indians in the vicinity, they built a chapel of their own, the precursor of the present Saint Mark's in-the-Bouwerie. Out of Guthrie's active brain had come the notion that this sort of a memorial would be in the nature of an *amende honorable* for what had been done subsequently to the whole redskin race or, as he put it: "Had we understood the Indian as he was understood by both Quaker and Jesuit missionary there would have been no such danger to either Dutch or English worshippers, and placing these monuments is a kind of *amende honorable* and the expression of a spirit of catholic reconciliation among the common children of one Father."

Solon Borglum was greatly attracted to the project.

He had his own long background of memories to draw upon. Interest in Indians was not a new thing for him but older than his art. From the time his playmates had been Indian children and his father had taken him on long drives across the prairie to call on Indian patients, he had been deeply concerned and his sympathy had greatly matured over the years. The summer he and Emma had spent their deferred honeymoon with the Sioux had been a milestone, widening his horizon so that he could contribute to the enthusiasm of the ardent clergyman.

At least a dozen Indian figures can be counted among Borglum's work. In 1915 he was acknowledged as one of the best sculptors of the American Indian in the country. His Indians were not the stereotyped portrayals of the race that could legitimately consider itself America's forgotten people. Nothing points up the difference so clearly as the two figures he conceived for Dr. Guthrie.

The traditional portrayals of the Indian as a savage, complete with paint and feathers, though these had figured in some of his past work, was not now of interest to Solon. He wanted to show, with all the power and insight of which he was capable, the redman as a human being with the same dignity as any other and with the same aspirations to nobility of the spirit. It was as though at a single stroke of a well-ordered mind, the sculptor cut through the layers of history to reveal the fundamental truth of the oneness of mankind in the eyes of its Creator.

Guthrie wrote his "dear new friends," January 11, 1917: "We had a very good time at your wee house and big barn and are most eager to see the youngsters that were desirous of inspecting us. As a compromise between the wild west and Paris they must themselves be interesting, both as specimens and as persons . . .

"I am very greatly encouraged in my plan of setting up two great symbols in Indian style right and left of the entrance at St. Mark's Church. It is a very rare experience to me to meet a man with whom I can share my deepest convictions. Mr. Borglum and I seem to have arrived at the identical spot starting as we did from such different points of departure, and travelling such different ways, that it is truly amazing.

"To feel that I have met the man who will conceive better than I can the thing that I greatly desire is surely very comforting. To see that he can both originate and sublimely conceive and as firmly and nobly execute, gives me the sense of perfect security in pursuing my course. I have only to win the consent of the donor to a scheme that I can now absolutely endorse . . ."

The fact that Guthrie could offer the artist so little in the way of remuneration was the last thing Solon cared about. Six hundred dollars was the actual amount of the advance. Solon's mind was on the opportunity to create a religious masterpiece embodying the American spirit, the lines of which would be strictly American.

When he saw the completed models Dr. Guthrie was equally enthusiastic. He was sure now that Saint Mark's would not only break new religious ground but would become a place of aesthetic pilgrimage. Visitors would be attracted to it as Europeans to their shrines. Art would once more become "the handmaid of religion." At the same time he was apprehensive of their reception.

The feast of Saint Nicholas, December 6, 1917, was the time chosen for public viewing of the models. The rector felt that the situation called for a special service designed to educate the public and he wrote the sculptor:

"Suppose we make the entertainment of the festival take on an Indian character — the Dance of Payatumi and the Corn Maidens (Zuni). The music will also be Indian. Suppose we invite, you and I, through some friends, all the artists that are worth-while, to come and see these sketches, and a few of us keep up our educational propaganda, drawing out the artists and putting on record all their appreciation and see that it reaches whom it most concerns."

The "sacrilegious" incursion of savages onto consecrated soil passed off without incident, the day of demonstrations being not yet! Even the comment was not too unfavorable. And there the matter rested for the time being. The clergyman went on scheming how to defeat the Philistines and the artist went off to a different war.

After Solon's departure from American shores Guthrie wrote to Emma to assure her that in his opinion her husband was "the most vital, lovable, primitive soul" he had ever met.

A high point was reached in the life of the Silvermine community with the arrival in 1915 of Harold Paget with a brand of leadership that blended with and extended that of its founder. In many respects the antithesis of Solon Borglum, the scholarly, slightly built Englishman, veteran of the Boer War, was able to work with Solon because they had so much in common. Both had gay spirits and hearty laughs, which punctuated their conversation; both had an infectious sense of fun, and both enjoyed the free, unconventional life of Silvermine. "H," as he was known to his friends, gave a more sophisticated air to the renamed Neighbors Club, now the Village Room, and wrote and directed numerous skits and playlets for its enlarged activities. A popular collaborator who often took a lead part was Alice King. Her musical talent, an added attraction, helped to keep the Village Room a lively place.

The Flahertys joined the colony at a later date but their name merges into the Silvermine story of these years. Here a bit of history can be told, for the original ancestor of the documentary film, "Nanook of the North," was shown in Silvermine on that same lawn which had witnessed the previously told vigilante frolic. Charming, happy-go-lucky Bob Flaherty had just returned from a trip with the arctic explorer, Vilhjamur Stefansson. He was full of his experiences and had the means to prove them! Following the showing of that film, it became clear to everyone that a new star had come to Silvermine. The novelty of the film, the captivating story that it told of a distant people, known to most only through history books, together with the fact that Bob was a natural raconteur, was an experience that none would forget. Later, in what proved a fortunate accident the film was destroyed by fire, but enough people had seen it to gain Flaherty a sponsor who financed a well equipped expedition back to the Esquimaux country, which produced the world-famous "Nanook of the North."

Doctor and Mrs. Byard bought the Gruelle place, an expansive river property near the bridge from Mill Road to Borglum Road. Kenneth Byard, Dr. Byard's brother, bought properties near the Four Corners and remodeled one of the homes into the Silvermine Tavern. Dorothy, his talented wife, became a charter member of the Silvermine Guild of Artists. Others were Albert Jacobson, the sculptor, former student of Solon's; the G. F. Scotson-Clarks, he the editor and noted food and diet expert; David Robinson, the painter, and his gifted actress wife Adele Klahr; the Clarence Kings, who became permanent residents by exchanging summer rentals of the Millar cottage for a home of their own.

Another whose name deserves mention became a close friend of Solon and Emma and was a familiar figure at Rocky Ranch in the summertime, the devoted bird-lover and indefatigable secretary of the Connecticut Audubon Society, Frances Hurd. Solon built a blind especially for her by the stream that ran through the woods. She camped all one summer in a tent pitched in the meadow. Great was the excitement she caused on the day she discovered the Great Blue Heron. As a frequent lecturer in the schools she came to be known as "the Bird Woman."

As the war clouds became more ominous on the eastern horizon, a very different spirit invaded the Silvermine community and began to shatter its idyllic life. Change started the day it dawned on the members that Silvermine lay within a strategic area that embraced the prime industrial and munitions target of Bridgeport. Soon there were visions of German spies in Silvermine backyards. Fun and frolic gave way to more serious concerns: bazaars to raise money were substituted for fancy dress parties; Emma planned and directed a Belgian Fair at Rocky Ranch, which was spread out on both sides of the road, and long before the United States entered the war the neutrality that President Wilson demanded became non-existent. Tempers flared when military drill was added to the activities of the Village Room. A military corps followed. In Norwalk the Gallaher Battery was formed, whose bugler was the sixteen-year-old son of Solon, Paul Borglum. The carefree atmosphere was at an end.

CHAPTER XV

"L'Américain"

"When we entered this great war my sole wish in life was to get in and help. To go on with my sculpture was impossible." So reads Solon Borglum's first entry in his war diary. A simple enough statement, direct and to the point. There is no reason to enlarge upon it. As has been written about him, "all his life he has been riding across plains as the crow flies, to express the spirit in him . . ."

In his 50th year, Solon was not, of course, of military age; nor was he unemployed. He had never been busier than immediately before his enlistment. The room he had contrived out of the hayloft of his studio barn was seldom now without an occupant. Assistants and models were coming and going. Mildred Nash, his most valued assistant, came in 1913, boarding in the village but lunching every day with the family of which she became a beloved part. She earned Solon's special favor with her enthusiasm and willingness to turn her hand to anything. The publication of "Sound Construction" attests to this fact.

Only age prevented immediate enlistment in the army. He was not satisfied to be releasing a younger man by teaching twice a week at the Art Students' League, nor drilling with the Gallaher Battery in Norwalk, nor going to weekly drills at Governor's Island. Nothing would satisfy him save actual participation "over there".

His friend "Put" Brinley found the solution, telling him that the YMCA was looking for older men for overseas service with the troops. He himself, with writer John Erskine, a Wilton friend of Solon's, were about to leave.

Solon applied and was accepted. His medical examiner wrote on his application, "Send him anywhere." He packed his deepest feelings into the simple statement, "I am exceedingly happy that I am going to be of some use in this war."

Quickly he finished up a group — men and horses called "Back 'em Up" which he was doing for the Aeolian Company to be placed in their Fifth Avenue store window as part of the publicity for a Liberty Bond drive. He put his affairs in order, entrusting his family in his absence to his brother August. Since her husband's allowance with the YMCA had to be supplemented by a part-time job, Emma chose to teach French at the New Canaan Community School. Solon made his wife promise not to overtax her strength by teaching more than three times a week. Within a matter of days he was in Princeton getting intensive training.

Solon noted in his diary the points stressed at Princeton: "Every man has the chance to do a Christ job — Adaptability — Be ready to do anything. In all cases, resourcefulness, moral stamina, Christian conviction; Loyalty to Country; How to hold prayer meetings, how to conduct ourselves in a strange country, what to drink."

June 11 found him aboard the *Megantic* bound for Liverpool. On the transport he and his buddy, Jimmy Hubbell, a Minnesotan, organized entertainment. Solon's specialty was naturally a Wild West show with nurses and Red Cross girls smuggled in from their segregated quarters for the parts of Indian squaws. To Emma's amusement he also organized French classes. Her husband, she said, would stop at nothing!

Passing through London, Solon saw Westminster Abbey and Saint Paul's. The Gothic architecture of the first appealed to him more than the classical lines of the second. He heard Lloyd George address the House of Commons and was impressed. On the Cross-Channel boat he encountered the already famous but then fugitive, Alexander Kerensky, and noticed that Kerensky seemed "to look around him with his mind rather than with his eyes."

In Paris there were inevitable delays, which Solon filled in various ways. Pastor Vignal had recently died so his son-in-law took a pot of geraniums to the grave, sending Emma a sprig. He revisited old haunts, wrote of the Latin Quarter that students were no longer "lounging around" for all had gone to war. He ran into Gutzon's brother-in-law, the Reverend James Montgomery, in France with the Red Cross, and with him visited hospitals, overcrowded with wounded from the great German offensives. He also worked on his French. Yet all the while he was restless and impatient.

At last orders came, sending him to the French Third Army with headquarters at Meaux. Here, with a retired French veteran, he was to run a *Foyer du Soldat*.

This, he reflected, meant that some knowledge of the language had put him where he most wanted to be. But knowledge of the human heart was a language he knew better. *Foyer* is a pleasing word meaning a place to gather and relax. Literally, it means the "hearth," the heart of a man's home, that intangible something for which a man will fight. Solon Borglum needed no one to instruct him here. He had the idea of trying to *be* that hearth, providing its substance in ways that would be understood, handing out a cup of coffee or chocolate, a cigarette, a cheery word, a warm handshake, at times and in places where these things would mean the most to a fighting man. In his khaki uniform with his special identification tag, his happy smile, he became *l'Américain* for countless French soldiers.

Solon wrote in his diary: "One is impressed more and more with the enormity of the great burden the world is carrying; how happy we all are that we are to have a small part in lessening that burden!"

Some of Solon's colleagues were angling for desk jobs. Some were expecting to have an orderly for the hard work and when none was forthcoming, did none of it themselves. Others were concerned with getting their three square meals a day. Solon had only contempt for such men, which he expressed in his letters home. Nor did he care for the sky pilot who interpreted his job as "bringing men to Christ." In his book, the young men who were fighting and dying were not "sinners," but heroes, deserving only a compassionate ministry from their church. If his role at times approximated that of chaplain, he wanted to serve the living, not the dying, and he did not feel equipped to prepare men to die. The kind of chaplain that impressed him was one old padre who was always hanging around behind the fighting, just on the chance that he could be of help. One entry in the diary reads: "I had the great pleasure of telling the men when they came back from leave that the old padre was still among the living, waiting to welcome them."

Solon's first assignment near the Front was Montmirail. Here his knowledge of French was put to good use, since it was where the allied armies joined up. For the moment he and his buddy became extremely busy as the second battle of the Marne was being fought. But almost immediately this satisfaction faded, the sector becoming quiet with the failure of the German attack. Solon found himself in what resembled rest camps, occupied chiefly by his countrymen.

His diary notes that doughboys did not appear as much in need of rest as the *poilus*, who had been fighting for three years. The French were more serious and knew what the war was about. The American boys seemed only to want amusement, distraction, anything to take their minds off an unpleasant job; but entertainment was not what Solon had come to provide.

A pass arrived that would take him closer to the fighting and his spirits at once revived. Quickly filling his shoulder-bag with supplies, he was on his way, this time alone.

The tide of the war had just receded as he passed through Château-Thierry and he saw for the first time the real meaning of war.

From Château-Thierry he was sent to Epernay, and a little later he was joined by a French colleague. The two had to make their way forward by hitchhiking, for by some strange quirk of official decision the French army did not furnish Y-workers with either transportation or food. The first they had to improvise, the second to purchase. Yet, by a wondrous inconsistency, they were held liable to court-martial!

So almost anything on wheels, as long as it was moving in the right direction, served the Y-men's purpose. Usually it was an ambulance or camion, but once it was a *poilu* with a pair of donkeys. With their baskets and pots of coffee and chocolate and packs of cigarettes strapped to the sides of the animals, they were able to move along, but the man with the donkeys soon reached his destination and they were on their own again, forced to thumb a ride. They still managed.

It became Solon Borglum's distinction to be the first of his countrymen to enter the city of Rheims after the German retreat from before its walls. For hours as he trudged toward the city he had been aware of the great mass of the cathedral against the sky, "like one great mountain with twin peaks, clearly outlined in the gray mist of the evening which was hanging over the valley. I could not take my eyes from its towers, still sending out its messages of power far beyond the destruction caused by the world's greatest of wars." Entering the city

Solon and Emma in front of the "little" house, now somewhat enlarged. June 1918, before going overseas with the Y.M.C.A. for his war service.

Solon H. Borglum, (right) in uniform with his "buddy", Jimmy (standing left), an instructor, and an unidentified helper; his first *Foyer du Soldat*, Montmirail, France, 1918.

he still felt that awesome presence dominating everything around and below, the razed houses and rubble-filled streets. One day he made a mental note that he would return and sketch its shattered beauty; he did so several times. At Rheims the best spot for the *foyer* happened to be right in front of the great cathedral. In the lulls when not serving the endless lines of men, he was able to glance up and find inspiration and strength in the thought of all that the shrine had meant to the French nation and the world. He had discovered that the best time to open a *foyer* was at night when troops were on the move. Sleep was something to be caught up on during the day, which became his routine. In case someone came along while he was asleep, he would leave a pot on the stove with a note inviting people to help themselves.

For days the battle raged just beyond the city, and through all the nights Solon handed out his mugs of hot refreshment under the shadow of the huge, shattered structure. He became a well-remembered sight, many of the *poilus* who passed through Rheims recalling *L'Américain*. He ran into them constantly in the days and weeks that followed. Their expression of surprise and delight at finding the khaki uniform and the emblem of the Y so near the front was always a cherished reward. He also discovered, a little later, that he had unwittingly committed a serious faux pas in depriving some important organization of the honor of being the first to open canteens in the beleaguered city.

The German retreat, however, brought on more dissatisfaction. His pleas for permission to enter the combat zone were then at last heeded. His next orders "turned him loose" and for nine weeks he was allowed to cut himself off from communication.

As he and his French companion, Angeneur, who shared Solon's ardor, made their way forward, with Asfeld as their objective, the devastation of war hit them with fullest force. The American was reminded of what he had seen on the Plains when a tornado struck, except that all the tornadoes put together could not produce such wholesale death and destruction as he saw that day! "Over the whole breadth of the valley was spread a blanket of death, destruction and emptiness, beaten together by rain and mud." For the first time he saw war-shocked inhabitants emerging from their holes, too numb to react to their liberation.

Raymond Ingersoll, his superior, saw Solon at this time and reported to Emma: "We were working with the Fifth French Army along the Marne, south of Rheims. Most of the time Borglum was with a front-line regiment, sleeping in battered buildings and dugouts, sharing with a spirit of positive enthusiasm the hard work and the danger of the soldiers and going on foot with them in their night marches as the enemy fell back. I remember seeing him one day mudstained and completely exhausted. He had been tramping alone all night through strange and shell-torn roads in search of needed supplies for the men. That, and like experiences, he took as a matter of course."

Another glimpse is recorded by the commander of the 38th Division, signed "Michaud." It was sent to Solon's companion, Angeneur, to be shared by both men.

> ". . . I remember well your presence and that of your colleague, M. Borglum, amongst us during those October days of 1918 . . . I remember very well your precarious installation in a humble hut in the woods of Asfeld-la-ville over which the shells passed . . . you prepared and distributed with a tranquil courage, smiling, the cups of chocolate, near which congregated my Zouaves, who joyfully told me of their happiness at finding such a feast even in battle! . . . veritably you brought them in this manner a moral strengthening, when they had need of it, more perhaps than material . . .
>
> "And that is why, it is with all my heart that I thank you both, M. Borglum and you, for contributing and maintaining the forces' very high morale, the good humor, the gaiety of those troops and at the peril of your lives in spite of the extraordinary difficulties of obtaining supplies . . ."

The area, as General Michaud said, was being heavily shelled by the retreating Germans. Inexperience betrayed Solon into selecting a crossroads for his canteen. He was unhurt only because a quick-witted soldier persuaded him to move into a dugout for the night. In the morning, on observing the demolished canteen, his comrades asked, "Was *L'Américain* scared?" "Not a bit," came the reply. "He didn't even wake up."

When a gasmask became a necessity of life as well as a nuisance, *L'Américain* was twice caught without his mask. Neither time, however, was his gassing bad enough to require hospitalization though it could have shortened his life.

A feverish ardor possessed him in the last weeks before the Armistice. He snatched food and sleep as he could, depending for the first time on scraps from the regimental mess. He hadn't taken his clothes off for days and his uniform was in shreds. The accounts which, according to regulations, he was supposed to keep meticulously, were reduced to a hopeless jumble. He had his own system with them, just as he had his own idea about running a *foyer*. At the front he simply threw the rule-book away, refusing to charge men straight out of the trenches. On a lieutenant arriving, leading the 60 survivors of a battalion, this Y-man did not ask to see their money before serving them. On checking his accounts an accountant found that Solon had thrown in his own allowance, and actually was owed three hundred francs!

After the Armistice the French unit to which Solon was attached, the 158th Infantry Regiment, began to move toward Germany as part of the army of occupation. Solon's life changed abruptly, and with the change came an almost total ebbing of his ardor. Nothing so effectually doused his fire as the boring, fatiguing routine of erecting his canteen one day only to have to tear it down the next as the advance proceeded. Duties became chores instead of joys. Even the privilege of dining with the colonel in the officers' mess, which he was invited to do, gave no real satisfaction since it meant separation from the men. But he appreciated the fellowship of the officers and their very evident esteem. Colonel LeRoy's loan to Solon of his horses enabled him to get around with much greater ease to all the *foyers* for which he was now responsible.

Solon had the strong feeling that the work he had come to do in France was finished. His unusually lengthy letters home showed that his thoughts had never been far away from his loved ones and he expressed keen disappointment when he did not hear from them. His thoughts of home redoubled: of Rocky Ranch, his work, Emma's valiant effort to keep things going in his absence, his children — Paul just finishing high school, and Monica with her passion for horses. All at once it came over him: Home was where he wanted to be. To the pleas of his commanding officer that his services were needed as much now as before, demobilization being bound to be a slow tedious process, and combating boredom would take all a *foyer* director's skill, Solon turned an unsympathetic ear.

One thing only made him pause — the approach of Christmas. He, the homebuilder, the sentimentalist, simply could not bear the thought of "his" troops being without means for proper celebration of the feast. Accordingly, the week preceding the holiday he became obsessed with the notion of staging for his French friends a real American Christmas, complete with all the trimmings.

The task took ingenuity. It could have been the most demanding project of his entire overseas service! Where could he hope to find gifts for an entire regiment? He went first to his organization's headquarters. There he obtained 800 articles — pocket-knives, pipes, tobacco pouches and chocolate bars. But what were these among so many? He needed at least twice that number.

Where and how he discovered and collected everything, only Solon Borglum knew. His 50th birthday, December 22, 1918, found him spending the night in a currier's office waiting for the driver of a van who was to transport him and his acquisitions back to his regiment, but the van did not arrive. In the morning he phoned for help and, against all probability, received it. On Christmas morning no less than 1,750 separate gifts lay spread out in front of four huge Christmas trees at the 158th's temporary billet.

With the New Year there was time to relax. The sculptor's thoughts returned to art with greater compulsion, but before he was allowed to depart he was due for a surprise.

A special meeting of all the officers of the regiment was called. Champagne and cake were served in the large dining room of their hotel billet, decorated with Allied flags, for a very special occasion indeed. Colonel LeRoy presided. As an ex-prisoner of war he told of some of his experiences, laying special stress on the sacrifices of the ordinary French soldier who had given up years of his life to serve his country. Abruptly his tone changed. He spoke of one who had been serving, voluntarily, at the risk of his life for a country not his own, an American. Then he named the one American present and asked him to step forward. At first Solon thought he was being called on to speak and recoiled from the thought. Someone took him by the arm and led him forward. Only as the War Cross of France was pinned on the breast of his American uniform did he realize that the celebration was in his own honor. And when the Colonel put his hands on his shoulders and kissed him on both cheeks in traditional manner and the strains of the American and French anthems rang out, emotion overcame him.

The honor, as the Colonel pointed out, was a unique one; the Croix de Guerre was not given to civilians, it was reserved for soldiers in the actual fighting line.

Several weeks later, Emma received a long letter from the Colonel, enclosing a transcript of the citation:

> "Solon Borglum, Esq. American citizen . . . who has put himself at the disposal of the Regiment as a member of the great work, Foyer du Soldat . . . has not ceased for several months to put into this work his entire Apostle's soul, organizing Foyers behind the front lines, even in bombarded villages. He has rendered and continues to render the best of services to the soldiers of the regiment with all his great capacity for organization, generosity, and qualities of heart.
>
> January 6, 1919"

Solon accepted the honor as a recognition of the work of the Y-men. But Ingersoll wrote to tell Emma how they were all delighted that the honor had come to her husband, whose work he said, "has been such that he has had less support in it than have most directors. What he has done has been entirely an individual accomplishment; and he would have been our first choice for honors had we any voice in the matter.

"Yesterday I had the pleasure of seeing Mr. Borglum at his picturesque village in Luxembourg. You will be glad to know that he is looking exceptionally well. He has worked very hard, and at times has appeared tired, but now he is in splendid condition."

"RÉGIMENT DE"
LORETTE

Extrait de l'ordre du Régiment n° 7.

—

Le Lieutenant-Colonel Cite à l'ordre
du Régiment :

Monsieur Solon H. Borglum, citoyen américain.

« Est venu se mettre à la disposition du Régiment,
comme membre de la belle œuvre Le Foyer du Soldat.

N'a cessé depuis plusieurs mois, en y mettant
toute son âme d'apôtre, d'organiser des Foyers
derrière les premières lignes, même dans des villages
bombardés - a rendu et continue à rendre les meilleurs
services aux soldats du Régiment, par ses facultés
d'organisateur, sa générosité et ses qualités de cœur » -

Croix de Guerre -

Le 6 Janvier 1919
Le Lᵗ Colonel Le Roy, cᵗᵏ 158ᵉ Régᵗ Infⁱᵉ

Le Roy.

A photocopy of the citation announcing Solon's Croix de Guerre.

CHAPTER XVI

"A Scheme Without Precedent"

On Solon's return from France his advice was frequently sought concerning the best way to commemorate the heroic dead. He was not unprepared for, nor unsympathetic to the great change of national mood which was sweeping the country, causing the drying up of that spate of bronze and stone monuments which had made his first return from France so memorable. To one such inquiry he cautioned against erection of "the old standardized statues and tablets," saying "It is not the bigness[1] of a bronze or marble which brings out the greatest ideal."

The thought is a keynote of his art, with its preference for the small over the large, the universal over the particular, the anonymous over the big name. But it has a deeper meaning, which Laura Gardin Fraser, fellow-sculptor, put into words when she called Solon Borglum's work "small in size but big in effect." [2]

The words could apply to Solon's war service, which also could scarcely be described as big or "important". He had neither been an officer nor a combatant, and this could have been one of the things that caused Gutzon to embroider the facts out of all resemblance to the truth. The feeling is also evident in what Major Hellman at Y headquarters said when Solon told him what he had been doing: "Was *that* the best[3] they could give you?" The question has the sting of scorn. To which Solon replied, "It was the best work I have ever had."

Again the words could have wider application. The impact on the French mind, on the consciousness and thinking of our Allies, of that lone friendly figure in their midst, must have been considerable. It too could have been "small in size but big in effect."

Before Solon left France a colleague borrowed the handsome hard-cover notebook issued by "les Foyers du Soldat, the Union Franco-Américaine," his "Livre d'Or," [4] containing the thirteen pencil and ink sketches he had made, all signed "Solon H. Borglum, Sculptor." On its return over a hundred signatures had been added.

All sorts of people had come into contact with this Y man in the past months. Frenchmen, from Colonel LeRoy down, Africans serving in the French Army, Belgians, and a few Englishmen. Some used a half page to express their gratitude, some but a sentence, like *"Mon rêve: passer un instant au foyer du soldat."* A soldier whose name was Carnilaf-Vel described himself as "Poète-Chansonnier" and wrote lines that fill a page. Others merely expressed thanks for hospitality received on their way to or from the front. *Vive l'Amérique* was added by quite a number.

A few American names appear: John Sherman Hoyt ("War Work Council"), C. V. Hibbard ("International Committee, YMCA New York City"). F. B. Kirkbride, who gives his address as New York and Rowayton, Connecticut, wrote: "To express my admiration for the worth and genius of a neighbor whom I have first had the pleasure of meeting in war-ridden France." Major Samuel M. Wilson, of the Judge-Advocate's Office of the U.S. Army, gave utterance to the thought, "The drive that we started at Château-Thierry we will finish in Berlin — 17 September, 1918."

On dugouts being exchanged for billets Solon expressed to Emma strong reservations about his change of status. He did not mind the improvement in his physical comfort, but he questioned in his heart the separation it entailed from those he had crossed the Atlantic to serve. At the same time, he enthusiastically recounted the most exciting of his new experiences, boar hunting in the forest. Nor was he insensitive to the importance of his position in the French army, in the larger sense. In one letter he speaks of his meticulousness in shining his shoes, something he seldom did at home. He said he knew the French would attach importance to such details, since he was the representative of his country among these officers.

Nor had he lost any of his humor. His drawing of his buddy Jimmy Hubbell, according to Monica who met Jimmy, was a wonderful likeness. He was short and tubby, a bit like Fiorello La Guardia, but straight as a ramrod, his cigar in a holder held at the cockiest angle. It is captioned by the artist, "A man, but a YMCA man, my friend Jimmie."

Among his drawings one sketch shows a canteen in operation. In bold lettering over the door appear the words "FOYER DU SOLDAT," along with the Tricolor and the Stars and Stripes. In front there is a line of soldiers; an NCO at attention holds a cup; on the right there are benches and a table, with men in all stages of exhaustion. Other sketches show scenes of the devastation the artist has witnessed.

In Paris on his way to get his discharge, Solon ran into Putnam Brinley. "Put" told him that his friend Lloyd Warren, the New York architect, was looking everywhere for him. He had a job for Solon Borglum.

Solon shook his head. He had at that moment only one desire, to get home as quickly as possible. He had not realized until then how tired he was.

Yet he could not refuse the unusual opportunity which he was offered and hoped to be so busy time would pass quickly, a wish that was to be granted.

The A. E. F. Art Training Center in Bellevue, suburb of Paris, functioned only as long as was required to find shipping to get the boys home. It opened its doors March 5, 1919, and closed them again, for lack of students, June 15. But it must rank as one of the most imaginative, inspiring and inspired ventures in education ever undertaken by the United States Government. As its commandant, Major George H. Gray, stated: "Our army of citizen-soldiers found itself at the end of the campaign in a foreign land which is a veritable treasure house of art of every description, [one] whose whole history is intricately laced with the history of art, a land which for ages has been producing masters and masterworks, a land replete with museums, schools and instructors of great gifts."

A benevolent government was providing these citizen-soldiers before discharge with the opportunity to take up once more the tools of their arts and crafts. Solon shared the major's enthusiasm, calling it "a scheme without precedent."

The School of Fine Arts for advanced students was housed under one roof. A good site was obtained within easy reach of Paris and the French government rendered every assistance. The master artists opened their studios to the Americans so that, in the words of the commandant, "the young student could see with his own eyes great works in the process of making." Gray added, "the mind of the soldier was ready to receive and the unselfish effort to give and help in this work was a joy and a privilege to the teachers. With this spirit permeating the faculty the students were quickly assigned to their respective classes as soon as they reported."

Solon was appointed head of the sculpture department, located in the former school of Isadora Duncan. He was made an honorary captain, given a Sam Brown belt and assigned the dancer's private apartment. His students, all advanced, numbered 16. He was delighted with their seriousness and dedication and was enthusiastic about the whole venture. He noted that while there was just enough military snap to be stimulating, "the soldier-student upon arrival was first astonished, then overjoyed. He would throw down his pack at the door and wonder if it was really true," soon becoming as absorbed in his work as the man ahead. "No thought of dreamy idleness, nor questioning of military orders could possibly enter his mind for he soon realized that the Government had planned three short months for him, and was not only giving him the instructors, but also the time and the tools." On entering his classroom the student found all necessary supplies. "Each architect was given a new drawing-board, mathematical instruments, and pencils; the painter, a fresh paintbox, tubes of paint, canvas and easels; the sculptor his clay and modeling stands." The students were not only able to study, but actually were paid "to study the profession they loved and which they had willingly shelved to enter the war."

Solon, who himself had had so little in his student days, was quick to appreciate what all this meant to the citizen-soldier. "No one can realize the great joy of the soldier who had staked everything and won and who suddenly found himself in a well-equipped studio, one of hundreds of comrades, some working over their drawing boards, some on their canvases and others with clay, each trying to recapture ideals which he thought he had lost."

Visits were made to the leading ateliers and museums of Paris and the class helped to embellish the grounds of the *pavillon* and made a tablet for the new Pershing Stadium for the 1920 Olympics.

Solon now had the chance to return to Rheims, which he did many times in order to make sketches of the cathedral he planned to etch. His colleague, Robert Logan, painted the great edifice as it stood amid the rubble, and this painting was also among Solon's cherished possessions.

On one of these trips,[5] Solon was accompanied by the sculptor and art

My Corner,

"My Corner." Solon's room at Bellevue. He has just received the photographs of his work from Emma. Spring 1919.

The A.E.F. School of Fine Arts, Bellevue, Seine-et-Oise, near Paris, 1919. Sculpture class.

historian, Lorado Taft, who described the occasion. They arrived at 2 a.m., intending to spend the night at the Y., but found every bed taken, with men sleeping on the floor. Instead they walked the deserted streets, which were flooded with moonlight: "I never saw or felt anything so thrilling," Taft wrote. "The silent streets with ruins everywhere. Not a person to be seen or heard, just shattered walls and piles of stone. Then all of a sudden, an open space, and that majestic building reaching into the sky! Oh, but it was wonderful! I was tempted to steal away this morning and not spoil the vision with anything more precise and literal. We stayed around there almost an hour and the only sound I heard was an occasional sigh from the pinnacles, or was it from the very heart of the structure? Borglum explained that it was the calls of the young rooks nesting in the recesses. The building kept sighing and it was like the melancholy soughing of the wind in the treetops . . ."

Solon stepped off the *Imperator* at Hoboken to be greeted by his son Paul, just graduated from high school. His return was celebrated by his neighbors in traditional style. They gave him a surprise party, inspired and led by Harold Paget and Clarence 'Jim' King, bursting into the living room that same evening. The joshing of his neighbors was familiar: "You look wonderful . . . the picture of health . . . ," as were the returning hero's replies: "Why not? I've had a wonderful rest." "The gassing, how many times? three?" "Nothing, nothing." With Bertha's help Emma had canned immense quantities of vegetables and fruit. She had knitted piles of garments and taught many hours at the New Canaan Community School, not heeding her husband's admonition to spare herself. The winter of 1918–1919 had been particularly rigorous. Many were the mornings Emma had been compelled to get to her teaching in New Canaan by the round-about way of the New Haven Railroad, with her neighbors, the Pagets or the Kings, picking her up and driving her to South Norwalk, where she took the train to Stamford, and thence by the branch line back to New Canaan, only two and a half miles by roads, rendered impassable by ice and snow, from Rocky Ranch.

The change that in time was to render everything different, the Great Revolution of the Twentieth Century, had already begun. The old life which Solon had loved so well, with its beautiful simplicities, its character of a veritable

Eden, was a sure victim. Commuting had arrived and with it the automobile. The steadily shrinking process of communication between town and country had begun. Also, the sylvan retreat that Solon had found for himself and his family had been discovered. More and more summer residents stayed the year round, and Emma, whose reaction to it all would be so different from Solon's, would no longer suffer the agonies she had once suffered on the approach of winter.

What was uppermost in Solon's mind at the moment, however, was the need of taking care of his children's education. He frequently spoke to Paul of his own great handicap due to his lack of schooling. He had so much he wanted to say now. He did not wish his children to repeat his own mistake and have to spend a lifetime catching up. More convinced than ever that both should have a college education, he saw to it that Paul entered Dartmouth in the Fall; while Monica went to Simmons College in Boston, several years later.

He was unprepared for the change he found in his children. It seemed to him that both had seized the opportunity of his absence to grow up and not always in a way he approved. Compared to his own teen-age years, young people seemed to him altogether too frivolous, "the generation gap" being apparent then as now.

But the greatest change could have been in himself. One Silvermine friend who knew him well described the change he saw in Solon as "mellowing". Jim King meant that Solon had become more tolerant. This would not be surprising in one who had just witnessed the breakdown of the escalator of Progress. Solon had once again rubbed shoulders with all manner of men. He had witnessed a leveling process at work, which he hoped would continue. He had had his fill of hostility, and was sick of it.

If Solon believed that he would have the contract for the Huntington project to tide him over the difficult stage of readjustment, if he expected to receive final payment for that ambitious scheme, he was disappointed. The chairman, on Solon's disembarkation, was nowhere to be seen. Gutzon had disappeared, without, apparently, even completing the first stage of his assignment. All that Solon had in the way of work when he stepped off the S.S. *Imperator* were his two figures for Saint Mark's . . .

The summer of Solon's return was spent on the literary material to be published in the *Century* magazine, describing the unique, imaginative and totally extraordinary government experiment, the AEF School of Fine Arts at Bellevue. August Borglum, who had brought his family to Silvermine to welcome Solon, lent his assistance, devoting hours of work to helping Solon gather together and put into readable shape his rough notes.

Solon gave two talks that summer, one was to a group in Washington, D.C. that was organizing an exhibit of Scandinavian art, the other to a group interested in planning a school for industrial design. To both he gave encouragement. His concern now, however, was with the neglect of fundamentals he found in so much of the teaching. Teachers were beginning, he thought, at the wrong end, giving to their pupils cake instead of bread and he felt deep concern. "Remember," he told his audiences, "that Michelangelo went through the minutest apprenticeship of drawing, painting, modeling and marble carving, and still had plenty of time to produce and leave us the greatest pieces of personal work in sculpture, architecture, and industrial art."

But the tragic thing was that the speaker himself was not to have in his remaining days anything like that amount of time.

"The Dinner Bell." A carved door which was Solon Borglum's own secret passage to the dining room. *E. Irving Blomstrann.*

CHAPTER XVII

Teacher

Six months after Solon Borglum's return home his "School of American Sculpture" opened in New York.

It was predictable that some day Solon would want to have his own school. He had always shown interest in youth and in teaching. At Loup River he taught his eight-year-old brother Frank how to draw. The student of J. Laurie Wallace in Omaha occasionally visited the Sioux and taught their children to draw. The Paris student helped the future Mrs. Paul Manship in modeling a horse's head. The Rocky Ranch sculptor did not refuse requests for help from the art schools so long as teaching did not encroach too much upon time needed in the studio. At Cooper Union, the Art Students' League and the Beaux-Arts Institute of Design he was a familiar figure before going overseas; the last elected him to honorary membership for his devotion to the principle of the free school.

There was new eloquence and assurance in Solon's delivery as he considered the future of American art. If the present moment was unpropitious the future was bright. He denounced imitators and plagiarists who "merely masqueraded as artists while remaining blind to all the marvelous materials for great art that lay before them from America's history and culture," castigating their failure, from laziness or habit, to select and design in harmony with American ideals. He contrasted them to artists of the Renaissance, who, he said, traveled around Europe recording and adapting what they found to their own concepts. He felt that the American artist should be "the interpreter of his country's ideals" and summoned him to leadership.

In this situation Solon Borglum's first thought was to have the AEF School of Fine Arts at Bellevue transferred to Washington as a government-sponsored art school. While colleagues wholeheartedly supported this proposal Solon did not meet with success. His idea was ahead of his day. Nevertheless, the thought of dismantlement, the loss of all the school's fine equipment, the dispersal of its staff and the dissipation of valuable experience, especially when it was so needed at home, was acutely distressing to him. There was no way — unless he did it himself and in New York. A manual of instruction at least was ready, his *Sound Construction*. F. Tolles Chamberlin, Fellow of the American Academy in Rome, recalls with pleasure the visit he had with the book's author and how impressed he was by the drawings Solon displayed on the walls of his studio. To Chamberlin, both the school and the manual had about them a feel of inevitability. As Louise Eberle wrote, "One could scarcely imagine him[1] not doing that, for so deep a believer in his country's destiny in art, and so right-minded a pioneer therein, would naturally labor to pass on his faith to a succeeding generation."

Instruction of the French soldier followed the Armistice. Ingersoll recalled how he had come upon Solon, busy with classes for interested French soldiers in the mountains of Luxembourg. The Bellevue experience was certainly a decisive event in his mature life. The drive to communicate and defend his convictions cut through the man's innate modesty and reticence.

So, almost at the close of his life, Solon Borglum comes alive in a new way. He is more assertive in his manner of promoting ideas. Recent experiences, the distinction of the Croix de Guerre on his civilian breast, his success as director in an American Army art school near Paris, released in him a force that circumstance had often needed though it had never caused it to surface in the same fashion.

The name he chose for his school is significant. It was not to be the Solon H. Borglum School, nor the "American School." Since the art, not the school was to be American, it was *The School of American Sculpture*.

The broad objective of the School was stated in a brochure: "To provide a means for raising sculpture in America to its proper position, using American ideals and models, and not copying the classic."

Solon wrote Robert Fulton Logan (January 12, 1920): "Have started the school at last, been open one month, rather late, but we have seven very serious

Studio portrait taken in the Rocky Ranch studio by Gertrude K. Lathrop, sculptor. A serious man on a serious venture. 1921

Happy To Be Home Again   Solon Borglum, c. 1920, modeling the "Columbus" bell

students. We are going to make it grow by doing continually serious hard study."

A little later he informed Jimmy Hubbell that the school was "going on fine": "If we can get through this summer it seems to me that this is going to grow into a great big problem. It is continually pushing itself out of cramped quarters. If you see the young man who said this school is too swell for him, tell him he's wrong. The tuition is high, but it is the most serious school in the country and the only thing swell about it is that everybody must work."

The success of the school from the day of opening was phenomenal. Numbers doubled and redoubled. The first location was the Colonial Studios on West 57th Street; the larger quarters, which it soon had to find, was on East 59th, close to Fifth Avenue. By the end of the second year, enrollment for the next semester had climbed to 90. As its founder and director said, success was based on seriousness. The high fees — $50 a month was not cheap in 1919 — kept the dabbler and the frivolous away. Every student had to sign up for at least six months, and the stiffness of the course, for which a high school diploma was a prerequisite, did the rest. There was no paid advertising during Solon's lifetime, the school becoming known only by word of mouth. Each month parents and interested friends were invited to see the student's work. The remainder of the explanation for the school's success is that Solon was a born teacher.

Solon Borglum's teaching methods were not spectacular. He neither attracted attention to himself, nor tried to impose his own ideas. What he wanted, what he sought for most, was for each student to develop his own potential and create his own "masterpieces," uninfluenced by anything that had been done in the past. The teacher defined what he meant by a masterpiece, "a creation developed and finished to the highest understanding in the period in which it is done." The dream on which he founded the school did not seem wholly unrealistic because he automatically imparted a portion of his own "drive" to his students, engendering in them their own individual ambitions. In this way "masterpieces" *were* possible. He set no limit to what was attainable. Solon's view of America's future was as optimistic as it was about himself and the capabilities of his students.

As a teacher Solon used few words, and still fewer compliments. This could be one secret of his success, for compliments can easily be mistaken for flattery, and all that Solon is reputed to have awarded his pupils' best efforts was to give them a quiet smile of encouragement. "Peg away" would tell them there was still

work to be done before they could feel the piece was finished. Just as "use what
you have" was a maxim of his own life, so it was in frequent use in the
classroom. There it would refer to some experience, or circumstance, or theme;
for what the teacher wanted had to come from the head and the heart; cleverness
with the fingers was not enough. Much more was required than mere accurate
observation of surfaces, the student had to know what lay underneath. In his
homely way he reduced the thought to the simplest terms: "It only takes a
moment to put the skin on." The goal was ever thoroughness. A former student
recalls his keeping a model at one pose for as long as four weeks. "You must
draw," says the posthumously published manual, "until you see form in its right
place. You must study construction until you work in fine, large lines, which will
represent deep knowledge, and you will have complete confidence in yourself.
This is the big thing in sculpture. If you do not learn construction now, you will
be struggling with it always."

The method, in effect, was a blending of great authority with modest
charm, seriousness with a smile, demand with honest encouragement. These were
the qualities that his students never forgot. At Solon's last rites, the spokesman
for a delegation from the School stated that "his teaching was simple, vivid,
strong and true; his patience, courtesy and generosity, unending. He gave to the
School without reserve his tremendous energy, high courage, and unfailing
interest. Big, simple and real, his was a great spirit."

One day Solon received a letter from the director of the Tulane (Louisiana)
School of Art. Mr. Woodward wrote him: "We do not teach sculpture in this
school from lack of a proper instructor and because the appeal for that form of art
has not yet been especially pressed upon us. Occasionally, however, I am called
upon for advice by prospective students of sculpture. In the absence of other
opportunity I have been accustomed to advise that the student would be well
employed in the study of drawing. My eye was caught by the statement in your
circular relating to drawing. I am accordingly writing to inquire just what part
exercises in form drawing have in your course leading to sculpture."

Solon replied: "It gives me great pleasure to help anyone who is trying to
show the right road. According to my experience with young students, it is a fact
that they *want* to know the right way. They are very easily carried away by
movement; that is, when there may be some student that seems to be clever, this
cleverness is only faking the surface and soon runs out, but careful study of

structure by drawing gives one a sound foundation, which soon outstrips all cleverness or bluff. The student must study structure of the human form, horse and plants in the School, and when the figure cannot be had, there is no excuse because the structures of flowers, leaves and all parts of plants can be had so easily, and will develop one's mind so much, and it is the true road to confidence."

Solon was teaching again at the Beaux-Arts and for a period of time he substituted for another teacher at Cooper Union. One former student, who became an artist of note, recalls how excited the class was on learning that this eminent sculptor was to be their teacher. "He was my last teacher before I went to Rome on a scholarship." Another recalls his gaiety, how they loved to see him coming. He was still blunt and outspoken. Awe creeps into the voice of a third, a former Beaux-Arts student, as he speaks of his experience of having been taught by Solon Borglum. With the same blend of modesty and distinction, Solon enjoyed a monthly meeting for lunch in New York with former Bellevue colleagues including Peixotto, Hellman and Warren, in happy fellowship. But surely only Solon would have forgotten until the very last minute one reunion in particular, a banquet at which the guest of honor was to be none other than General Pershing, or have gone in an old business suit!

Guthrie's war with the traditionalists of Saint Mark's reached its foreseeable dénouement when word leaked out that a nude female and two nearly nude savages were about to invade "the oldest piece of consecrated ground on Manhattan," giving the ghosts of Peter Stuyvesant and other worthies lying in the vaults a most terrible shock. Solon found himself tagged a radical along with the rector. This was in no way alarming, being almost as old a situation as art itself, nor was it in the least detrimental to an artist's reputation. Live art has always been controversial, and there are those who say that controversy is a sign of being alive. But Solon's reaction was to shun the publicity more than ever. He wanted only to get on with his work. It needed the urging of his friend and close neighbor, John Cassel, to give him a different slant and become agreeable to granting an interview to Cassel's colleague, Will B. Johnstone on the *Evening World*. The controversial statues were about to start their journey from studio to church when Johnstone arrived, but Solon was still reluctant and the facts had to be dragged out of him.

Johnstone described the artist[4] as "dressed in sculptor's smock, his muscular arms bare . . ." calling him "the loved and respected Solon of art in this talented community" who, like Grieg, sought "the inspiring solitude of nature for his important works." He called the studio "a littered museum," citing the many statues he saw there — the General Gordon and the Bucky O'Neill, Fighting Bulls, the two eagles for the Pan-American Building in Washington, D.C., the Washington, the Napoleon, and the models for the Geographic project of Archer M. Huntington — a generous collection of Solon Borglum's later work.

Solon was emphatic about the appropriateness of his two Indian figures, repeating that "The Indian belongs as much in a church as in front of a wigwam. We pride ourselves that we have the only germ of aspiration and inspiration. Didn't the Indian commune with heaven through the eagle?"

"Aspiration" showed the primitive man "without fear but feeling for the first time something beyond the physical, coming from within yet separate, call it what you will — soul, love, worthy deeds. He is the monument to that feeling which all of us have." As for "Inspiration," that figure depicts the first "soul-elevating discovery" of the savage, the notes that come from a rude whistle made from a turkey wing bone symbolize the beginning of the arts, music. A smile plays about his lips as he listens.

"I could not use Greek or Roman figures, or angels," he said. In speaking to Americans, the American idiom was necessary. "It is of the soil, and I merely speak in terms of the Indian, the only unhyphenated American, to convey the human traits of aspiration and inspiration, repeated today in all of us," by the man in the street, "the poor of the East side who live in dirty rooms, who aspire to leave that and in the end achieve degrees at Columbia; we all suffer, we aspire, and work for betterment."

These were Solon's last important works, created for a man who believed so fervently in the union of religion and art that he said, "We should live, fight and die for beauty." Into "Aspiration" with its depiction of tremendous vital energy, physical strength, yet with massive hands hanging helpless and imploring, the sculptor poured all that he had learned about life and the meaning of art in those last experience-packed months of his career. He is on record as saying he never stopped thinking about Guthrie's idea all the time he was in France. If

"Aspiration" does not represent the peak for this gifted sculptor, there is no peak, his life just ended. . . .

Despite the artist's explanation and defense the *Evening World*'s headline proclaimed;

STATUE OF NUDE WOMAN AND TWO INDIANS IN SAINT MARK'S CHURCH A RADICAL INNOVATION

How the 'nude woman' got into the act requires a word of explanation, since she formed no part of the rector's original scheme and the sculptor himself did not want to part with her. It happened this way: On one of his visits to Rocky Ranch Guthrie caught sight of the little white marble figure. And if we remember that he was both esthete and cleric, we are not surprised to learn that it was love at first sight. The little kneeling figure with outstretched arm and hair to receive the dew was Solon's design for "The Waters" in Huntington's project,* and became almost as popular as the Indians were puzzling. Everybody loved the little nude, including the man who made it. Solon had been so enamoured with his design that after the vote of the other sculptors assigning the idea to another sculptor he had carved it in marble to give it permanence. But Guthrie being a persuasive and persistent man managed to prevail upon the sculptor to part with the statue and allow him to include it in his own plan.

To Solon, Guthrie wrote a characteristic letter explaining what he had in mind. It began, "Dear Solon the Wise," [5] and continued:

> I leave the changes and the chances to you so we have the two 8 foot Redmen in their beauty in plaster looking OK by the 15th of October on their guard. As to the beloved "Water" I've got a better plan for her exhibition in the recess of greenery between the brick wall and the Rectory by making a shallow birdbath to which water drips from a rockery or rough pedestal 4 feet high and to the right and left a stone bench and about the birdbath a mass of blue flowers — forget-me-nots or lobelia or ageratum, and on guard a row of little red cedars or spired boxwoods . . .

---

* It will be recalled that each sculptor designed a model to represent Earth, Waters, the Heavens, Man. After the selection each sculptor was free to use his other designs as he wished.

The two heroic plasters were duly unveiled and dedicated on the 125th anniversary of St. Mark's in-the-Bouwerie's incorporation, the tenth anniversary, as it happened, of its rector's own pastorate. Those announced as having a part in the service included the rector of Trinity Church, the Reverend William T. Manning, shortly to be elevated to head the diocese.

"The nude female" quickly won approval and acceptance. Guthrie had renamed it, "The Little Lady of the Dew," describing it as "an exquisite depiction of beauty, innocence and chastity." The two other figures did not fare as well. They still appeared to some as huge, unprepossessing savages that had no right to "hang around" as charming an entrance as St. Mark's. "It is certain," wrote one reporter, "that their arrival on East 10th Street has caused a sensation in the neighborhood. All day yesterday the neighbors trooped by and stopped to gaze upon the massive Borglum creations through the bars of the ancient iron fence." When it was suggested that the parish might have to bow to the storm and remove the offending Indians to a less prominent position, the artist jumped to their defense. He reaffirmed his belief in their propriety, not only within the precincts of a church, but even beside the altar itself; they represented, he believed, the highest possible expression of "the religious spirit in art." He resented very much the preference being shown for "The Little Lady of the Dew," regarding it as a repudiation of his whole aim as an artist. "Aspiration" and "Inspiration" were, for him, "the culmination of years of study and the best that is in me."

As 1921 moved toward its end Solon tried to maintain an impossible schedule. His two studios, in New York and Silvermine, were 45 miles apart. Just as he had foreseen, the success of the school created its own problems. He needed a staff. He had no assistant to help with the instruction and lacked even a good business manager. His hope was to develop a teacher assistant from among the members of the night class, which was reserved for men. No doubt he would have, given time.

The serene skies of success the school represented for his family were of course pleasant, especially for one faced with college expenses. It was an agreeable thought that Emma would no longer have to worry about her "precipice"!

Meanwhile, it was difficult, much too difficult, trying to run the school

"The Waters." Saint Mark's Church in-the-Bouwerie, New York City. This marble figure depicting the waters of the earth was orginally done in a 13½ in. size model for the Archer Huntington project for the American Geographical Society. When the marble figure joined Solon Borglum's "Aspiration" and "Inspiration" in 1920, its name was changed to "The Little Lady of the Dew". *Keystone View Co. Inc.*

Nine foot Indians create a furor in New York City. Statue of "Aspiration" at the entrance to St. Mark's in-the-Bouwerie. *Gertrude K. Lathrop.*

alone. In the Silvermine studio, carving of the figures for Saint Mark's got underway in the summer. As he helped in the difficult operation of cutting and moving the great blocks of limestone for the carving, Paul was enormously impressed by his father's skill and resourcefulness.

Every day now the problem was the same, how to get enough time for his own work. Solon had a great distaste for staying in town, but with night classes three times a week lasting until 10 o'clock, commuting became more than a problem. He usually caught the midnight train home. In order to get any work done at all he tried to keep up his old routine of rising before dawn, which made the pace a killing one.

The Silvermine artists saw less and less of him. There were no more exhibitions in the Borglum studio, which in any case had been outgrown. The last, number 13, was in 1920. That things had changed was the general feeling. On an invitation arriving for the Silvermine Group of Artists to be represented at the American Federation of Arts' opening session, Solon asked protesting architect Boring to represent the Silverminers, an utterly unheard of thing in the old days.

Christmas was celebrated with a childrens' party for which a huge tree was set up in the Studio. Several days later there was a teen-age dance. After the holidays Solon went south to give a lecture in Norfolk, Va. and on his return served on a jury for the National Arts Club's annual art exhibition, opening January 5.

Three weeks after the New Year, which was unseasonably mild, Solon and Emma held the usual monthly reception at the School and both returned home in time for the funeral of their long-time friend and neighbor, Austin W. Lord, an occasion which brought out the community in full strength. Who could have guessed that only two weeks later all would gather again for a similar sad reason at the Borglum Studio?

Solon's brief illness, confused with occasional attacks of indigestion and migraine, was misdiagnosed by his doctor, a new man who did not know his patient and first accepted Solon's own diagnosis of his condition. It turned out to be appendicitis, culminating in a ruptured appendix. After a hurried operation at the Stamford Hospital his condition was not at first considered critical, everyone, including the surgeon, expecting him to pull through. Distant relatives were not called and Gutzon, living nearby in Stamford, was notified but asked not to come and see his brother lest the visit alarm the patient. Sunday was a good day for all. Relief and a gentle gaiety permeated the usual hospital atmosphere. But early Monday morning Solon's condition suddenly grew worse. Paul was summoned from Dartmouth; Monica, who had stayed at Rocky Ranch, joined her mother at the hospital.

It was in the middle of the afternoon when Emma and Monica had, at the nurse's suggestion, left Solon's room for a moment. Solon was in a very deep sleep.

Gutzon arrived in time for his brother's last sleep. A replay of familiar words sounded from the room where Solon lay: *"We shall do great works together!"* "Wake up, Solon! Wake up!" The distraught man's cries could be heard down the corridor. But it was too late for that old dream of "two brothers." Much too late. . . .

Death came a few hours later, on the afternoon of January 30, 1922, nine days after the first brief sign of illness, five weeks after Solon's 53rd birthday.

The funeral was an intimate service, held in the Studio at Rocky Ranch as Solon would have wished it. Unbelieving neighbors and friends came offering help. Students from the New York school asked to be allowed to arrange the workshop of their master, suddenly become large and empty. Statues were wheeled aside, leaving only the towering plaster model of "Aspiration," which was placed beside the unfinished stone figure.

The bier was put at the foot of these statues. The hammer and chisel were left at the base where the sculptor had last put them down. A soft brush on the shoulder, used for dusting off the marble chips, remained where he had left it. On the casket was placed the American uniform of *L'Américain* with the Croix de Guerre. When all the wreaths and floral displays had been brought in, there was scarce room enough for the many who wished to crowd in. The rector of Saint Mark's in-the-Bouwerie officiated. William Norman Guthrie concluded a brief service with words expressed with deepest feeling: "Solon Hannibal Borglum believed profoundly in spiritual reality, and therefore he could conceive greatly, at times sublimely, and execute with austere audacity and brave tenderness." Then followed the familiar lines from Browning:

> "One who never turned his back but marched breast forward,
>   Never doubted clouds would break,

Never dreamed, though right were worsted, wrong would triumph,
   Held, we fall to rise, are baffled to fight better;
      Sleep to wake . . .
No, at noonday in the bustle of man's work-time
     Greet the unseen with a cheer!

As a final act, Dr. Guthrie asked Solon's son to place against the unfinished statue of "Aspiration" a large wreath of arborvitae and evergreens, gift of Saint Mark's in-the-Bouwerie, symbol of life everlasting.

Chronology

1868	Born in Ogden, Utah, December 22, son of Jens Møller Haugaard Borglum and Christina Mikkelsen Borglum.
1869–1882	Childhood in Fremont (Nebraska), Omaha, St. Louis, and nearby towns; chiefly Fremont, where his father sets up practice as a doctor and where Solon obtains his grammar schooling.
1882–1883	One year of high school at Creighton College, Omaha.
1883–1884	Ranch hand in southern California. From time to time sees his brother, Johnny (Gutzon) who is studying art in Los Angeles, sharing an interest with him in art.
1884	Back in Omaha, Nebraska.
1885	Listed in Omaha City Directory as "painter, residence 2415 Caldwell," his father's home address. Plans for the development of his father's newly acquired land in central Nebraska, some six thousand acres.
1885–1893	Cowboy-ranchman on the Loup River.
1890	John Gutzon pays him a visit at the ranch and, seeing the rough sketches that he had made, says, "Solon, you should be an artist!"
1890–1893	Solon remains on the ranch but goes to Omaha from time to time to take lessons with the painter J. Laurie Wallace, former student of Thomas Eakins.
1893	Another visit from Gutzon who has dropped his first name and, on seeing Solon's work, persuades him to sell the ranch and set up a studio with him in Sierra Madre, California.
	Solon leaves the ranch and goes to Sierra Madre. Little of this period survives except the fact that the plan did not work out and Solon left.

1893-1895   Itinerant artist, going from Los Angeles, where he becomes a sidewalk painter, to Santa Ana, where he puts down stakes, renting a room for a studio and giving lessons on weekends. Between weekends he roams the mountains of the Santa Ana range, mixing with wanderers like himself and storing up memories for the future. Makes life-long friends of Daniel R. Wood, high school teacher, and Professor and Mrs. Perham, his hosts in Santa Ana.

1895   Exhibits his work in local YMCA which is reported in local newspaper. Nets enough money to go to Cincinnati to study. At the Cincinnati Art Academy he enters the classes in drawing, painting and sculpture.

1895-1897   Studies under Louis T. Rebisso at the Cincinnati Art Academy. Wins attention and special scholarships. Exhibition of his sculpture nets money for a trip to Paris "to look around."

1897   Meets Augustus Saint-Gaudens and other American artists who encourage him, persuading him to stay in Paris for further study. Frémiet, who becomes his master, tells him, "*Mon ami,* you are lucky! You lived. You had something to say before you studied art." He studies the human form at the Académie Julian under Denys Puech.

1898   Exhibits "Lassoing Wild Horses" at the Salon; given Place of Honor. Also exhibits "Winter," which is purchased by well-wishers in Cincinnati who present it to the Cincinnati Art Museum. December 10 marries Emma Vignal, daughter of a Paris Protestant minister.

1899   Spring: Exhibits life-size group "Stampede of Wild Horses" at the Salon; Honorable Mention. Also exhibits "In the Wind."
Summer: Returns to the West with his bride and spends four months at the Crow Creek Reservation, South Dakota, guests of the Reverend Hackeliah Burt and his wife, Episcopal missionaries to the Indians. Some of Solon's finest groups result from studies made during this summer. On way back to France exhibits new work at Hospe Auditorium in Omaha.

1900   "Stampede of Wild Horses" requested for entrance to United States Pavilion at *Exposition Universelle,* Paris. "Buffalo" also shown, given a bronze medal. Unfinished group "On the Border of White Man's Land" requested by the committee, which holds a place for it until finished. Titled "The Scout" it receives a silver medal.
Lilli, Solon's first child, born in May.

1901   Solon learns to carve marble. Carves small marble bust of Lilli.
Exhibits life-size plaster of "Sun Dance" and marble "Our Slave" (captured

wild horse) at the Salon. Begins carving "Snowdrift" and "The Last Roundup" in marble.

Pan-American Exposition in Buffalo, N.Y. Awarded silver medal for "Remarkable success of twelve bronzes and marbles."

Creates 44 in. high "One In A Thousand" after early group.

Elected to the National Sculpture Society in New York, sponsored by Augustus Saint-Gaudens and Frederick MacMonnies.

Sets up a permanent studio in New York. Emma remains in Paris with her parents. Paul Arnold, second child, born there December 29.

1902   Bas-relief of Thomas P. Ochiltree, member of Congress from Texas.

Summer: Emma joins Solon in New York with their two children.

Exhibited at the National Sculpture Society at Madison Square Garden.

1903   One-man show at Keppel Galleries, 20 East 16th Street, New York City: displays 32 bronzes, marbles and other sculptures.

First appearance in *Who's Who in America*.

Daughter Lilli dies in May.

Confusions begin between himself and his brother, Gutzon, who has dropped his career as a painter to become a sculptor.

Included in *American Masters of Sculpture* by Charles H. Caffin, Doubleday, Page and Co., New York, being one of eleven sculptors so listed; full, illustrated chapter.

Work and position described in *The History of American Sculpture* by Lorado Taft, The Macmillan Co., New York.

Daughter Monica born December 9.

1904   Elected to Council of the National Sculpture Society.

Four works depicting spread of white man into the West for the Louisiana Purchase Exposition in St. Louis. Works placed on the Plaza of St. Louis facing main launch landing.

Awarded gold medal for "In the Wind," one of nine works shown in Art Palace at World's Fair, St. Louis; others are "On the Trail," "Lame Horse," "The Bull Fight," "Just Born," "The Blizzard," "Deer Killing a Snake," "Dancing Horse," "Our Slave."

1905   Serves as juror for the Edmund Stewardson Prize at the Pennsylvania Academy of The Fine Arts.

May: Contract for General John B. Gordon Monument for Atlanta, Georgia.

Revisits Paris with Emma and children.

Paul Manship becomes student helper, beginning in Mamaroneck and accompanying him to Connecticut, living with the family.

Record book shows sale of 40 bronzes to date.

Exhibits his four great works from St. Louis at Lewis and Clark Exposition, Portland, Oregon. Also exhibits a "speaking" likeness of Major William Hancock Clark.

1906   Becomes Honorary Member of Portland Commercial Club, March 17, 1906, "in token of its admiration of his superb artistic ability and as a partial expression of its deep appreciation of his work now adorning its home."

April: Contract for the Bucky O'Neill Monument for Prescott, Arizona.

Purchases farm in Connecticut, "Rocky Ranch," first used as a summer home, 30 East 14th Street remaining Solon's New York Studio address.

1907   The Metropolitan Museum of Art purchases "On the Border of White Man's Land" and "The Bull Fight," (conflict between Civilization and the Savage.)

May 25, General John B. Gordon Monument unveiled.

July 3, Bucky O'Neill, the "Rough Rider" Monument, unveiled.

1908   Erects giant bronze steer's head façade, on the Schieren Building, Ferry Street, Manhattan, New York, now at the Brooklyn Museum.

"Eagle" and "Condor" for the Pan-American Building, Washington, D.C., representing North and South America. Erected above and on each side of main entrance.

Erects cement under life-size group of oxen on large rock in front of Rocky Ranch Studio entitled "Clearing Old New England."

August-September: First Exhibition of The Knockers Club at Rocky Ranch, forerunner of the Silvermine Group of Artists, subsequently The Silvermine Guild of Artists, following Solon Borglum's death in 1922.

1909   Portrait busts of the astronomer Simon Newcomb of Washington, D.C., and Ex-mayor Charles A. Schieren of Brooklyn, New York.

Unveils large bronze bas-relief as memorial to educator T. J. Backus at Packer Institute, Brooklyn, New York.

Publishes "Impressions of Simon Newcomb," *The Independent*, July 22.

Bust of James Edwin Hurley, General Manager of Atchison, Topeka and Santa Fe Railroad, erected in Terminal Building, Topeka, Kansas.

1910   Exhibits "Pushing Ahead — Washington, 1753" at the National Academy of Design Exhibition, New York City.

Sends "Lassoing Wild Horses" to the *Exposition Internacional de Arte, 1810–1910*, in Buenos Aires, Argentina. Silver medal.

Starts work on "The Command of God — Napoleon at Moscow."

1911   May: Unveils "Taps," a bronze tablet mounted on marble in Soldiers and Sailors Memorial Cemetery, Danbury, Connecticut.

First meeting of Boy Scouts in Solon's Silvermine Studio.

Portrait relief bust of General Joseph A. Mower placed in Museum Building, Vicksburg National Military Park, Vicksburg, Mississippi.

Unveils two under-life-size "Private Jones" statues at Lynchburg, Virginia, one in front of the Jones Memorial Library, the other in front of East Hall, Randolph-Macon Woman's College.

Member of special committee of National Sculpture Society to amend constitution relating to competitions.

Exhibits "Pushing Ahead — Washington, 1753" and several large framed photos ("Cowboy at Rest" and "Bucky O'Neill") at International Exposition of Art and History, Rome.

1912   Bronze "Little Boy with Fish" sold to Mr. J. T. Lovett, Monmouth Nursery, Little Silver, New Jersey.

Vice President, National Sculpture Society.

Associate, The National Academy of Design.

1913   Erects colossal busts of Confederate Generals Giles A. Smith, W. Sooy Smith and Edward D. Tracy in Vicksburg National Military Park.

Erects heroic-size monument to Jacob Leisler in Huguenot Park, New Rochelle, New York.

Canadian Government purchases "Pushing Ahead — Washington, 1753" for The National Art Gallery, Ottawa.

Contract with Archer Huntington for sculptural decoration on projected Court of the American Geographical Society grounds at West 155th Street, New York City. Four sculptors engaged in work, Chester Beach, Charles Harley, Solon Borglum, and Gutzon Borglum, Chairman.

Membership, *Union Internationale des Beaux-Arts* indicated by payment of dues. Election date not known.

1914   Erects colossal busts of Generals Francis J. Herron, and John Gregg for entrance to Vicksburg National Military Park.

Visits to Atlanta: Stone Mountain prospects emerge.

Solon has a marble cutter teach him how to carve without pointing. Does "Paul," "The Command of God — Napoleon at Moscow"; "The Waters" (female figure under life size); starts "Monica."

1915   Solon's symbolical monument to the American Pioneer for the Panama-

Pacific World's Fair in San Francisco placed at entrance to "Court of Flowers." Secretary of Interior Franklin K. Lane bases his opening words on Solon's unusual group, which was causing much comment.

Three-foot-high "The Heavens" cast into plaster; it is the selected model for his work on the Huntington project for the American Geographic Society.

Bronze tablet to the 71st Regiment in New York City and andirons.

1916   The Schieren Memorial ("The Gentle Closing of Two Lives"), Greenwood Cemetery, Brooklyn, on the grave of his dear friends, the Schierens, who died within a few hours of each other.

Frank Purdy arranges a traveling exhibit west together with work by Gutzon Borglum.

The Joslyn Museum in Omaha acquires two works, "On the Trail" and "Just Born."

Teaches at Beaux-Arts Institute of Design, New York, 1916–1917; develops ideas for *Sound Construction,* posthumously published art textbook, 1923. Mildred Archer Nash, his student helper for many years, is assistant in this work, her name appearing on the book.

Detroit Institute of Arts acquires the following bronzes: "Tamed," "Lassoing Wild Horses," "Blizzard," "Snowdrift," "Intelligent Broncho," "Rough Rider" (not to be confused with the "Rough Rider" Monument).

1917   Honorary Member, Beaux-Arts Institute of Design, New York. Continues work on *Sound Construction* and "The Heavens."

Becomes involved in the Saint Mark's in-the-Bouwerie project for the creation of two giant statues representing "Aspiration" and "Inspiration".

1918   Elected Life Member, The National Arts Club, New York, N.Y.

Elected Member, The Players, New York, N.Y.

Accepted May 20 by the American YMCA for overseas war work. Attends Fourth Congress for Overseas War Work and for Secretaries, Princeton, May 22–29. Sails for England June 11 on *Megantic* over submarine-infested waters. Paris, attached to Third French Army, later to Fifth French Army, to establish and direct *Foyer du Soldat* positions behind the firing lines. Later given complete discretion, goes to the front, where his work is independent and personal.

1919   Decorated with the *Croix de Guerre* in recognition of his ". . . great powers of organization, generosity of spirit, and apostle's heart . . ." he continues service with the French Army, riding, thanks to two horses belonging to his Colonel, into recently occupied villages in France and Belgium. In Luxembourg work with the French is finished.

March-June: Director of Sculpture at the specially organized A. E. F. Art Training Center at Bellevue, Seine-et-Oise, suburb of Paris, for American soldiers waiting for transport home. Returned on the *Imperator,* later renamed *Berengaria.*

Master Mason, Grand Lodge of Free and Accepted Masons for the State of New York, No. 5, September 6, 1919.

Organized exhibition of work done in Paris A. E. F. Art School at Corcoran Gallery, Washington.

Failing to sell idea of reestablishing the A. E. F. Art Training Center in New York or Washington, establishes his own School of American Sculpture in December at the Colonial Studios, 39 West 57th Street, New York.

Lectures on art and describes the work that had been done in Paris at the Art Training Center. Completes his notes on his experiences overseas and publishes article in the *Century* magazine, A. E. F. School of Fine Arts I.

1920   Publishes second article on the A. E. F. Art Training Center in Paris, *Century.*

Completes work on full scale heroic figures of "Aspiration" and "Inspiration". Accepts request to serve as substitute teacher at Cooper Union and at the Beaux-Arts Institute.

October 24, "Aspiration" and "Inspiration" full-scale plaster models unveiled at Saint Mark's in-the-Bouwerie, New York, together with marble figure, "The Waters," renamed "The Little Lady of The Dew."

The School of American Sculpture moves to larger quarters, 9 East 59th Street.

Last exhibition of the Silvermine Group of Artists held in Solon Borglum's studio.

1921   The last year of his life is spent trying to run the school whose success boomerangs, requiring more and more of his time. Rocky Ranch becomes a hive of industry at the same time as he works on the cutting into stone of his giant figures "Aspiration" and "Inspiration," with the help of his son, Paul. Vainly seeks a new studio helper, Mildred Nash having married.

Delivers last lecture on art at Norfolk Society of Arts Building, Virginia, December.

1922   Acts as juror for the last time, National Arts Club Exhibition opening, January 5.

Dies suddenly Monday, January 30, following an appendectomy in
Stamford Hospital. Funeral services held in Rocky Ranch studio, Dr.
William Norman Guthrie officiating. Memorial Services held in New York
at Saint Mark's in-the-Bouwerie, in the Fine Arts Building, New York,
arranged by the National Sculpture Society, and in Omaha.

References

Chapter I *The Borglum Brothers*

1. "an originally Mormon family": Andrew Jenson, Office of Church Historian of the Church of Jesus Christ of Latter Day Saints, Salt Lake City, Utah, to Frank Borglum, Feb. 10, 1936, — copy sent to Harriet Borglum Faidy (cited hereafter HBF Chicago) from Alvin F. Smith, Librarian, Church of Jesus Christ of Latter Day Saints, Salt Lake City, Utah, Oct. 27, 1947; verified, Idaho State Historical Society, Boise, Idaho, May 14, 1970. Solon H. Borglum papers, Studio (cited hereafter SHB Studio).

2. "his 'little brother' " *Give the Man Room*, (cited hereafter GMR) pp. 28, 68: "The boy to whom Gutzon frequently referred as his little brother." "and his policy of never competing with him", "he could never consider himself free to accept any commission in which he thought that his brother might have an interest."

3. "The clash at Sierra Madre": Douglas M. Perham to Monica Borglum Davies (cited hereafter MBD) Sept. 18, 1961, Solon Borglum Papers, Library of Congress, (cited hereafter SHB Library of Congress); Conversations and interviews between Douglas M. Perham and the author and MBD, New Almaden, Calif. (1962); Interviews with Mrs. Pictor Nelson, Sierra Madre, Calif. 1962; Emma Vignal Borglum, *Account of the life of Solon H. Borglum;* "doing great things together . . ." conversations HBF and MBD. Gutzon Borglum's own words heard at the Stamford Hospital when Solon was there, recalled by MBD, 1922.

4. "but frequently oblivious to factual accuracy": revealed in the correspondence between HBF and August Borglum (cited hereafter AB) following their reading of the manuscript GMR; repeated to MBD and the author by HBF after the publication of the book, GMR; Examples: Gutzon changed his birthplace from Idaho to California when writing to an inquirer, "I am a Pacific Coaster born and bred out there," Sept. 12, 1911, Gutzon Borglum Papers, Library of Congress (cited hereafter GB Library of Congress);

"Yet the biographical sketch in *Who's Who in America*, which he himself wrote says that he was born in Idaho on March 25, 1871." GMR p. 24 (This particular change of his birthdate to 1871 has been picked up so frequently by biographical encyclopedias, *etc.* that it has almost become standard!). Gutzon advanced Solon's return to America to "early 1900" in a widely read *Letter to the Editor* of *New York Times*, March 1, 1922, following Solon's death. Gutzon wrote that he and Solon had "volunteered together and were among the first two hundred registered before the draft." [World War I] The following statements are typical errors of fact: "Solon intrigued his way and by conspiracies of one sort or another landed at Verdun . . . and at Château Thierry, forgot his Red Cross duties, picked up from the dead the tools of death and ammunition . . . was arrested, courtmartialed, and given the Croix-de-Guerre!" Letter to Wm. C. Langdon, October 27, 1927, GB Library of Congress.

5. "Gutzon Borglum — A Sculptor of the West": *Los Angeles Times*, April 2, 1922, p. 23.

6. "The Plainsman": "Gutzon Borglum spent much of his life on the Plains. . . ." Mari Sandoz, *Love Song to The Plains*, University of Nebraska Press, 1966, p. 233.

7. "Solon Borglum, The Sculptor, Once A Cowboy" New York *Sun*, Oct. 27, 1912.

8. "awarded a gold medal for a small group, 'Return of the Boer' ": The Missouri Historical Society — *St. Louis Official Record* lists Gutzon Borglum among the winners of the gold medal for "No. 2047" "The Boer".

9. "The critics were generous in their judgment": New York *Sun*, Nov. 4, 1902, Sculpture Society's Exhibition: ". . . we shall find a stimulus to it [enthusiasm] in the work of Solon Borglum . . . and there are some . . . not represented here, all small statuettes, yet big with truth, and with familiarity with the larger, sterner aspects of nature that is so rare in art."; *Louisiana Purchase Exposition Official Handbook*, The Art Department, St. Louis Museum, gives the following biographical data about Solon: ". . . an artist at heart and practically grown up from childhood in the saddle, it is not surprising that Mr. Borglum should have become the most forceful exponent of Western life in American sculpture. Mr. Borglum's art studies did not begin systematically until he was twenty-seven years of age. The following year he obtained a prize which enabled him to go to Paris, where he soon attracted widespread attention. With his series of bronze statuettes and groups he struck such a new and truthful note in American Art that Mr. Borglum may serenely look forward to the verdict of posterity, which undoubtedly will confirm the admiration of his contemporaries." (p. 359); Also *The Art Interchange*: "The fact of his recognition at Paris is in a measure indicative of his achievements." Vol. CLVI, 1901, No. 1, p. 2.

10. "Oh, he was . . . a go-getter." Paul Manship, not long before his death, to the author.

11. "Borglum? I won't discuss him." quotation *Mount Rushmore*, Gilbert C. Fite, p. 21.

12. "I see that Borglum is making molehills": quote taken from a lecture series on *American Monumental Sculpture*, Laura Gardin Fraser, Part II, p. 23, SHB Studio.

13. "Do you see Mr. Borglum very often?" Fite, *op. cit.,* p. 105.

14. "Stanley King's biographer, Claude M. Fuess, relating . . ." Claude Moore Fuess, *Stanley King of Amherst*, Columbia University Press, 1955, pp. 90–93.

15. "Gutzon went down to Atlanta": GMR, p. 177.

16. "was originally to have been a joint enterprise . . ." Sam Venable's two sisters, at Memorial Exhibit at Union League Club, New York, spoke frankly to MBD about Stone Mountain, one of them making the memorable statement, "Do not forget, Miss Borglum, when our family gave the land at Stone Mountain for a memorial to the army of the Confederacy, we believed that both Solon and Gutzon would work on it together." (Nov. 13, 1924.) Solon was well known to the Venable family from the time of the contracting for and the unveiling of the Gen. John B. Gordon monument in Atlanta. A reference to the fact of their working together is seen in the following partial quote published in Norfolk, Va., when he was introduced as a lecturer on Art: "Solon Borglum, noted sculptor, who, in association with his brother, was working upon the colossal monument to the army of the Confederacy, at Stone Mountain near Atlanta, until the entrance of the United States into the great war terminated all work there" The lecture was given at the Norfolk Society of Arts several weeks before he (Solon), died. Scrapbook SHB Studio. Another reference: "He (Gutzon) had also gotten his brother Solon to give talks to publicize the project:" Price, *Gutzon Borglum,* p. 107.

17. "as distinctly opposite as two persons could be": Fraser, *op. cit.,* p. 23.

18. "Though Solon Borglum was a most unassuming man": Raymond Ingersoll, Letter to *New York Times*, Feb. 6, 1922.

19. "one of America's best loved artists": Lorado Taft, Commemorative Service, Saint Mark's in-the-Bouwerie, April 15, 1922.

20. "under the influence of the Old World." Lorado Taft, *The History of American Sculpture*, Macmillan & Co., NYC, 1903, p. 468.

21. "Charles H. Caffin devoted . . ." Charles Caffin, *American Masters of Sculpture*, Doubleday Page & Co., NYC, 1903.

22. "powerful bias toward Italian art," GMR, p. 37.

23. "those belonging to the clique of painters . . ." *St. John's Wood Artists —* Gutzon Borglum is not listed as a member, although it was formed in the 1890s, and was famous in that day, holding an important place in Academy Exhibitions. Raymond Lester & Clarkson N. Potter, *Victorians Narrative Paintings*, 1966, p. 28.

24. "great by the time he was thirty": Gutzon's first entry in his diary, Nov. 11, 1897. GB Library of Congress.

25. "Solon across the Channel": Bibliothèque Nationale, Office de Documentation, Paris, France; Solon's success was reflected in the press, e.g. "1898, sends 'Lassoing Wild Horses' to the Paris Salon and receives favorable criticism in 17 Parisian papers." This was published in a chronology of events in Solon's early life, "A Nebraska Sculptor — World Famous", Omaha *World-Herald*, April 12, 1903; flattering attention was paid his work by French President Laubert, SHB Studio.

26. "Lisa, an artist in her own right": *Los Angeles Sunday Times*, Sept. 15, 1889, p. 12, *Los Angeles Times,* Oct. 28, 1889, p. 5: *Who's Who in the Pacific Southwest*, a compilation of Authentic Biographical sketches of Citizens of Southern California and Arizona, The Times Mirror Printing and Binding House, Los Angeles, California, 1913, pp. 50–51.

27. "An impending contract with the Midland Railway": GB Library of Congress.

28. "Royal Society of British Artists, London": Listed in catalogues of members and exhibitions 1901–1902. Gutzon's name is listed as a member through 1905. No exhibits.

29. "Solon did not condemn his brother's behavior": Miller Borglum to August Borglum following Solon's death, 1922, AB Detroit.

30. "the end of an era": GMR, pp. 64–65.

31. "Oh, he admired Solon's work": HBF conversation with author.

32. "who was jealous of Solon": Mrs. F. E. Perham to Solon in Paris at the end of the Summer of 1897, quoted in part, "Solon, you are no match for a designing jealous woman — are you convinced of that? You have received ill treatment enough from that woman to teach you that your plans ought to be kept secret as possible from her and from her husband who seems to be a tool in her hands, to work whatever she sees fit to propose . . . if you rise to distinction in spite of their efforts to drag you down, those who have treated you worst will be the first to claim consideration from you." SHB Library of Congress.

33. "But what does Solon know about art?" August Borglum to Gutzon, following Solon's death, March 15, 1922, AB Detroit.

34. "one of the outstanding phenomena": Fite, *op. cit., passim.*

35. "He believed profoundly and therefore he could conceive greatly": Dr. Guthrie, Commemorative Service, Saint Mark's in-the-Bouwerie, April 15, 1922.

Chapter II   *A Child of the West*

1. "Legend has it", — this is not altogether a legend. The meticulous attention

given to the heredity of the Borglum family is shown in the letters written from time to time following Dr. Borglum's return to Denmark in 1908, during which time he searched the Royal Archives for data relating to the early branches of the family. SHB Studio.

2. "The American story begins": Letter to HBF October 27, 1947 from Alvin F. Smith, Librarian, Church of Jesus Christ of Latter Day Saints, Salt Lake City, Utah, SHB studio; Idaho State Historical Society, May, 1970, letter to Phil Kovinick, SHB Studio.

3. "very studious person": letter from Dr. Borglum to Solon, July 31, 1903. SHB Studio.

4. "a man of good address": Alvin F. Smith to HBF, October 27, 1947. SHB Studio.

5. "Christina re-joined her parents", HBF to MBD conversation.

6. "insatiable curiosity": Gutzon Borglum, letter to *The N.Y. Times*, Mar. 1, 1922.

7. "hardy and quick and clearheaded": *World's Work*, Goodrich, p. 1858.

8. "The records of Creighton College": Wm. O'Donnell S.J. to MBD Feb. 19, 1954. SHB Studio.

9. "had given up St. Mary's Academy in Kansas City": Contrary to published data concerning Gutzon the following was sent to MBD by the Archivist, Registrar of Saint Mary's College, dated August 15, 1957: "John Gutson (*sic*) Borglum was born 25 March 1866 (*sic*). He entered St. Mary's College 9th. January, 1882. He left St. Mary's College in 1882, presumably in June." SHB Studio.

10. "a green serious lad": Charles Lummis, *Land of Sunshine*, p. 34.

11. "On a ranch somewhere in the vicinity": GMR, p. 39.

12. "Solon now helped Gutzon": Louise Durant Rice — MBD, conversation.

13. "This could be the basis of a later claim": after exhaustive research this writer has been unable to find any other tenable basis for this claim.

Chapter III   *The "Epic of the Plains"*

1. "It was merely": *World's Work, op. cit.*, pp. 1861–3.

2. "Many a time": *ibid.*, pp. 1863–4.

3. *Youth's Companion,* Nov. 24, 1910.

4. SHB Studio.

Chapter IV   *The Vital Decision*

1. "Solon, you should be an artist": the idea has been variously expressed, but the sense is always the same, i.e. that Solon should drop ranching and become an artist. *World's Work, op. cit.*, p. 1865.

2. "Elizabeth Jaynes Putnam": *Annals of Early Sierra Madre*, p. 108. Los Angeles *Times*, September 15, 1889. The wedding was prominently reported as a social event with the names of many important Los Angeles people present: "A notable wedding took place in this city last Tuesday morning at the Unitarian Church. The high contracting parties were the artists J. G. Borglum and Mrs. L. Jaynes-Putnam. Dr. Fay performed the ceremony. . . ."

3. "Henry Bargy": *L'Illustration*, p. 262 — No. 3216. October 15, 1904.

4. "warned his father": Price, *op. cit.*, p. 38.

5. "There were pictures everywhere": conversations, John Mack — Jean Borglum Brinkema, with MBD.

6. "spoke of it years later": Gutzon Borglum, letter to *New York Times, op. cit.*

7. "sturdy, energetic and interesting": *Annals of Early Sierra Madre*, p. 108.

8. "Old Saddleback": *Shadows of Old Saddleback*, p. 198.

9. "You are lucky, Sir": New York *Sun*, 1912, Oct. 27: *Solon Borglum, Sculptor, Once a Cowboy.*

10. "His early years": *New York Times*, Dec. 10, 1922: *Artists Create Solon Borglum Memorial Fund.*

11. "Another visitor": *World's Work, op. cit.*, p. 1869.

12. "most pleasing personality": Douglas Perham to MBD Jan. 16, 1962. SHB Studio.

13. "exhibited": *Orange County Herald*, Sept. 14, 1895, p. 5 col. 1: "Solon H. Borglum, a young artist of this city, has arranged a number of his best pictures in the Y.M.C.A. rooms in the Kimball block on Fourth Street for exhibition today. The public should see them."

14. "If I had known": this incident is included in most stories of Solon's early life.

15. "It is generally felt": Cincinnati *Commercial Tribune*, June 20, 1897.

Chapter V *Why Paris?*

1. "a strange mixture of irony and dedication": New York *World*, Dec. 10, 1922.

2. "I set out": Selene Ayer Armstrong, *The Craftsman; Solon Borglum, Sculptor of American Life.* Vol. 12, July 1907.

3. "did not touch brushes again": Louise Eberle, *Scribner's Magazine*, Vol. 72; July-Sept. 1922.

4. "There was not a thought wave": Caffin, *American Masters of Sculpture*, ix.

5. "In breadth of handling": *ibid.*, p. 158.

6. "as Mrs. Proske aptly put it": Proske, *Brookgreen Gardens Sculpture,* 1968, p. xxv.

7. "Thus Charles Caffin in his appreciation": Caffin, *op. cit.,* p. 158.

8. "he told the story": Robert Alexander Horwood, *Los Angeles Times,* Illustrated Magazine, April 2, 1922, p. 23.

9. "Solon conceded": Selene Armstrong, *The Craftsman, op. cit.*

10. "All art. . .": (Henry Kirke Brown quote.) *Amer. Art Journal,* Vol. IV, Nov. 1972, p. 58.

11. "I wish I could tell you": Selene Armstrong, *The Craftsman, op. cit.*

12. "daring, decorative, prolific": Wayne Craven, *Sculpture in America,* p. 420.

13. "a statue about which": Craven, *op. cit.,* p. 422.

14. "one of the finest sculptors": *ibid.,* p. 495.

15. "All the time": Emma's Journal. SHB Studio.

16. "Say, boys, come out here," New York *Sun, op. cit.,* p. 11.

17. "The group 'Lassoing Wild Horses' ": *ibid.*

18. "Joanne Holbein, daughter of Phimister Proctor"; notes for the author. SHB Studio.

Chapter VI   *A Paris Bride in Indian Country*

Much of this chapter, which deals especially with the personality of Emma, is based on the account she wrote of her Summer with the Sioux Indians in South Dakota which left so indelible an impression on her mind. As her son-in-law I well remember the impromptu narrations she often gave of these experiences. Thirty-five years later she re-told bits of this "amazing honeymoon" for the last time to a group of enraptured visitors. That night Emma Borglum died.

1. "Solon is busy and in love": Lisa Borglum to August Borglum, AB papers.

2. "Clement Barnhorn . . . was responsible": This fact is referred to in Emma's Journal which must be accepted, although a mutual friend, Alphaeus Cole, thought that Solon and Emma had met through members of his family. Letter to MBD from Alphaeus Cole, SHB Studio.

3. "Borglum sculpture is spirited, alive, authentic": Conversations among visitors to the Solon H. Borglum Centennial Exhibit, Silvermine, and AMD. Also, ". . . refreshes the spirit as a thing of health." Pach, *Ananias or the False Artist,* p. 146.

4. "It depicts the unity of humanity and nature": Letter to MBD from Alan E. Hugg, Adult Education Consultant, State Department of Education, Hartford, Conn., May 14, 1970.

5. "To gain new friends": To cite another recent new friend in New Jersey, *The*

Home and Store News (June 23, 1971) speaks of "Lassoing Wild Horses" recently acquired at auction as "exciting sculpture," "the handsome bronze," "a beautiful creation," "wonderful example of American art."

6. "ruined her work": Mrs. Mildred Nash Bly to author.

7. "unfinished passages": Caffin, *American Masters of Sculpture,* p. 158.

8. "It cannot be claimed. . . .": Taft, *op. cit.,* 541.

9. "The advice he now gives his son": Dr. Borglum to Solon in reply to Solon's request for family data to give to "Who's Who". SHB Studio.

Chapter VII   *New York*

1. "quiet, unassuming": *World's Work, op. cit.,* p. 1874.

2. "the U. S. Grant competition": There is much about this in Gutzon Borglum's biography. Willadene Price quotes a letter to Lisa; "this is an opportunity too good to miss. The government has allotted two hundred and fifty thousand dollars for the work. Besides the money, this would establish me as a sculptor in America if I could win. Solon is competing too. If I don't win, I hope he does." (Price, *op. cit.,* p. 52) GMR uses it as a peg for the incredible statement that Gutzon never competed with his brother. (GMR, p. 68).

3. "has immortalised": Taft, *op. cit.,* p. 468.

4. "Borglum horse": SHB Library of Congress; SHB Scrapbook, Studio.

5. "letter from Saint-Gaudens": SHB Library of Congress.

6. "F. W. Ruckstull": for sake of consistency I have adhered to that spelling. Ruckstull was born Ruckstuhl.

7. "gold medal"; This 'unique' bronze, originally called "In the Wind" shares the title "Snowdrift" with the marble group, carved in 1902.

8. "Bargy": ". . . il semble évoluer sans cesse vers une conception de plus en plus sereine et de plus en plus classique de la sculpture. Ses premier groupes, originaux et puissants, mais violents et tourmentés, expriment la lutte de l'homme et du cheval. C'est la 'vie intense' mise en sculpture; on y sent le dresseur et le dompteur sous l'artiste; il bataille a la fois contre l'argile qu'il sent entre ses mains et contre la bête qu'il imagine entre ses jambes; il veut exprimer l'inexprimable." *L'Illustration,* 15 Octobre 1904, 202. No. 3216.

9. "Johansen": *Kundst,* Denmark, Med 8; Bulleder 7; Aarag-Haefte 10.

10. *"The Art Interchange": op. cit.*

11. *New York Herald,* June 28, 1903. *Denver Times,* Mar. 7, 1903. Omaha *World-Herald,* April 12, 1903.

12. "Century": *Century Magazine,* June 1904.

Chapter VIII *Monumental Work*

1. "Saint-Gaudens cautioned him": SHB Library of Congress.

2. "the relative merits": SHB Library of Congress.

3. "eloquently defending": Report of the Gordon Monument Commission, p. 8. SHB Library of Congress.

4. "Solon Borglum was an artist": *Dictionary of American Biography.*

5. "in every window": Atlanta *Constitution,* May 26, 1907.

6. "The genius which could so catch": Mrs. C. O. Brown to Solon, SHB Library of Congress.

7. "An Atlanta newspaper": *Atlanta Georgian,* Feb. 4, 1907.

8. "A knock at the door": The story of this incident is reported in *The Arizona Rough Rider Monument and Captain W. O. O'Neill,* a booklet published by *Prescott Evening Courier* (Old Capitol Booklets). SHB Studio.

9. "Were you called upon": The unveiling of the Rough Rider Monument, Omaha *World-Herald,* July, 1907.

10. "Paul K. Thomas": *Cincinnati Times-Star,* Dec. 6, 1908.

11. "Another writer": *The Craftsman,* Vol. 12; July 1907. pp. 382–9.

12. "America's Rough Rider": SHB Library of Congress.

Chapter IX *Second "Borglum The Sculptor"*

1. "on which he had just signed a three-year lease": July 1, 1901. "Un grand atelier d'artiste au fond du jardin dépendant d'une maison sise à Paris, boulevard du Port Royal numero 31 — (trente et un.)" There was a renewal clause for six or nine years. GB Library of Congress.

2. "volte face": ". . . this would establish me as a sculptor in America . . ." Price, *op. cit.,* 52. Gutzon left Paris Nov. 14, 1901, shortly after Solon. That Gutzon left Europe so soon after Solon is not generally recognized. It is indicated in a letter Emma wrote Lucy who was in Omaha, dated Oct. 14, 1901 "We are very busy, preparing for the departure of Solon, his trunk is in the diningroom. . . ." In a letter to August dated Mar. 31, 1900, Solon tells of his intention to gradually enter the field of competitive monumental work in America, "there is much of that kind going up in America . . . now I think I stand a chance. . . ." AB papers, Detroit.

3. Gutzon hopes Solon wins it if he does not. Price, *op. cit.,* p. 52.

4. "resumed her teaching": *Who's Who in the Pacific Southwest,* Times-Mirror Printing and Binding House, Los Angeles, p. 50, 1913.

5. "I am tired and old": Price, *op. cit.,* 78.

6. "companion and housekeeper": Conversation HBF and MBD.

7. "a second artist to expedite the work": GB Library of Congress.

8. "He had made a bust of Mrs. Jessie Frémont": Price, *op. cit.,* 42.

9. "He had been a student of Mercié": Office de Documentation de la Société des Amis de la *Bibliothèque Nationale,* Paris.

10. "I had to live abroad and I had to live": GB Library of Congress.

11. "quite returned": GB Library of Congress.

12. "criticized by his teacher": Price, *op. cit.,* p. 23.

13. "deserve very serious study": New York *Sun,* Nov. 4, 1902.

14. "was apt to be calamitous": The story of Gutzon's resignation from the National Sculpture Society comes directly from the lips of Mrs. James Earle Fraser (*vide* my preface, p. 13). She had earlier told the story to MBD, interrupting herself frequently with the question, "You never heard about this?" to which MBD would reply, "No!" When my wife and I returned to Connecticut and I began working on the Solon Borglum biography I asked Mrs. Fraser to retell the story to me, which she did.

15. Letter to MBD, SHB Studio.

16. "straight from a witness": James Earle Fraser, a member of the NSS present at this stormy meeting, was engaged to Laura Gardin and reflected the indignation of the members present. The clashes that had occurred and continued to occur between Gutzon and the sculptors left a marked impression upon her which she did not forget.

17. "They would be artists, distinct in their individual fields": This agreement was well-known within the family. It is referred to in a letter from HBF to AB dated Oct. 15, 1947: ". . . . That was the time when the controversy was going on about painting and sculpture of the two boys." AB papers, Detroit.

18. "upon his (Solon's) return from Europe" SHB Studio; AB Detroit.

19. "Although the work is the product of my brother's hand": *The Arizona Rough Rider Monument* and Captain W. O. O'Neill, *Prescott Evening Courier,* Prescott (no publication date).

20. "destroying letters from his enemies." Recollections MBD.

21. "Gutzon Borglum calls": New York *Tribune,* Jan. 13, 1904.

22. "he displayed insurgency among insurgents": Fite, *op. cit.,* p. 21.

23. "gold medal", the fact has been confirmed by the records of the Missouri Historical Society. SHB Studio.

24. "Gutzon usually had a name for his statues": Price, *op. cit.,* p. 61.

25. "Gutzon himself": McSpadden, *Famous Sculptors of America,* p. 223; Proske, *Brookgreen Gardens,* p. 63–64.

26. "Albert TenEyck Gardner": A. T. Gardner, *American Sculpture,* p. 101.

27. "Clement Barnhorn": SHB Library of Congress.

28. "You seem to have such": Price, *op. cit.,* p. 74.

Chapter **X** *Collision*

The account here given will be unfamiliar to the reader. This is because it is built upon new material. The value of the biographical method as applied to the life and career of Solon Borglum is at this point most fully demonstrated.

The greater authenticity of this account is guaranteed by the fact that it incorporates two points of view, Solon's as well as Gutzon's, not just one as previous accounts have done. Neither sculptor as it happened got the Custer commission. This could explain the omission of it from previous accounts, all written from Gutzon's standpoint. Though the Gutzon Borglum files in the Library of Congress are amply supplied with material, previous writers may well have considered it a meaningless incident. But when the point of view is switched to Solon Borglum the situation changes completely: it then becomes an acutely poignant episode in the clash of two brothers.

The same is true precisely of the Lincoln, Nebraska, clash with which the chapter concludes. The scattering of letters preserved over the years in Solon's files throws a flood of light on the whole chapter.

1. "I'm making a hell of a lot of money": Gutzon to Mrs. Dodge as told in a letter to Lucy written by Emma. AB papers, Detroit.

2. "letter initialed CHD to Gutzon": GB Library of Congress.

3. "He also had an exhibition in Paris": GB Library of Congress. This statement can be looked upon as deliberately made to reduce Solon's success in Paris to "an exhibition." The latter part of Gutzon's letter reveals his desire to restrict his brother's achievement to the creation of Western work, cowboys and Indians, at the same time as he establishes himself as the sculptor of monumental work: "Of late years I have given up the doing of Indians leaving that particular field to him (Solon) and confining myself more directly to monumental work." Implicit in this letter is the very plausible thought that Davis, like Mrs. Custer, was confused. He was ascribing the international fame of the one to the other, describing Gutzon as, ". . . unquestionably the greatest sculptor in America today." A preposterous claim for either brother.

4. "another sculptor in the running": SHB Studio. It is possible that Solon Borglum asked for copies of letters exchanged between members of the firm of Harrison Granite Company, but more likely that the letters were sent to Solon for his files: SHB Studio.

5. "is supplied by the following": AB papers, Emma to Lucy.

6. "mistaken identity": GB Library of Congress. SHB Studio.

Chapter XI   *The Finding of Rocky Ranch*

1. "in token of its appreciation": SHB Library of Congress.

2. "appraisal of Solon's work": *ibid.*

3. "broad approach": Letter to MBD, *ibid.*

4. "In the autumn": The crossing on the *S.S. Rotterdam* is authenticated by a program for a concert given on November 6, 1905. In the margin and at the top are drawings of sea horses, a mermaid with trumpet and chains . . . A tiny sea horse carries on its back the initials, S.H.B. Mrs. S. H. Borglum appears opposite no. 8 "Song selection." SHB Studio.

5. "Paul Manship wrote": SHB Library of Congress.

Chapter XII   *Silvermine: A Measure of Heaven*

1. "A delightful drive": Paul K. M. Thomas, *Cincinnati Times-Star*, Dec. 6, 1908.

2. "Our special neighborhood": W. W. Matthews, *The Country Gentleman*, Sept. 30, 1909.

3. "Cars from all over": Notes about the early Silvermine and the Silvermine Group of Artists, Dorothy Ashe Thompson. SHB Studio.

4. "However vague": *Christian Science Monitor*, Sept. 4, 1915.

5. "One of his poems reads": *Everybody's Magazine*, reprinted in *The Craftsman*, Vol. xxix, No. 5, Feb. 1916.

6. "Use what you have": Mrs. Louise Durant Rice, former student of Solon Borglum at The School of American Sculpture, to MBD.

7. "My years as apprentice": SHB Library of Congress.

Chapter XIII   *The Mature Man*

1. "The mature man": Robert Alexander Horwood, *Los Angeles Times*, April 2, 1922.

2. "You are very intense in your work": SHB Studio.

3. "Here is the universal significance": New York *World*, Sunday, Dec. 10, 1922.

4. "purchased in 1913 by the Canadian Government": *The Globe*, Toronto, Oct. 25, 1913.

5. "a good story for The Herald": SHB Library of Congress.

6. "Solon's Pioneer caused a flurry of comment"; *Sculpture of the Exposition Palace and Courts*, H. S. Crocker Co. Publishers, San Francisco, 1915.

7. "History of a later period": *The Sculpture and Mural Decoration of the Exposition,* introduction by A. Stirling Calder, Paul Elder & Co. Publishers, San Francisco. 1915.

8. "Were this gentleman a Frenchman": review, The National Sculpture Society Exhibition, New York *Sun,* Nov. 4, 1902.

9. "Keep fresh in the minds" *The Daily Standard Union,* Nov. 11, 1907 S.H.B. Studio.

10. "It is a book": Edgar J. Hesselein, *New York Times,* Nov. 18, 1923.

Chapter XIV   *"A Man Who Stands Alone"*

1. "the philosophy by which he lived": SHB Studio; AB Detroit.

2. "Vanishing Types": *Youth's Companion, op. cit.*

3. "For the purpose of executing": SHB Studio.

4. "I think we should get together": SHB Studio.

5. "A friendship that ended only with the life of Solon Borglum": The section dealing with Dr. W. N. Guthrie is written from personal acquaintance.

The correspondence referred to is in the Library of Congress, SHB papers.

Chapter XV   *"L'Américain"*

The chief source of this chapter is Solon Borglum. From the time he left home to take his week-long course at Princeton until the end of the war he carried a small notebook in which he jotted down brief accounts and descriptions, together with ideas as they came to him and as he was able to record them. Subsequently his brother, August, helped him to put together and enlarge upon these fragmentary notes. The completed account is now in the Library of Congress among the SHB papers, together with all letters quoted with the exception of his personal letters to Emma and the children, which are in the Studio.

Chapter XVI   *"A Scheme Without Precedent"*

1. "It is not the bigness": SHB replying to Charles A. Gusman's inquiry about appropriate statues to memorialize the soldiers, January 31, 1921. SHB Library of Congress.

2. "small in size": Laura Gardin Fraser, *Lecture on Art,* SHB Studio.

3. "Was that the best": Major George Hellman to Solon, SHB Studio.

4. "Livre d'Or": SHB Studio.

5. "On one of these trips": SHB to Emma, SHB Studio; Mary Taft Smith, *Lorado Taft, Sculptor and Citizen,* privately published, Greensboro, N.C., 1946.

Chapter XVII   *Teacher*

1. "One could scarcely imagine him": Louise Eberle, *In Recognition of an American Sculptor*, Scribner's Magazine, July–September, 1922.

2. "You must draw": SHB *Sound Construction*, p. 5; notes especially prepared for one of his students, who was deaf. SHB Studio.

3. "His teaching was": *Borglum as a Teacher*, Helen Avery Robinson, Jr., for the Student Committee, Letter to the Editor, *The Sun*, New York, Feb. 8, 1922.

4. "Johnstone described the artist": Will B. Johnstone, *Evening World*, New York, Oct. 19, 1920.

5. "Dear Solon the Wise": Letter from Guthrie to Solon, SHB Library of Congress.

Bibliography

PUBLISHED MATERIAL

BOOKS

ART AND SCULPTURE

Ainsworth, Ed. *The Cowboy in Art*. New York and Cleveland: World Publishing Co. 1968.

Borglum, Solon H. *Sound Construction*. New York: Privately. 1923.

Caffin, Charles H. *American Masters of Sculpture*. New York: Doubleday, Page. 1903.

Calder, A. Stirling. *The Sculpture and Mural Decorations of the Exposition*. San Francisco: Paul Elder. 1915.

Centennial Exhibition National Academy of Design 1825–1925. Catalogue, Washington and New York. 1925.

Chase, George H. and Post, Chandler R. *A History of Sculpture*. New York: Harper. 1924.

Craven, Wayne. *Sculpture in America*. New York: Crowell. 1968.

Cresson, Margaret French. *Journey into Fame*. Boston: Harvard. 1947.

Cortissoz, Royal. *Augustus Saint-Gaudens*. Boston: Houghton Mifflin. 1907.

Dean, Robert J. *Living Granite*. New York: Viking. 1949.

Dennis, James M. *Karl Bitter*. Madison: University of Wisconsin. 1967.

Dodd, Loring Holmes. *The Golden Age of American Sculpture*. Boston: Chapman & Grimes. 1936.

Fite, Gilbert C. *Mount Rushmore*. Norman, Oklahoma: University of Oklahoma Press. 1952.

The Forest City of 1904. St. Louis: Thompson. 1906.

Francis, David R. *The Universal Exposition of 1904.* 2 Vs. St. Louis: Louisiana Purchase Exposition. 1913.

Gardner, Albert TenEyck. *American Sculpture.* A Catalogue of the Collection of the Metropolitan Museum of Art. Greenwich, Conn.: New York Graphic Society. 1965.

James, Juliet. *Sculpture of the Exposition Palaces and Courts.* San Francisco: Crocker. 1915.

Krakel, Dean. *End of the Trail.* Norman: University of Oklahoma. 1973.

Larkin, Oliver W. *Art and Life in America.* New York: Holt, Rinehart & Winston. 1960.

Lombardo, Vincent Joseph. *Piccirilli, Life of an American Sculptor.* New York and Chicago: Pitman. 1944.

Low, Will H. *A Chronicle of Friendships,* 1873–1900. New York: Scribner. 1908.

McCracken, Harold. *Frederic Remington.* Philadelphia and New York: Doubleday. 1947.

McCracken, Harold. *The Frederic Remington Book.* New York: Doubleday. 1966.

McSpadden, Joseph Walker. *Famous Sculptors of America.* New York: Dodd Mead. 1927.

Murtha, Edwin. *Paul Manship.* New York: Macmillan. 1957.

Neuhaus, Eugen. *The Art of the Exposition.* San Francisco: Paul Elder. 1915.

Post, Chandler. *A History of European and American Sculpture From the Early Christian Period to the Present Day.* 2 Vs. Cambridge: Harvard. 1921.

Price, Willadene. *Gutzon Borglum.* Chicago: Rand McNally. 1961.

Proctor, Alexander Phimister. *Sculptor in Buckskin.* Norman, Oklahoma: University of Oklahoma. 1971.

Proske, Beatrice G. *Brookgreen Gardens Sculpture.* Brookgreen Gardens, South Carolina. 1943. Revised 1968.

Rathbone, Perry T., Editor, *Westward the Way.* St. Louis: City Art Museum. 1954.

Read, Herbert. *A Concise History of Modern Sculpture.* New York: Praeger. 1966.

Rodin Sculptures. Greenwich, Connecticut: Phaidon. 1964.

Ruckstull, F. W. *Great Works of Art and What Makes Them Great.* New York: Putnam. 1925.

Saint-Gaudens, Homer. *The Reminiscences of Augustus Saint-Gaudens.* New York: Century. 1913.

Saint-Gaudens, Homer. *The American Artist and His Times.* New York: Dodd Mead. 1941.

Sculpture and Mural Paintings. Official Guide to Panama-Pacific International Exposition at San Francisco. 1914.

Taft, Lorado. *History of American Sculpture.* New York: Macmillan. 1903.

Taft, Ada B. *Lorado Taft, Sculptor and Citizen.* Greensboro, N.C.: Privately. 1946.

Tharp, Louise Hall. *Saint-Gaudens and the Gilded Era.* Boston: Little Brown. 1969.

MISCELLANEOUS

American Heritage History of the Great West. New York: American Heritage Publishing Co. 1965.

American Heritage Book of the Pioneer Spirit. New York: American Heritage. 1959.

Bates, William O. *Jacob Leisler.* New York: Mitchell Kennerley. 1913.

Bowen, Edith Blumer. *Annals of Early Sierra Madre.* Sierra Madre, California: Privately, 1950.

Casey, Robert J. and Borglum, Mary. *Give The Man Room.* New York and Indianapolis: Bobbs-Merrill. 1952.

Fletcher, Alice C. *Indian Story and Song.* Boston: Small, Maynard. 1907.

Guthrie, William Norman. *Offices of Mystical Religion.* New York: Century. 1927.

Hafen, LeRoy R. and Ann W. *Handcarts to Zion.* Glendale, California: Clark. 1960.

Hawkes, Adeline. *The Broom Behind the Door.* Boston: Meador. 1949.

Howe, M. A. DeWolfe. *Life and Labors of Bishop Hare.* New York: Sturgis and Walton. 1913.

La Farge, Oliver. *The American Indian, A Pictorial History.* New York: Crown. 1956.

Landmarks of New Canaan. New Canaan, Conn., Historical Society. 1951.

Mulder, Willa and Mortensen, A. Russell, Editors. *Among the Mormons.* New York: Knopf. 1958.

Roosevelt, Theodore. *The Rough Riders.* New York: Scribner. 1905.

Sandoz, Mari. *Old Jules.* New York: Hastings. 1935.

Schmitt, Martin F. and Brown, Dee. *The Settler's West.* New York: Scribner. 1955.

Sorensen, Virginia. *Kingdom Come.* New York: Harcourt Brace. 1960.

Smith, Joseph Fielding. *Essentials of Church History.* Salt Lake City: Deseret News Press. 1922.

Spencer, Clarissa Young and Homer, Mabel. *Brigham Young at Home.* Salt Lake City: Deseret Book Company.

Stephenson, Terry E. and Thomas E. Williams. *Shadows of Old Saddleback.* Santa Ana, California: Privately. 1931.

Swanner, Charles D. *Santa Ana.* Claremont, California: Saunder. 1953.

Washington, George. *Facsimile of 1754 Journal.* Williamsburg, Va. 1959.

West, Ray B. Jr. *Kingdom of the Saints.* New York: Viking. 1957.

MAGAZINES AND ARTICLES

Adams, Adeline. *The Spirit of American Sculpture.* The National Sculpture Society. 1933.

Adams, Adeline, Article on *Solon Borglum*. Dictionary of American Biography. Vol. 2.

American Art Journal. *Symposium on Nineteenth Century American Sculptors*. November 1972.

Armstrong, Selene Ayer. *Solon Borglum: Sculptor of American Life*. The Craftsman, Vol. 12. July 1907.

Bargy, Henry. *Le Sculpteur de la Prairie*. Paris. L'Illustration No. 3216. October 1904.

Borglum, Gutzon de la Mothe. *Solon H. Borglum*. The American Magazine of Art. Vol. 13. November 1922.

Borglum, Solon H. *Some Impressions of Simon Newcomb*. The Independent Magazine. Vol. 67. July 1909.

Borglum, Solon H. *The A. E. F. School of Fine Arts*. Sculpture and Architecture. Century Magazine, Vol. 99 November-April 1920.

Borglum, Solon H. *The A. E. F. School of Fine Arts*. Painting and Illustrating. Century Magazine. April-December 1920. Vol. 99.

Borglum, Solon H. *Our Vanishing Types*. The Youth's Companion, No. 47. November 1910.

Borglum, Solon H. *Report on the Department of Sculpture*. Report of The American Training Centre, Bellevue, Seine-et-Oise. March-June 1919.

Bowdoin, W. G. *S. Borglum and His Work*. The Art Interchange. Vol. CLVI No. 1. January 1901.

Bronzes by Solon Borglum A. N. A. In the Detroit Museum of Art Bulletin, Vol. 10, No. 7. March 1916.

Caffin, Charles H. *Solon Borglum and His Work*. The International Studio, Vol. 19. June 1903.

Caffin, Charles H. *The World's Fair at Saint Louis*. The World's Work. August 1904.

Carrington, M. Marquette. *Solon Borglum, Artist, Soldier, Patriot*. Washington, D.C. Art and Archaeology. March 1922. Vol. 13.

Eberle, Louise. *In Recognition of an American Sculptor*. Scribner's Magazine, Vol. 72. July-September 1922.

Goodrich, Arthur. *The Frontier in Sculpture*. The World's Work, March, 1902.

Harper's Weekly. *Mr. Borglum's Bronchos and Broncho-Busters*. Vol. 47. May 16, 1903.

Johansen, P. *Solon H. Borglum*. Denmark. Kundst (Art) Med 8, Bulleder 7, Aarag-Haefte 10.

Keppel, Frederick and Co. New York. *Catalogue* of exhibition of bronzes and other sculpture by Solon H. Borglum, with an introduction by Charles H. Caffin. 1904.

Kovinick, Phil. *South Dakota's 'Other' Borglum*. South Dakota History. Summer 1971. Vol. 1, No. 3.

Laurvick, J. Nielsen. *Solon Borglum*. Scandinavian-American Review. May-June 1915.

Messenger, V. E. *Arizona's Hero Memorial.* The Great Southwest; The New Southwest Publishing Co. Denver, Colorado. August 1907.

Peixotto, Ernest C. *An American Fine Arts Academy Near Paris.* Scribner's Magazine. No. 1, Vol. VLXVII. January 1920.

Sewall, Frank. *A Sculptor of the Prairie, Solon H. Borglum.* Century Magazine. Vol. 68. June 1904.

White, Elmer. *Bucky O'Neill.* Phoenix, Arizona, Arizona Magazine Co. March 1907.

Bibliography

UNPUBLISHED MATERIAL

As I made clear in my preface and acknowledgments, research stemming from personal interviews and much unpublished material in the possession of institutions, friends and members of the Borglum family have played a conspicuous part in this study.

This is true, for instance, in the area of genealogy and general family background, the data being repeated in some instances. In 1908 Dr. James (Jens) Borglum visited Denmark with his wife and two daughters, Theodora and Harriet, for an extended stay in the course of which he did considerable research into family history. The stay yielded much source material for the first Borglum, to our knowledge, to migrate to these shores, which is included in "The Harriet Borglum Faidy Papers", making them of first importance in any family history.

The Library of Congress has both the Solon H. Borglum Papers — with the exception of a small bundle being held back by the family for the time being — and the Gutzon Borglum Papers, the latter in a hundred or so boxes. Much use has been made of both collections. And another collection of first importance I have drawn on is that in possession of Professor and Mrs. George Borglum of Royal Oak, Michigan — "The August Borglum Papers".

In addition, mention should be made of the invaluable "Solon Borglum Scrapbook", four copies of which exist, in the Library of Congress, the Nebraska State Historical Society, Mrs. Paul Borglum, with my wife keeping one for her own use. Measuring 24 inches by 20, this is a unique record of Solon's life. It has been microfilmed by the Archives of American Art.

In Chicago, The Harriet Borglum Faidy Papers include such items as data relating to the origins of the De La Mothe and Borglum family names, and her father's research into the Royal Archives of Copenhagen. She accompanied her parents to the Borglum Kløster in Jutland and saw the names of numerous ancestors on tombstones. In this connection, I would add the name of Miss Lillian Field of Chicago, who supplied much material on the early family history, and Wendell Borglum's recent study.

The Hegsted family's unpublished journal of Hans Hegsted contains references to Jens Borglum when the two young men labored together as Mormon missionaries in Denmark. Hans married Maren Borglum, Jens' sister, and kept a journal which covers their move to Salt Lake; some of their descendants are to be found in Utah. Hans and Maren, unlike Jens, remained inside the Church of Jesus Christ of the Latter Day Saints.

Further light on this early period is provided by a letter of Alvin F. Smith, librarian at the Mormon Tabernacle, which contains a brief biography of Jens, the later Dr. James Borglum, dealing with his traveling elder years as he moved into positions of increasing responsibility in the Mormon Church.

The Faidy papers also contain illuminating facts on the lives and activities of various members of the Borglum family in that Omaha home, with a wealth of data regarding dates and addresses, etc. There is an account book, for instance, kept by Ida, Senior, which not only provides information relating to the various children but includes sums sent by Arnold for the purpose of helping Solon and August in their studies. A paragraph here and there provides the researcher with an insight into family life and the mutual concern of members of the Borglum family for one another.

Ranking in importance are the private letters contained among the August Borglum Papers. They cover some forty years and fall naturally into two groups. The first bears on the whereabouts and the activities of the young members of the Borglum family, in school and later when they were making their own way in life. The second group concerns the Vignal sisters, Emma and Lucy, after they were married to Solon and August Borglum. The double relationship became particularly important after both couples established homes in America at the turn of the century. Frequent visits and a regular exchange of letters preserved their mutual affection. Emma's letters to Lucy are uninhibited, revealing her likes and dislikes, reflecting their interest in music, art and literature. Some of these letters illuminate the troubled relationship between Gutzon and Solon. Of special pertinence here are letters exchanged between August and Harriet and August and Mary at the time of the publication of *"Give the Man Room"* by Robert Casey and Mary Borglum, Gutzon's widow.

Re the Solon H. Borglum Papers which are in the Library of Congress, the key importance of these papers is clearly evident throughout my book. I have drawn from them freely as my notes amply prove. Among the papers still in the possession of the family are the following: data relating to the genealogy and the background of the family; a copy of "Fragmentary Biographical Sketch of Grandfather Gutzon N. Borglum, 1754–1808;" Memoir of the Mothe-Borglum family including an "etymology" of the name, and other interesting data; an account of one day's experience on the ranch during a blizzard in 1887 written in long hand by Solon; and nearly all Solon's letters to Emma and the family during his overseas service in World War I, together with his account of experiences.

Solon H. Borglum's Monuments and Other Sculpture

	Material	Approx. Height	Location
1. General John B. Gordon	bronze	monumental	Atlanta, Georgia
2. Captain William O'Neill (Rough Rider Memorial)	bronze	monumental	Prescott, Arizona
3. Jacob Leisler Memorial	bronze	monumental	New Rochelle, New York
4. Private Jones	bronze	under life size	Lynchburg, Virginia
5. Major William Clark	bronze	life size bust	Portland, Oregon
6. Professor Simon Newcomb		life size bust	
7. Mayor Charles A. Schieren	bronze	life size bust	Brooklyn Museum, New York
8. General Joseph A. Mower	bronze	portrait relief bust, life size	Vicksburg, Miss. National Military Park
9. General Giles A. Smith	bronze	colossal bust	Vicksburg National Military Park
10. General William S. Smith	bronze	colossal bust	Vicksburg National Military Park
11. General Edward D. Tracy	bronze	colossal bust	Vicksburg National Military Park
12. General John Gregg	bronze	colossal bust	Vicksburg National Military Park

	Material	Approx. Height	Location
13. General Francis J. Herron	bronze	colossal bust	Vicksburg National Military Park
14. Honorable Michael Glen Cunniff	bronze	memorial panel life size	Phoenix, Arizona Capitol Building
15. Colonel Bates Tablet	bronze	bas relief	New York, N.Y.
16. Taps (Soldiers and Sailors Memorial)	bronze	bas relief	Danbury, Connecticut Wooster Cemetery
17. The Schieren Memorial	bronze	life size	Brooklyn, N.Y. Greenwood Cemetery
18. Truman J. Backus Memorial	bronze	bas relief	Brooklyn, N.Y. Packer Institute
19. Hamilton Hamilton N.A.		monumental life size bust	
20. James Edwin Hurley	bronze	portrait relief bust, life size	Topeka, Kansas
21. Honorable Thomas P. Ochiltree	bronze	medallion	
22. 71st Regiment Trophy (andirons)			New York, N.Y.
23. Lilli	marble		
24. Paul	bronze	life size bust	Mrs. Paul Borglum, New Canaan, Conn.
25. Paul	marble	life size bust	New Britain Museum of American Art, New Britain, Conn.
26. Monica	bronze	life size bust	New Britain Museum of American Art, New Britain, Conn.

	Material	Approx. Height	Location
27. Eagle	marble	6 feet	Washington, D.C. Pan-American Bldg.
28. Condor	marble	6 feet	Washington, D.C. Pan-American Bldg.
29. Clearing Old New England	cement	under life size	Borglum Road, Wilton, Conn.
30. Lady (dog)	Indiana limestone	life size	S.H.B. Studio
31. Benjamin Franklin	plaster	17 in.	New Britain Museum of American Art, New Britain, Conn.
32. American Seal			
33. Pushing Ahead — Washington 1753	bronze	16 in.	State University of Iowa Iowa City, Iowa; National Gallery of Canada, Ottawa
34. The Command of God — Napoleon at Moscow	bronze	28 in.	The National Collection of Fine Arts, Washington, D.C. New Britain

	Material	Approx. Height	Location
			Museum of American Art New Britain, Conn.
35. The Command of God — Napoleon at Moscow	marble	30 in.	George F. Harding Museum Chicago, Illinois
36. The Heavens	plaster	monumental	Disappeared
37. The Heavens (model)	bronze	40 in.	The National Collection of Fine Arts, Washington, D.C.
38. The Little Lady of the Dew (original title, The Waters)	marble	under life size	Saint Mark's in-the-Bouwerie, New York
39. The Waters (model for above)	bronze	13 in.	The National Collection of Fine Arts, Washington, D.C. New Britain Museum of American Art, New Britain, Conn.
40. The Earth	plaster	13 in.	S.H.B. Studio
41. Man	plaster	38 in.	S.H.B. Studio
42. The Bells of History	plaster	38 in.	S.H.B. Studio
43. Aspiration	limestone	heroic	Saint Mark's in-the-Bouwerie, New York

	Material	Approx. Height	Location
44. Inspiration	limestone	heroic	Saint Mark's in-the-Bouwerie, New York
45. Aspiration	plaster	40 in.	destroyed in foundry fire
46. Inspiration	plaster	40 in.	destroyed in foundry fire
47. Back 'Em Up	plaster	34 in.	S.H.B. Studio
48. The Nativity	plaster	20 in.	Saint Mark's Church New Canaan, Conn.

Garden Sculpture

	Material	Approx. Height	Location
49. Boy with Fish (fountain)	bronze	life size	Florida
50. Boy with Fish (lying down)	cement	life size	S.H.B. Studio
51. Vase with Figures (depicting two sides of life)	lead	40 in.	Silvermine Cemetery

Wood Carvings

	Material		Location
52. Young Pioneers	carved on fireplace panels		S.H.B. Studio
53. The Seasons	carved on fireplace panels		
54. The Dinner Bell	carved oak door		Mrs. Linda Fry Wilton, Conn.
55. "The Prayer" — an old man and child	clay	life size	Unknown

Solon H. Borglum's Sculpture of the West

		Material	Approx. Height
1.	Bust of Joe Andrews	plaster	5 in.
2.	Bust of a child (no title)	plaster	5 in.
3.	Bronchos Frightened by Saddle	bronze	6 in.
4.	Great Dane "Titan"	plaster	7 in.
5.	Horse Pawing a Dead Horse	plaster	
6.	Buffalo	bronze	5 in.
7.	Just Born	bronze	4 in.
8.	Deer Killing a Snake	bronze	6½ in.
9.	Charging Bull	bronze	7 in.
10.	Winter (horse suffering from cold)	bronze	7 in.
11.	Buffalo	bronze	14 in.
12.	Buffalo (variation)	bronze	14 in.
13.	Lassoing Wild Horses	bronze	20 in.
14.	Lassoing Wild Horses (variation)	bronze	20 in.
15.	In the Wind, also titled, Snowdrift	bronze	12 in.
16.	Snowdrift	marble	11 in.
17.	Single horse (no title)	bronze	6⅛ in.
18.	Broncho	bronze	7 in.
19.	Single horse (no title)	bronze	10 in.
20.	The Intelligent Broncho	bronze	20¾ in.
21.	The Bucking Broncho	bronze	8 in.
22.	Blizzard	bronze	6 in.
23.	Blizzard (variation)	carved oak	25 in.
24.	Savage Broncho and its Mother	plaster	10¼ in.
25.	Nighthawking on the Plains	bronze	12 in.
26.	Tamed (horse tamed)	bronze	7¾ in.
27.	The Lame Horse	bronze	6 in.
28.	Cowboy		

	Material	Approx. Height
29. Our Slave	marble	15 in.
30. Our Slave	bronze	7 in.
31. The Rough Rider (not to be confused with the memorial monument to Captain Bucky O'Neill)	bronze	19¼ in.
32. Burial on the Plains (sometimes called Desolation)	bronze	15½ in.
33. Burial on the Plains (sometimes called Desolation)	marble	16 in.
34. The Bull Fight	bronze	3 in.
35. The Last Roundup	plaster	13½ in.
36. The Last Roundup		
37. The Last Roundup	marble	13½ in.
38. On the Trail	bronze	15 in.
39. Stampede of Wild Horses	plaster	life size
40. Stallions Fighting	plaster	life size
41. Stallions Fighting	marble	12 in.
42. The Indian Sun Dance	plaster	life size
43. The Indian Sun Dance	plaster	12 in.
44. The Indian Love Chase	bronze	38 in.
45. Evening	bronze	22 in.
46. One in a Thousand	bronze	44 in.
47. One in a Thousand	bronze	24 in.
48. On the Border of White Man's Land	bronze	20 in.
49. The Scout (original study)		
50. Bear 1	bronze	12 in.
51. Bear 2	bronze	8¾ in.
52. Bear 3	bronze	3¼ in.
53. The Indian (a study)	bronze	18 in.
54. The Prospector	bronze	19 in.
55. The Prospector	marble	19 in.
56. The Prospector (fragment)	plaster	9¼ in.
57. The Dance	plaster	12 in.
58. Eagle Dog	plaster	12 in.
59. Indian braves (done in South Dakota in 1899 now lost)		

		Material	Approx. Height
60.	Indian brave		
61.	Indian brave		
62.	Indian brave		
63.	The Secret	plaster	
64.	The Perfect Horse	plaster	
65.	Dancing Horse	bronze	17 in.
66.	The Sandstorm	bronze	11 in.
67.	The Indian Buffalo Dance	staff	12 ft.
68.	The Indian Buffalo Dance (model)	bronze	36 in.
69.	The Indian Drummer (fragment)	plaster	19 in.
70.	The Indian Dancer (fragment)	bronze	26 in.
71.	The Pioneer in a Storm	staff	12 ft.
72.	The Pioneer in a Storm (model)	bronze	36 in.
73.	The Cowboy at Rest (sometimes called "At Rest" or "The Outlook")	staff	12 ft.
74.	The Cowboy at Rest (sometimes called "At Rest" or "The Outlook") (model)	bronze	36 in.
75.	The Cowboy at Rest (sometimes called "At Rest" or "The Outlook")	bronze	15 in.
76.	A Step Toward Civilisation	staff	12 ft.
77.	The Chief (fragment)	plaster	18 in.
78.	Sorrow on the Plains (fragment)	plaster	18 in.
79.	The American Pioneer — A Reverie	staff	12 ft.
80.	The American Pioneer — A Reverie	plaster	12 in.

The circumstances of Solon Borglum's life render peculiarly difficult this listing of his work. The reader is warned that these lists are necessarily incomplete. For years his hand-to-mouth existence was made possible by the sale of plasters at a nominal price, and he was notoriously generous in giving away these and later plasters, frequently unsigned. Two single unnamed horses have already turned up. More seem likely. In 1896 Borglum presented his California hosts, the Perhams, with four intaglios. The whereabouts of only two of these, signed S.H.B., are known.

A.M.D.

Museums and Institutions where Solon H. Borglum is represented

1.	Connecticut, New Britain	New Britain Museum of American Art
2.	Georgia, Atlanta	Atlanta Historical Society
3.	Georgia, Stone Mountain	Stone Mountain Park Museum
4.	Illinois, Chicago	George F. Harding Museum
5.	Iowa, Iowa City	State University of Iowa
6.	Louisiana, Shreveport	R. W. Norton Art Gallery
7.	Michigan, Detroit	Detroit Institute of Arts
8.	Missouri, Clayton	Clayton Public Library
9.	Nebraska, Omaha	Joslyn Museum
10.	New York, New Rochelle	Thomas Paine Cottage
11.	New York, New York	Packer Institute
12.	New York, New York	Brooklyn Museum
13.	New York, New York	Metropolitan Museum of Art
14.	Ohio, Cincinnati	Cincinnati Art Museum
15.	Oklahoma, Oklahoma City	National Cowboy Hall of Fame
16.	Oklahoma, Tulsa	Thomas Gilcrease Institute of American History and Art
17.	Rhode Island, Westerly	Westerly Public Library
18.	South Carolina, Murrells Inlet	Brookgreen Gardens
19.	Washington, D.C.	National Collection of Fine Arts, Smithsonian Institution
20.	Wyoming, Cody	Gertrude Vanderbilt Whitney Gallery of Western Art
21.	Canada, Ottawa	National Art Gallery
22.	Texas, Austin	University of Texas Museum

This list does not include monuments or private collections.

Index